Lyn's l

Lyn Madden

First published in 2007 by
Cork University Press
Youngline Industrial Estate
Pouladuff Road, Togher
Cork, Ireland

British Library Cataloguing in Publication Data
A CIP catalogue record for this book is available from the British Library.

ISBN 978-1-85594-207-3

Typesetting by Red Barn Publishing, Skeagh, Skibbereen, Co. Cork
Printed by JH Haynes & Co Ltd, Sparkford, Yeovil, Somerset, BA22 7JJ, UK

www.corkuniversitypress.com

Lyn's Escape

Dedication
To Po. Who painted me with a loving eye.

Acknowledgements
Without June Levine this book would not exist. Appalled at her suggestion that I should write an update—I had no wish to dip my toe in the sewer again—'I have a life now' I responded. But things can change. There were times during the last year when we argued, sometimes violently, mainly about content, and my use of the F word, that she must have regretted ever suggesting this second effort. It is a testament to her good heart and unstinting loyalty to our friendship that she is still talking to me!

Warm thanks are due to Ann Heath, fount of wisdom, friend, guardian of the original MS (in a Tigger folder) who approached her duties with all the ingenuity, proficiency, inventivenes of a POW. We made it Ann—in spite of the American!

Preface

I am often asked 'Whatever happened to that woman?' They could only mean Lyn and my reply is always the same: 'Lyn? Doing fine, up and down like the rest of us.' Except that the rest of us never had so many obstacles to face as Lyn Madden.

She is now almost sixty, retired from a respectable job and has written this book about her journey to date and her battle with her son Joey's heroin addiction. Hers is a story of survival against enormous odds. It is also a shocking story of exploited workers in modern England. The jobs Lyn was able to get were done in Dickensian conditions, for a pittance, but she stuck with them because they made her feel part of 'normal society', and freed her from dependence on Social Welfare. She must have moved a dozen times in as many years in an effort to feel safe, and with each move came another job.

This book is not a happily-ever-after story—how could it be? On the other hand, after what happened to bring her before the public eye in Dublin, Lyn never expected to make old bones.

Twenty years ago, a Dublin pimp, John Cullen, slipped a fire bomb into the unlocked window of a young woman's home at 15 Hammond Street, Dublin. The fire killed three women, Dolores Lynch for whom it was intended and her mother and Aunt Hannah. The motive was vengeance. Seven years earlier Dolores' evidence had sent John Cullen to prison for three years. In the language of Dublin gangland she had 'grassed him up' and it was well known among the prostitutes who worked on the banks of Dublin's Grand Canal that he was out to 'get her'. On that fated night, Cullen dragged Lyn Madden along with him on his mission to destroy Dolores. Lyn was terrified to even insist on knowing where they were going, until she realised what was happening, and it was too late. Later she became state witness for the prosecution in his murder trial. In so doing, she believed that she had signed her own death warrant.

The Lynches were a respectable working-class family. Mrs Lynch was born Kathleen King in the house in which she perished. It had been her mother's house and her grandmother's before that. Mrs Lynch worked in Dorene's Fashion Clothing factory for 35 years. That had been her mother's trade too and Mrs Lynch apprenticed two of her daughters, Kathleen and Dolores, to the factory when they left school. Dolores could not settle in that job. Two other daughters worked in a hotel. Mrs Lynch had a hard time rearing the four girls after her husband died, but a month before she was killed by the fire, the family of women were delighted with an outing they made to town to buy their mother a fur coat.

Dolores, who was the youngest of the Lynch family, was a quiet child until she reached fourteen years or so, but then became a cause of great anxiety for her mother and her eldest sister, Nora. Although strong willed, Dolores was easily led. Nora believed that it was through her association with The Legion of Mary that Dolores had fallen into bad company. The Legion, a group of nuns committed to saving 'fallen women', had a junior branch which Dolores joined while she was still in school. At seventeen, Dolores was working on the Canal in 1967 when Lyn Madden arrived from England. The women who worked on Dublin's Grand Canal used to go into the Legion House nearby, out of the cold for a cup of coffee. Lyn recalls that Dolores was the only one willing to kneel down to say the Rosary with the nuns.

Lyn claims that there was not another woman on the Canal less interested in doing business than Dolores. She just enjoyed the buzz and chat with the women. Her personality was larger than life. Dolores lived for excitement, wanting to be part of whatever was happening in other people's lives. She had to be in on things and she became a feminist as well as joining other activists of the time. 'She was enormously generous,' recalls Lyn, but she never had a bean and her family often ended up funding her charitable endeavours.

Though easily led, Dolores would not be driven. No pimp would get away with bullying Dolores, which was how she ran foul of Cullen. On the Canal, she moved from one woman to another as she exhausted their store of stories. Lyn says Dolores cost her a fortune in lost business. 'She would root me to the path with her chubby little hand on my sleeve and she'd giggle and look up at me and say: 'Wait till I tell you.' And she did that with all of the women.

She was a great storyteller, never missing a detail. She never mentioned her family or told anyone where she lived, although she knew all about everybody else's family. And she was a good listener, warm and sympathetic. She was also a compulsive giggler and even giggled when she came into court. Eventually, a judge told her to get a job. She obeyed that order, but first she told her prospective boss all about herself. This squashed the worry that haunts any prostitute who tries to go straight, that of her employer finding out about her past. However, she missed her friends from the Canal and after work, Dolores went to hear the gossip and be part of any excitement.

It was in the same spirit of camaraderie that Dolores got involved with feminists, and other activists in the mid-seventies. Her family turned on the television one evening to catch sight of Dolores marching behind a republican banner in the North of Ireland. She joined feminists who believed that women in prostitution should be shown solidarity by the sisterhood. She became extremely exercised about how women in prostitution were treated by society as a whole and attended many meetings on the subject. She wrote to politicians with several demands on behalf of 'girls on the street'. She wrote to the Minister for Justice saying: 'the girls who make their living on the streets of Dublin are very annoyed and disappointed that you have refused to meet us . . . '

She wanted the law changed, she wanted to get women off the streets, she demanded a rehabilitation centre for women who attempted to come off the game. There was horrendous violence against prostitutes in the late seventies and Dolores spoke out on their behalf at meetings, gatherings and marches. However, many of the women on the Canal denied that she represented them. Nor did that stop her talking on their behalf.

In 1979, Pope John Paul was coming to Ireland. Catholics of all ages planned picnic parties for his visit to the Phoenix Park. Dolores was bound to get involved in such an occasion, but she also saw it as a heaven-sent personal opportunity. She had managed to quit prostitution, but felt ashamed of her past and the hurt she had caused her mother. And so she wrote to the Pope and told him all about herself. He replied to her letter by inviting her to visit him at Castle Gondolfo. Her mother and her Auntie Hannah gave Dolores £500 to go and visit the Pope. More than anything Dolores wanted to be forgiven for her past life and she showed everyone the picture of herself with Pope John Paul. Lyn recalls that when she told John Cullen about the snapshot, he sniggered dismissively.

During the last year of her life, Dolores changed as John Cullen's threats reached her ears. John Cullen was brooding and in a state of rage while people who had anything to fear from him ran scared. Nor did he stop after the Lynches house went up in flames. Dolores' mother and aunt perished in the smoke of their home and Dolores survived for 24 hours with 80 degree burns. In her agony, did Dolores realise that it was Cullen who put the fire bomb through the window of her home?

Everyone else around the Canal knew that Cullen was on a rampage both before and after the death of the three women. He brutally raped Lyn's best friend Roisin O'Connor because he guessed that Lyn had told Roisin what had happened to the Lynches. Roisin promised Lyn that she would give evidence in the murder trial, but withdrew that promise when Willy O'Donnell, Roisin's boyfriend, warned her against it for fear that Cullen would escape conviction through some quirk of the law and come after them both.

When Lyn first met John Cullen, Roisin and other women warned her against him. But still, she ended up with him as her lover and pimp. She says that she thought he would protect her from other men. Besides she had a history of choosing violent, impossible men. We explored the reasons for this in *Lyn: a story of prostitution* published by Attic Press in 1987. To Lyn, being in love meant being in extreme pain, because she had never known any other kind of love. Nor could she easily leave that kind of relationship because in so doing, she would prove herself a failure and undeserving of love. So, when her relationship with Cullen began to disintegrate, Lyn felt fear, a paralysing fear. She wanted to get away, but she was afraid to go. John Cullen was dangerously violent, treacherous, unpredictable, quick with a knife or bottle. And he brooded long and hard over vengeance and how he would exact it.

Cullen was one of seven children. His father died when he was nine years old and he seemed to go off the rails as a result of that. He refused to go to school and his first contact with the law was for stealing sweets. His mother sent him to relatives in England in an attempt to keep him out of trouble but she had to take him home again. He still would not go to school and was sent to Upton Reform School for truancy. Lyn told me how he and his criminal friends used to talk about their days in the reform school and the terrible treatment they received there. They recalled every mole or other minor characteristic of the men who reared them.

The religious brothers who took on Cullen's care and education cruelly dominated every day of his life until he was released as a teenager. His body was marked from beatings. He recalled beatings with a twisted towel rung out in cold water when he was naked in the shower. The only education he received at Upton had to do with inflicting grievous bodily harm as a result of which he vowed that when he was free no one would ever again get away with hurting him.

John Cullen was in and out of jail all his life. He was married and supported his family on the earnings of Lyn and other women. Violence or the threat of violence was his only way of negotiating with people, and a broken arm, a face gouged with a broken bottle or skull broken with the leg of a chair were all in a night's work for him. He drove Lyn into taking an overdose, promised to kill her himself. Before he went to jail he set up a contract on her life. That is why when it came to it, Roisin broke her promise Lyn. She was sure that if Cullen walked free, he would come after her and kill her.

Through the years I have not always been in touch with Lyn although I would sometimes receive a note or a card from her. She was too afraid that if I knew where she was that it would be 'easy to get it out of you'. She believed that Cullen could still seek vengeance through his gangland connections. She insisted that I had an alarm button in my bedroom. Things have eased up a bit in the last few years what with emails and mobiles.

Lyn went back to school for a while during those years. and did extremely well. And she moved often, always terrified of being recognised and the word getting back to Dublin. Always looking over her shoulder. Always afraid that someone would blow her cover. If prostitution is a sin, then Lyn has paid dearly for the years she spent on Dublin's streets. But that is like saying that the slave should be punished for slavery, isn't it?

Several years ago Lyn went into a charity shop with her mother and while there she was offered a job. She loved that job and eventually was amazed to be promoted to a position of trust. For health reasons, Lyn retired more than a year ago and she remains friends with the people she worked with and a few of the customers who came into the charity shop.

She deeply regrets the effect that her life in prostitution had on her children. Nowadays, she tries to make it up to them, but who can relive the past? And yet Lyn does relive the past, every time she thinks of the Lynch family. That night with Cullen as he set the fire bomb comes back to her mercilessly. Every January as the anniversary of the Lynches' death approaches, she feels ill, unable to go out. It is useless to remind her of how Cullen terrified her. This January I reminded her that Dolores' sister Kathleen thanked her in the courtroom and said how much the family appreciated that she turned police witness. 'I know,' Lyn said, 'it was good of Kathleen, but . . .'.

June Levine
Editor

1

Two plainclothes police officers followed me up the gangplank lugging a cabin trunk I was taking with me. I waited nervously while they went to find a home for it; watchful in case someone came chasing after me, even though logically I knew it wouldn't happen.

When they returned, we stood making awkward small talk until the call came for anyone not travelling to leave the ferry, then we said our goodbyes; with sadness and regret on my part, and, I suppose, a feeling of relief on theirs. Owing to dreadful storms, we'd been hanging around the terminal for four hours waiting for the ferry to arrive from Holyhead.

As I watched them walking back down the gangplank I felt a sinking feeling of loss. They, and other members of the Garda Síochána, had given me round-the-clock armed police protection as part of a witness protection programme for a year and a half. I had grown accustomed to sharing my life with them. We'd become friends, I would miss them, every one of them.

The second I lost sight of them, the fear set in. I kept my head down as I set about finding somewhere to sit whilst simultaneously trying to spot who was on board without making eye contact.

I managed to find a seat near a window, settled myself in, and tried to make myself inconspicuous. I spread a newspaper on the seat next to me to discourage anyone from sitting beside me, and opened a book. Books are my only passion—I never forget one—but for the life of me I can't remember the title. I only pretended to read, hoping to go unnoticed.

The stark fact that I was never going to make old bones leading the life I had chosen was something I had previously acknowledged and pushed to the back of my mind. I had long known that the only way to change destiny was to get out of Dublin, but had been too cowed to make the choice. Now, watching the Emerald Isle slip away, here I was, still in one piece, physically at least. I had cheated death. My survival had come at a terrible cost to three women.

I kept looking over the top of the page every so often, to make sure no one was observing me. When anybody passed by my seat I froze.

Too nervous to think of food I'd skipped dinner and though the ferry had been long overdue, no one in authority at the ferry terminal had seen fit to lay on as much as a cup of coffee for the weary travellers. Irish people were used to the primitive ferry terminal back then, but a party of Canadians were quite vocal, for all the good it did them.

By then I had a raging thirst so I had no option but to leave the safety of my seat and make my way to the buffet. My back was rigid with tension. The storm still lashed the ferry, as I tried not to spill my coffee while surreptitiously looking at passengers, hoping not to see someone who knew me. I kept expecting someone to tap me on the shoulder and say 'Gotcha!'

It was a nightmare of a crossing in more ways than one. The storm hadn't lessened at all, and people were getting seasick. There was vomit in the aisles, and all over the floors of the washrooms. The toilets were overflowing, the stench was overpowering. Green-faced people with their hands clamped over their mouths were rushing to make it in time before they emptied the contents of their stomachs. Normally I'd have been one of them and though I did my share of retching, with no food in my stomach it was unproductive. Seasickness would have been an escape. It would have given me something else to think about, rather than dwelling on the fear of what lay ahead.

I had lived in Dublin for about sixteen years or so and had earned a small fortune by the standards of the times, but had with me just £80, which wouldn't go far. I wasn't too worried about that, though I did give a thought to all the money I'd given away, both willingly and under duress.

My cabin trunk contained an odd assortment of stuff. My clothes, of course, and silly things, items you wouldn't normally bother to transport from one country to another: bathroom scales, ornaments, cutlery, books, portable typewriter, a small table lamp and the like. I'd sold my TV and video to raise the fare for the ferry; everything else I'd given away, furniture, carpets, paintings, kitchen appliances, linens, bedding etc.

I had police protection right up to the minute I left the country, but I knew it could not continue indefinitely, not that it was ever so much as hinted at it. The police would have called it off eventually and I would have been a sitting duck.

With John Cullen safely under lock and key serving a life sentence I might not have been murdered, but someone from Dublin's sub-culture would have got to me. At the very least I'd have been badly hurt.

I wasn't just leaving a country; I was leaving sixteen years of my life too. While I knew leaving was my only option if I wished to stay alive, I still felt lost. For better or worse the people with whom I'd spent the last sixteen years—the women I'd worked alongside on the streets, their pimps and other criminals—were my peers, my friends, were the only people I'd known, were who I was. In a way I felt I was leaving my identity behind.

Why I hadn't thought of it before I don't know, but as I looked at the coastline disappearing, it struck me that it was the second time I'd been exiled in disgrace from the land of my birth.

I got nicked for shoplifting in Belfast when I was a teenager. After a week on remand in Armagh jail (a grim place in the sixties), the court ordered I be deported to England. Identical scenario, two RUC men in full uniform escorted me up a gangplank on to a boat. Miserable bastards didn't bother to wave goodbye; I was only sixteen after all. Half the ferry had witnessed my humiliation; I'd buried my head in a book then too.

Time seemed to stand still. I thought the ferry would never reach its destination. I once read of an actor serving a jail term who had seen scrawled on the wall of his cell 'The darkest hour of your life only lasts for sixty minutes.' I loved that. But without the safety of police protection, I was exposed, vulnerable to my greatest fear: coming face-to-face with someone connected to the Lynches or the

Cullens. By the time the ferry docked, I was in such a state I concluded the prison philosopher was mistaken. Sixty minutes is not merely an hour, it can be an eternity.

*

I was ahead of the queue as we docked, extremely relieved to have arrived without incident. British Rail staff proved very helpful in getting my cabin trunk off the ferry and on to the waiting train. I pounced on a seat next to the window, sat down, gratefully leaned my head against the cold glass, and stared out of the window, idly watching people walking along the platform. A lot of them still looked a bit sick. A guy walking past did a double-take in my direction, then came towards me, looking at a spot just over my shoulder. I thought he was going to the seat behind me—there were two free—but no, he sat down on the seat opposite me, giving me his full attention. 'Oh, bloody hell,' I thought, because you just know, don't you? Don't forget, I was an expert.

He was smooth though and didn't go for the direct approach; instead, he opened up a conversation with a couple of New Zealanders who had joined us at the table. The women had 'done' Ireland and were starting a tour of Britain. They were the first Kiwis I'd ever met and I was drawn in to the conversation in spite of myself, because they were so interesting. Their country sounded rather quaint, all cricket and 'will there be honey for tea?' sort of thing, like England in the 1930s. I can't remember where they left the train but it was somewhere in Wales. I was sorry to see them go; I could have listened to them for hours.

As soon as they'd gone, the guy started by asking if I'd been on the ferry. I said I had. 'You?' He shook his head. I get nervous whenever a real dishy guy tries to hit on me so I tend to talk a lot as a cover-up. I can laugh now when I think about it, but there's me waffling on about the stormy crossing I'd just endured and other previous bad boat journeys, and all the while he's studying me, assessing me, his eyes trying to hold mine, his lips smiling. Then he told me about himself. He was an officer in the Royal Navy, on his way to hospital after being winched off his boat by helicopter in the Irish Sea, before being dropped near the railway station at Holyhead. I think he said he was going for tests of some kind. I had a vision of him dangling on a rope in the middle of the gales. I don't know if I blushed but my face grew very hot with embarrassment. I felt such an idiot as I noticed the white shirt, the Navy sweater for the first time.

Then he asked me about myself. Was I married? 'No.' Involved? 'No.' Where was I going? Where had I come from? And so on. I was paralysed, incoherent. I hadn't planned what to say, wasn't expecting to be hit on within five minutes of setting foot on British soil. I didn't know who to say I was, didn't really know who I was myself. Or who I was going to be. I recall mumbling something along the lines of I wasn't sure what I was going to do. His eyes held mine.

'Come with me,' he said, brown eyes and teeth flashing. Quite gorgeous.

'Don't be silly,' I laughed nervously.

'Come on. Just do it,' he said, smiling seductively. 'You just said you weren't sure what you were doing.' He leaned across the table and lightly placed his hand on top of mine.

'The hospital business will only take a few hours. Come with me. Get off at the next stop with me.'

I didn't of course.

I trembled when he asked me, and I don't mean that frisson of sexual excitement you feel when you're attracted to someone. He asked for my phone number, I said I hadn't got one; this was pre-mobile phone days. He wrote his number on a page ripped from his notebook, and passed it across the table. 'Please call,' not begging, he was too classy for that. Leave me a contact number on the answer-phone, he smiled invitingly. I took the torn page but made no promises. He waited on the platform until my train pulled away and we waved to each other. As I looked back he blew me a kiss with his fingertips. I shook like a leaf until the train pulled in to the next station.

I wondered what was it about me that made him think I was game enough to just get off at the next stop if you please. What had he seen when he looked at me? I was attractive enough, I didn't look common, I was clean, nicely, conservatively dressed. The dyed black hair was long gone. Was it *so* transparent I didn't belong anywhere? Perhaps I had victim stamped on my forehead. I fretted over it for days afterwards.

It wasn't just what he said about getting off the train with him which has stuck in my mind for more than twenty years. It was the double-take he did as he was passing the window on the platform, that split second when our eyes had met and he'd decided he wanted me. The 'Brief Encounter' of Holyhead—instead of Hollywood—except I'm no Celia Johnson. My Navy captain was a bit of a hunk though, a million times better looking than Trevor Howard.

I've pondered more than a few times how it would have turned out if I'd gone with him, where I'd have been now. Since the murders and the psychiatric therapy I'd undergone as a way of coming to terms with them, I saw danger in every encounter with the opposite sex. It might sound as if I'm a few cents short of a Euro but I thought that my naval officer might have been intending to murder me, had I been foolish enough to get off the train with him. I know there had been a train full of people to witness our meeting but I had no friends in England, no home, no job and no work colleagues. No one would have known I was missing, rootless and stateless as I was. Like a backpacker, a backpacker travelling with a cabin trunk, full of useless chattels. I wonder what the murder squad detectives would have made of that little lot. I felt such a failure. I was forty years old, forty years of age and a refugee, again.

I know normal people won't understand why I see potential danger in everyday situations, but I mean, my last lover had killed three women, and the one before him had fatally stabbed his own brother.

As the ferry had been delayed the train was hours behind schedule too, and by the time I reached my destination I had to leave my cabin trunk at the railway left-luggage office because there was no-one at hand to help me with it. My mum's house was in darkness when I arrived. I rang the bell a few times but got no reply. I supposed she'd gone to bed. I started throwing stones at the window and shouting through the letterbox in a vain attempt at waking her. Then I realised I didn't know which bedroom she would be sleeping in—she had five of them—and if she was sleeping on the third floor she wouldn't hear me anyway. I tried throwing gravel again and it sounded very loud so I stopped, worried I'd break the window.

I crept round to the back alley where I found two milk crates which I placed one on top of the other and used them to raise myself up so that I could lean over the top of the gate and slide the bolt open. I sat on a garden chair with my head resting on my arms on the patio table. I knew it was going to be a long night. I could hear caterwauling tomcats not too far away and that dreadful sound they make which makes you think someone is being attacked. It was a rather eerie feeling sitting under the moon listening to them, just like an old alley-cat. But just like old times in a sense.

When I started going dancing as a fifteen-year-old, my mother imposed a curfew and if I was not home in time, she'd lock up and go to bed. The first couple of times she did it I tried knocking to get in but she ignored me, so I never bothered after that and spent many a night sitting in the back garden until daybreak. I'd left school and was working in a department store, so her 10.00 p.m. curfew was unrealistic. I tried really hard to adhere to it at the outset, which was difficult as all my friends had until 11.00 to get home. Then one day I woke up to the fact that my mum wasn't trying to protect me, she was just trying to impose her will on me, so I waited until the dance was over after that.

At sixteen I got in trouble with the law, shoplifting, and was placed in the care of the local authority and they sent me to a convent for a year. The day I left I got off the train expecting my mum to be waiting on the platform to welcome me home. More fool me, she'd gone to work as usual. I had no bus fare so I walked the four miles to the house and sat around for six hours waiting for her to come home. Going home to mother at forty years of age is a crushing experience for anybody. It was doubly hard for me as we hadn't lived under the same roof since I was seventeen; it hadn't been a bed of roses then and I wasn't hopeful now.

I tried to sleep but was too cold and uncomfortable. I kept looking at my watch, clocking the working girls in and out on the canal. The early birds who'd started around 8.00 p.m. would be going home around midnight; most of them had the school run in the morning. The telly addicts and the drinkers would start around 11.00 and begin wrapping it up at 2.30–3.00 a.m. I checked my watch at 3.45 and wondered how they had fared, had they had a good night? I hoped they'd had a safe one. I didn't envy them—what's to envy?—but I missed them. I missed the camaraderie, the wry humour. At least they knew their lot in life, knew who they were.

My past was like a battlefield, strewn with dead people, bereaved families, grief and suffering. I did my utmost not to linger there too long; I couldn't take the pain. But I couldn't go forward because I didn't know where forward was. I've never tried to shape my own destiny. I always wait for fate to throw the dice, and then react. As I waited for the dawn, I wondered what fate had in store for me.

My mother was glad of the company because she was in between husbands, having just divorced her third. The trouble was I didn't have a lot to do. She was at work during the day and she took her meals there so there wasn't much cooking to be done. I would just rustle up any old rubbish for myself because I don't have much interest in food. The cleaning, washing and ironing were soon sorted and apart from walking Wombie, her little Scotty dog, I was soon bored out of my mind. I didn't have a job. I didn't yet feel mentally capable of being with other people, didn't really feel a part of nice, civilised society. The years on the streets weren't the problem. I'm extremely resilient and adaptable and could fit in almost anywhere; I don't wear my past like an easily recognisable garment. I'd worked in a restaurant and in shops in the past when I'd had to go into hiding, so I knew I was capable of earning an honest crust. It was the deaths of the Lynches that made me feel unable to be around normal, decent folk.

Dave Black, an ex-boyfriend, always blamed me for his brother's death. Dave was a two-bit Dublin crook with aspirations to becoming a successful pimp. He was forever pulling a knife on me, and when I eventually got pissed off enough to go AWOL from him he borrowed his younger brother's car to come gunning for me. There was a fuel strike on at the time and he used up all the petrol in the car and when he got back home a row erupted between the three brothers, which culminated in Dave mortally wounding his elder brother.

Logic told me I wasn't responsible for the death of his brother. However with the passage of time I have taken some of the guilt on board because, with the benefit of hindsight, I can see that I was addicted to drama—having a row, storming off in a huff—and then having to hide, in fear of my life. I wonder if it's possible to be hooked on danger, on fear, on terror. I remember going to see *Dracula* as a teenager and (it being the days when most working-class people didn't have cars), having to walk home, and the feeling of abject terror as I walked under the railway bridge alone. A lot of women of my age-group say it affected them too, not like today when we're all rather de-sensitised to horror films. It wasn't the bat I feared; it was the sinister man in the black cloak. What I have yet to work out is why, then, I'm always attracted to the bastards in life, the man-in-the-black-cloak so to speak, the one who makes you shiver with fear when he looks at you.

If Dolores, her mother, and her aunt Hannah hadn't died I wouldn't have taken on the feelings of responsibility concerning the death of Dave's brother; his death would have been a separate, terrible tragedy. Though the death had taken place a couple of years before those of the Lynches, it was as if the two snowballed—had a cumulative effect on me—and I added it to my store-cupboard of guilt.

I'm one of a minority of people who have been present when human life has been taken. It's like belonging to some terrible secret society and it's always there in your thoughts, your heart, your tissues, your blood, your arteries, your very bones. I still flinch if someone looks too long into my eyes, as if they can see my soul. I always look away first.

So before I earned my stripes as a member of the human race I needed to heal my psyche, and try to adjust to a normal life. I was also afraid that I'd blow my cover by mentioning Dublin if I got into a conversation with anyone. So I kept at the cleaning, walking the dog and reading, reading, reading, while I waited, but I couldn't, if asked, have said what it was I waited for.

I can't recall when it first started, but all my adult life I've waited—with that butterfly feeling you get when something bad is coming your way—for some calamity to befall me. Like the Sword of Damocles hovering over me, it was never a wait for anything nice to happen.

Though my mum was glad to have some company, there was too much history between us for my stay to be enjoyable. She was blissfully unaware of the ambivalence of my feelings. I was only months away from the end of therapy when I'd had to come to terms with my father's sexual assaults on me, and my mother's part in that. All kinds of memories were surfacing and I wanted to get away before I said something I'd regret.

I've always been wary of my mother because she has a terrible temper and can turn on you in a flash; she's as strong as an ox too and only stops when she's exhausted. But though I was still scared of her enough to sleep with the light on, my own anger was simmering away near the surface like a cauldron and I felt quite violent towards her. I've been around enough to know that everyone one is capable of violence given the right, or rather the wrong circumstances, but the feeling was so alien to me; I was only used to being on the receiving end of violence.

I set about applying to various housing associations for a place of my own, but as my mother had plenty of space, I wasn't holding my breath. Still, my anger bubbled away and it got so bad I briefly contemplated sleeping rough.

My mother decided to have her kitchen extended which was to take around three weeks to complete. I wasn't looking forward to sharing my days with the builders, but fate works in mysterious ways, I got talking to the boss of the building firm and it transpired that he had a few houses, which he let out into flats. When I said I desperately needed somewhere he offered me one. I jumped at it. My mother was furious when I told her; she went on about my moving in on my own when I had a perfectly good room upstairs.

Once again, I packed my stuff; the guy at the grocery store across the road gave me some cardboard boxes, I'd acquired a lot more books since I'd been there. I was over the moon to be moving to my own place. I like my own company, love the solitude and knew I was extremely lucky to have secured somewhere of my own so quickly. When I'd finished packing my mother handed me a letter she'd 'forgotten' to give me. It was from a housing association offering me a brand new flat; I had to reply to within forty-eight hours. I looked at the date; my mother had sat on it for a week. Knowing my mother's skill at steaming peoples' letters open I knew she'd obviously read it and decided not to tell me until it was too late for me to act on it.

'What does it say?' She asked without a hint of embarrassment.

'You already know.'

She gave one of her innocent little-me looks.

'It doesn't matter,' I said tiredly. 'Forget about it. Let's get these in the car.'

2

On the day I moved I was up with the lark and carrying the last two bags into my new flat just as the milkman was delivering two doors away. At the time my sister's husband worked for the Milk Marketing Board—he owned three milk rounds—but as my mother couldn't stand him she always referred to him as 'the milkman'. Purely because I was on a high owing to the move, I made the mistake of saying to my mother, 'Hey Mum, *my* milkman's a bit of alright.' It was meant to be witty and I was mortified when my mother shouted . . .

'I say, milkman? Me daughter says you're a bit of all right!'

He laughed back at her. I dragged her into the hallway after me and shut the door.

When my mother had gone, I set about unpacking and putting things away. The place was unfurnished but I'd bought a bed, table, one chair, a fridge and a stove from a second-hand store for next to nothing. It looked bare but as soon as I'd stacked my books on the floor it had my stamp on it and I was 'well happy' as they say. I set my typewriter up on the table when I'd finished and, put a fresh sheet of paper in it. I was attempting to write a novel and was looking forward to having the luxury of working without interruption. At 10 p.m. I was as stiff as a board and the fingers of my right hand were quite painful from pounding the little portable, so I closed shop for the day.

After a bath, I made a cup of cocoa and climbed into bed contentedly happy. I lay awake for quite a long time listening to people walking by and familiarising myself with the sounds of the house. The place had nice vibes and I couldn't imagine anything bad happening there.

The next morning I woke up at the crack of dawn, full of the joys of spring as I realised where I was. Like most people who've been through the care system of children's homes, I love nesting and furniture, curtains, carpets, paint, wallpaper, anything that makes a place a home. One of the biggest highs I've ever experienced is that feeling of moving into a new place and it's all well . . . new. If I'd known how to whistle I would have done.

I took a quick shower, put my face on, made myself a cup of coffee, sat at the table and began typing. I'd only managed about two hundred words when the doorbell went. It was 6.10 a.m. Who the hell could it be at this time of the morning? I opened the front door warily to find the milkman standing on the doorstep with a smile on his face.

'Morning lovely lady,' he said, and handed me a pint of milk. 'Coffee please, two sugars.'

For a few seconds I was speechless. I looked down at the bottle of milk in my hand then back at him.

'Cheeky sod!' I said, recovering my wits. He was still smiling. Lovely smile actually.

'Oh well, for your sheer nerve I'll make you one.'

Well, he had called me 'lovely lady' and I'm such a sucker for any kind of affection.

As I busied myself in the kitchen I did question what I was doing, but thought 'what the hell, a cup of coffee is just a cup of coffee.' He said he'd only called because the light was on and he presumed I'd want a milk delivery. He smiled as he said it.

I smiled back and said, 'Yeah, and because of what my mother said.'

That too, he agreed.

I said I was sorry if he'd been misled, then explained about my sister's husband and the milk rounds.

He shrugged as if to say, so what, and then, 'Shall I go then, seeing as I'm here under false pretences?'

We smiled at one another again.

'Nah. May as well have your coffee.'

He nodded towards the typewriter and asked what the project was and I told him I was writing a book. He asked how many hours

I worked at it each day and was suitably impressed when I told him twelve. I said I didn't set out to spend that long at it but the time flew. He said I'd probably get along with his best friend, Roger, a schoolteacher, who'd had some short stories published. I changed the subject deftly before he had the chance to ask me had I ever had anything published before. He stayed for around fifteen minutes and it was only after he'd gone I realised we'd not exchanged names. I hardly gave him a thought afterwards, there hadn't been any sparks between us. I tended to be attracted to the mean and moody type only, whereas he'd been outgoing and cheerful.

Although I've always liked my own company I soon discovered that solitude is great when you use home as a bolthole to get away from people, but its not so hot when you never see a living soul from one week to the next, and I started to get bouts of loneliness. To counter it I went to the local park and sat on a bench talking to old ladies who were also there for the company. A half-hour stretch a couple of times a week filled my need for human contact There were places I could have gone, drop-in centres for women or the unemployed, but I'm not a joiner, though I can strike up a conversation with anyone when it's on my own terms. I saw my mum on Sundays when I'd cook dinner for us at the flat, but sitting chatting as if we were a normal family was something of an ordeal for me, and I was glad when she had gone.

Three weeks later the milkman called again for a cuppa. I was glad to see him really, he was someone to talk to. He stayed for around ten minutes and as he was leaving he asked if he could call again and I said I saw no reason why not, providing he at least told me his name. He laughed and promised, next time.

When I opened the door to him a week later he grinned and stretched out a hand in greeting.

'Hi, how are you? The name's Steve.'

'I'm well thank you.' I smiled back. 'The name's Lynda, friends call me Lyn.'

'Right, Lyn. I've bought some coffee.'

He handed me a big jar of Nescafé. I looked at the jar of coffee, then back to him. He was still smiling.

Steve was rather attractive with very thick black hair, turning grey, brown eyes and a moustache. He was a little chunky so he obviously liked his grub. He had an unpronounceable surname; his father was Polish and had fought for Britain in World War II.

Steve took to calling halfway through his round twice a week. A few weeks down the line, I used to quite look forward to seeing him. I was also glad of the diversion as it gave me an excuse to down tools and stop writing. My novel wasn't reading as I wanted it to. I kept changing the plot, and I realised all my characters were more than loosely based on people I knew—as most of my acquaintances were pimps, prostitutes and villains it was one dimensional to say the least.

I'd sent Julian, my literary agent, three chapters. He suggested that I introduce a mayor into the proceedings, which made me laugh. I thought mayors only featured in American novels. He was eager to know what happened next. Well, I was stumped, I knew nothing about mayors, or the machinations of mayoral office, or for that matter *any* normal people! I hadn't a clue about research at the time either. Now, of course, novels set solely in the underbelly of society are a genre, but they weren't fashionable then. As to what was going to happen next his guess was as good as mine.

Steve and I didn't have any in-depth conversations, just light casual chat as you would with a friend. Experience, however, had taught me that there's no such thing as a platonic relationship between the sexes—there's always a hidden agenda—which is such a shame because I like male company. Ok, so there are some right bastards out there, I've met more than my fair share, but at least you know where you stand with men. Most want sex, it's as simple as that. Get that out of the way and you can have a pleasant evening; no cattiness, no listening to someone being pulled to pieces, which is something I detest.

Whenever Steve turned the conversation round to me I was evasive; he once asked me jokingly if I was a spy for MI5, bound by the Official Secrets Act, due to my reluctance to answer questions. I can't say how the subtle change came, I wasn't conscious of it happening and I don't think I would have picked Steve out in a crowded dance hall, but affairs start between people who spend time together and his visits intensified until he was calling every day. Then one day he kissed me on the cheek as he was leaving, taking me by surprise.

A week later, our relationship changed and I discovered there was a dreadful drawback to becoming intimate with Steve; Steve liked plenty of affection, kisses, kisses, and more kisses, all accompanied by gallons of saliva, bucketfuls of the stuff. I don't know what Freud would have made of this oral fixation and the transfer of so much saliva, but I felt in danger of drowning. Luckily the event was over quickly.

I wouldn't be the first woman who looked on sex as something to be tolerated in a relationship. I never bother acting, never did as a working girl (they weren't paying me enough), and I wasn't going to start now. Most men I've known were quite happy with this state of affairs, selfishly relieved that they didn't have to waste time and energy trying to make sure I was enjoying myself. It has always bugged me that people think a low libido is a consequence of life on the game. It ain't so. Women and girls who arrive at prostitution with a healthy sex drive have no problem in switching off while they work, no different to the bored housewife. I can assure people that when a hooker's shift is over at the end of the night she sheds her street persona along with her working clothes, before switching her feelings back on for the person she cares about. I arrived at prostitution hating sex, so in a sense it was easier for me. I had already perfected the art of switching off all feeling below the waist as a child, thanks to my father mauling me. By the age of ten I'd learnt, even if subliminally, that sex was all to do with control and power. I hated having this knowledge because it robbed me of my childhood. I can't remember ever feeling carefree.

As I reached womanhood I never again wanted any man to have total power over me, so I used sex as a weapon, and for once I'm not being flippant. Because I was passive I allowed men to control my movements, my whereabouts, my actions, what I wore, the friends I kept, but no way was I going to let them control my sexuality; it was the one thing I had any control over.

I often wondered what it must feel like to have had a normal, happy childhood, no father waiting until you fell sleep so that you didn't have a chance to scream or cry out before he mutilated you, to have arrived at adulthood with a healthy attitude to sex. It must be nice. I have come across the odd woman who hasn't had some sort of sexual abuse and they seem unreal, like they come from a different planet. Part of me wished I was one of them, accepting at the same time that history can't be rewritten but in a perverse way I was glad it had happened; it enabled me to have the power to withhold my sexuality when I so chose. The thought of being at the mercy of my own desires horrified me. Although sex always left me cold I liked the affection, the kisses and the holding hands, the cuddles before and after.

Steve started calling at all odd hours after work in addition to the usual coffee breaks. He'd arrive wearing his tatty carpet slippers with his dog, Zach, whom he was ostensibly out walking. On reflection I can laugh at the carpet slippers, but you'd think he'd have made the effort to dress up for me. Poor Zach never did get his exercise, sometimes he was left sitting in the car while Steve came into the flat.

I was sitting on the bed reading late one night when I heard loud music coming from the direction of the back garden. It went on for quite a time and seemed to be getting louder so I went to investigate. I pulled the curtains to the French windows aside to find Steve strumming his guitar, grinning at me, and as I opened the doors I realised he was singing 'The Black Velvet Band'. I was laughing, but felt such a fool because he went on serenading me in spite of my plea for him to stop. I had to stand through another verse.

'What are you doing here at this time of night?' I asked when he finally stopped.

'I've come to ask if I can move in with you.'

Oh shit. He went on to say that he had been finding the deceit and the betrayal of his wife too difficult to cope with. He said he couldn't carry on going home to her when he wanted to be with me. He adored me, couldn't live without me etc., all the usual things people say to each other at the start of an affair.

What a dilemma. I didn't want him to move in with me, didn't want to have to 'do' for him, his washing, ironing and what-have-you. I was not a modern woman, and knew that before the day was out I would have signed up for a life of drudgery. More importantly, men are such space invaders and I didn't want my lovely little flat colonised. And have to swallow gallons of saliva on a regular basis.

I hadn't actually lived with a guy for six years or more. When I left Craig Nelson in 1979 I spent a lot of time enjoying being on my own, apart from missing my kids, before I met Dave Black. Though we saw each other on and off he lived at home with his mother. When I picked up with John Cullen I was glad that he was married. It was nice to be able to compartmentalise my life in that respect, get rid of them after a nice evening just chatting and whatever, lock the doors then climb in to bed with a cup of cocoa and a good book.

I don't know how to say 'No.' I'm fascinated by programmes on the television about women having self-assertiveness lessons, and have sat transfixed when they finally said 'No!' I'd never manage it even if I had a thousand lessons. So I couldn't give him an outright 'no'.

'Look Steve, this is all so sudden and unexpected. I have to tell you that you moving in would be a mistake. For starters I'm not who or what you think I am.'

He started to interrupt by saying he didn't care about anything he just wanted to be with me.

I put my hand up to stop him.

'There are things you don't know about me.'

He shook his head as if to say so what. I told him he'd better sit down.

'Don't look at me while I tell you.'

I spoke quickly, as if doing so would lessen the impact of what I had to tell him. I confessed the whole sordid mess that had been my life up to then. I told him about John Cullen, and the murders of the Lynches. I'd love to be able to sit here today and say I'd been ruthlessly honest with Steve and had held nothing back in the telling, but it's not true of course. I played it down a little. For instance, I told him I'd worked in a massage parlour, briefly.

Why pretend to be a masseuse, yet not admit to walking the streets? I don't know really. Well I do. I've got the cameras rolling in my head and can visualise myself loitering on the streets surrounding Dublin's Grand Canal, and I feel such shame. We all make distinctions anyway. Steve told me later that when I'd warned him that I'd something bad to tell him he'd been afraid I was going to tell him I'd taken part in blue movies.

'You cheeky, insulting swine!' I'd replied.

Distinctions again.

When I'd finished talking I could barely swallow, my mouth was so dry. Steve had turned grey; he wouldn't look me in the eye. He said something unintelligible, and then said he'd better go because it was getting late. He gave me a chaste kiss on the cheek as he left.

'See you Lyn.'

I don't think so, I said to myself. He must have been reeling with shock. The poor bastard had come a courting a 'lovely lady' novelist, only to discover that she was a retired hooker.

Although I didn't want Steve to move in with me I'd gotten used to his friendship and having him around, so I spent an anxious night wondering if I'd ever see him again. Steve would have cut his own hand off sooner than strike a woman and it was such a novelty to be with someone who was kind, thoughtful and romantic, sang me songs and called me 'lovely lady'. What more could I ask for?

Steve must have been made of much sterner stuff than I'd credited him with because early the following morning he arrived with a single red rose, which he handed me solemnly, wordlessly. He leaned towards me and looked into my eyes.

'I love you. I don't care about anything, I don't care about the past, I just want us to be together.'

I should, of course, have said no. Instinct told me to. I wasn't even grateful that he hadn't walked out as soon as he'd discovered the truth about me. My brain was saying 'No! No! No!' while my mouth betrayed me yet again and said 'OK, yes'.

Even as I was saying yes I was regretting it. My spirits sank as I looked around my tidy little flat and mentally superimposed Steve and all his belongings in it. He arrived the next day with two bags of dirty washing, his registered shotgun and guitar, my very own space invader. Another addition to the household was Zach, the black labrador.

3

Despite not really wanting Steve to move in, I decided to try to make the best of it. It wasn't to be an easy task, as it turned out. I resented the fact that not only had I Steve to look after, I also had his two children. It served me right for picking up with a married man. It was very hard to adapt to all of it though.

In my previous existence marriage counted for nothing. Everyone I knew had been married to someone other than the person they lived with, or like me, had never married at all. My own mother had been married three times. Still searching for the Holy Grail she married once more after I had moved to the flat. Ordinary people got their act together by getting divorced and then remarrying, thus legitimising their unions. My peer group lived outside the conventions of society and didn't bother with the niceties or the hypocrisy; they just moved their toothbrushes from one bathroom to another when the going got tough. Although the sanctity of marriage as a concept meant little to me I still felt a burden of guilt concerning Sue and the boys, and that, along with having my flat taken over by Steve and his wildlife, served as retribution of a sort.

At the weekends there were four of us in my tiny one-bedroomed flat. I adored Greg, Steve's youngest son. Greg had an infectious laugh and a lovely outgoing personality, but Glen, the eldest, I couldn't stand. Glen always seemed to just *be* there, with his resentful face. I couldn't blame him for resenting me but it was more than that. There was a personality clash also and we wouldn't have liked each had circumstances been different.

When the boys stayed over they slept in the bed with Steve and I made up a bed on the floor with spare blankets. It wasn't ideal, but I couldn't bring myself to share a bed with Steve while his kids were around. I wasn't alone on the nights I slept on the floor though, because Zach took advantage of the chance of a little kindness and snuggled up at my back. Like most dogs, Zach was very loving and, apart from being fed, sought nothing but a pat on the head, something Steve always refused him. He'd be sitting on the floor (because we only had the one chair), and Zach would be sitting beside him nuzzling at his arm in an attempt to get him to stroke him, but Steve always ignored him.

My heart went out to poor Zach; he never did get taken for a walk. I thought at the time how cruel that was, to own a dog purely to work it. Steve was a member of the hunting, shooting and fishing brigade and Zach's sole purpose in life was to fetch whatever Steve had killed, or shot out of the air. If I could go back in time I would have taken Zach for walks, but at the time I wasn't a dog lover and (apart from my mother's dog Wombie) I was totally ignorant of canine needs.

I only recall one dog in the family when I was growing up, Shandy, the Welsh collie who was barking mad. He bit everything and everybody in sight, much to my mother's amusement. The police were constantly calling to the house with complaints from the postman, the milkman and the neighbours. I remember standing at the kitchen sink washing dishes at my mother's house when I was eight months' pregnant with my first child and Shandy getting up from his bed growling and sinking his teeth into my backside, twice. I screamed to my mother to pull him off me but she was laughing too hard to respond. I was always scared of dogs because of Shandy.

Having to look after Steve's kids I accepted (I couldn't do much else), but one day I returned from the shops to find a Jack Russell running loose in the back garden, and a basket on the back doorstep, which Sue (the wronged wife) had deposited. Nice one, Sue. I suppose she'd decided that if I had the husband I may as well take the lot. I admire women like Sue; I wouldn't have had the gumption to do something like that. No matter what shit I took off people I never had the guts to react.

There was movement coming from the basket. I approached it

nervously, my hands holding my throat; I was relieved to see that there was a leather buckle holding it shut. A pair of eyes peered out at me through a small opening and I jumped back in fright. Being a townie I had no idea what the creature was and I was scared to death of it so I left it where it was, picked up the Jack Russell and walked round to the front door to get in to the flat. Steve laughed his head off when he got home and I pointed to the basket on the back step with a shaking hand.

'It's only a ferret. He's dead cute.'

He went to open the basket.

'Do you want to hold him?'

I was already running back indoors as I squealed. I refused point blank to have any truck with the ferret. I told Steve there was no way I would have it in the flat and he'd have to give it to one of his hunting friends. He agreed it was for the best. He put the basket in the shed and said he'd sort it.

Over the following few days I kept on at Steve to give the ferret away, and he kept saying he would. It was cruel to keep it in the outside shed in the dark but I was too scared to venture in and take the basket out. When I was sweeping the garden path or hanging the washing out I could hear it scrabbling about in the shed and I'd be shaking like a leaf until I got back indoors.

I soon realised Sue had come off best. Steve was monumentally lazy. There were now *two* dogs pissing and shitting in the back garden on a daily basis but Steve acted as if they belonged to someone else and made no attempt to clean up after them. Because I'm useless at confrontation I didn't say anything for ages. Instead, I took to standing at the French windows mentally playing chess because most of the slabs had mounds of dog shit on and the garden resembled a Damien-Hirst style chessboard. I was near to tears every time I looked out of the window, and dreaded to think what the guy in the upstairs flat made of the garden.

After four days I could bear it no longer and plucked up the courage to ask Steve to clean it up, and he did so. Once. No wonder Sue said she didn't want him back. Another week passed without him attempting it again and I erupted. I said that if he wasn't prepared to clean up after the dogs they'd have to go. I couldn't believe I'd done it, but it worked and he cleaned it up every day after that. Well, for a while. I didn't resent the dogs, just Steve's lack of consideration for them. Gemma, the Jack Russell, was a lovely little dog whom I nicknamed Lick-Lick because she was always licking my hand. Zach, the black Labrador, was as thick as two planks and just about the most slothful dog on the planet. Dogs do resemble their owners then!

Like a lot of women, I tried to embrace my new man's hobby. I went to gun-dog trials in me green Hunter wellies and a woolly hat, I ploughed through muddy fields, I sat on my frozen arse in a hide in the middle of winter with snot running from my nose, my hands too cold to reach into the pocket of my Barbour jacket for a tissue. I allowed my urban kitchen to be used for the skinning of a hare with a smell that lingered for weeks. I plucked pigeons and made rabbit stew. I hated all of it.

The crunch came one day when I'd been sitting in a hide for so long that I got severe cramp. When I climbed out to stretch my limbs Steve berated me for making him miss his shot. By that stage I was well and truly pissed off and I told him I wanted to go home now if he didn't mind. And who wants to spend all day pitting their wits against a poor bloody rabbit who'd never know what hit it?

Steve knew he'd blown it with me, and in an attempt to soothe me he persuaded me to take a shot at his hat, which he threw into the air, and I held the shotgun too near my face but the recoil almost knocked me out. To mollify me Steve put his finger through a hole in his hat to show me where my shot had peppered it. I hadn't taken my eye off the hat so I knew he lied. I saw his fib as an act of kindness, but I never again went out hunting with him.

We were sitting on the bed watching TV one day when the two boys walked through the French windows, followed by their mother. Should have locked them. I wanted the ground to open up and swallow me. We had no couch to sit on, hence the bed, but a bed is not the best place to be caught with your lover by the betrayed wife, and I was mortified.

Sue was magnificent. She didn't acknowledge me with as much as a flick of an eyelash. She stood at the foot of the bed with the boys like little soldiers, on either side of her and laid into Steve, listing every grievance she'd had since the day they'd met. I was too scared to sneak a look at Steve. I wasn't really listening to what she was saying; I was too busy taking stock of what she looked like and the only word that registered was divorce.

Sue must have tongue-lashed Steve for a good fifteen minutes and not once did she swear. I'd only seen her at a distance when we'd been collecting or dropping off the kids. I now saw that she was a green-eyed natural blonde with skin like alabaster. Sue was very beautiful. She was saying 'You did the dirt on me didn't you?' but Steve had lost his tongue. She was wearing shorts, and I'm thinking, 'Oh, she's got cat scratches all over her legs.' Her smooth-skinned, firm, ten-years-younger-than-my-legs.

When I forced myself to stop looking at Sue I noticed that Greg was staring at me intently.

'What? What is it?'

Finally he blurted it out.

'Why is your hair a different colour?'

I laughed self-consciously as I raised a hand to my carroty hair and muttered that I'd used the wrong hair dye. Sue turned her head and fixed her green eyes on me. I quaked in my boots.

'Can't you get it the colour you want?' she asked, not unkindly.

Phew!

Now that's style. Steve didn't utter a word. I felt a bit sorry for him but couldn't help but feel full of admiration for Sue. After her visit I couldn't stop thinking about her. Now I know why the trend of making the criminal come face to face with the victim has proven so successful in the fight against crime. I felt unclean, she was so *nice*. I said as much to Steve and tried to prod him to tell me what had gone wrong with the marriage; I wasn't the first woman he had had an affair with. He was pretty vague, but it seemed the rot had set in when she'd waited until they'd got married to tell him she didn't like the way he kissed. He said the marriage had deteriorated rapidly after that. That was his version.

They say two can live as cheaply as one but it isn't true. I was living on £30 a week unemployment benefit, though my rent was paid for me. Steve's moving in was catastrophic for me financially as all his money went to support Sue and the boys and to pay the mortgage on their house, because Sue had never worked. I had to somehow feed Steve as well as myself, and he could eat. I stopped buying cigarettes and went on to roll-ups instead which was something I hadn't done since I was in prison twenty years before.

Milkmen do a lot of walking and Steve's shoes were falling to bits so I broke into the rent money to buy him a new pair. The next month his car needed taxing so I used that month's rent to pay for it. Before I knew it I was up to my ears in debt, getting nasty letters and irate phone calls from my landlord. Although I only owed a couple of hundred pounds it may as well have been a million. I had the promise of *Lyn* being published but the wheels of publishing are grindingly slow. I had to look for new accommodation. Something was to happen which would make me speed up the search for a new place to live.

Because of the guilt I felt regarding Sue and the boys I got it into my head that I had to be seen, by them, to pay, and I decided I'd go out on the milk-round with Steve. I hated the thought that Sue would think I was a kept woman, even though I knew she'd be aware that he'd have nothing left over after paying for their household; she knew what his take-home pay was and she had no income of her own. But old habits die hard and I felt I had to earn my keep. Dumb I know, because it was me keeping him.

I don't know how I stuck it through the winter. It wasn't a bad round, as milk rounds go. A great deal of it consisted of Coronation Street type terraced houses, nice and close together. There were some rounds in the country where you could travel half a mile in between houses. I was scared going down the back alleys in the dark and nervous when I heard dogs bark, or saw a rat, as I did on more than one occasion. But it was the cold that got me. I'd sworn when I left Dublin I'd never put myself in a position of having to stand out in the cold again. My body clock took ages to adjust to the hours too. I was almost asleep when our round began at 3.45 a.m., though the cold soon put paid to that.

There's so much *stuff* delivered with the milk these days. In the good old times it would be milk and cream, and perhaps lemonade. I wasn't too bad with the milk, three pints for number three, two for number five, one for number seven and so on. But when it came to three pints of milk, two lemonades, and a bag of spuds for number twenty-two; one milk, two bags of spuds, a large carton of natural yogurt for number twenty-four; two milk, two double cream, a bottle of lemonade and a loaf of bread for number twenty-eight I was utterly confused. Bloody Co-op. It was all a novelty at first and I enjoyed it, I love to be active. I couldn't understand why Steve was always so reluctant to get up and out in the mornings. I later came to realise he was just a lazy sod.

Three months down the line I hated it. I hadn't even admitted it to myself and only woke up to the fact when I kept looking over my shoulder counting the full milk crates on the float and the stack was almost as high as it'd been at the start of the day. Whereas early on Steve had been pretty patient with me when I got the deliveries mixed up, now he'd started getting snotty about it.

I used to enjoy the call backs though. This was when we called back later in the day to collect the money. People were amazed to see a woman. A little Asian boy opened the door to me wide-eyed and shouted, 'Mama, mama, come quickly, it's a lady milkman!' Milkmen do quite well with their Christmas boxes, and Steve doubled his usual haul because he had a 'lady milkman' with him. I noticed a lot of generosity from the Asian people; one family left me out a silk scarf and a box of chocolates addressed to 'the lady'.

On Christmas Day, we doubled up on our deliveries so we wouldn't have to work on Boxing Day and by the time we got home we were both exhausted, and fell asleep before the Queen's speech, with no thoughts of food. We had Greg and Glen to stay with us for Boxing Day. Steve had pushed the boat out and spent all our Christmas tips on presents for them. I had told him not to get me a present, and he didn't.

One particularly cold winter morning I was walking up the driveway of a big house with three bottles in my frozen fingers, feeling mightily hard done-by, when I spotted a bunch of primroses poking through the frost. I stopped in my tracks, mesmerised by their beauty. I paused to admire them. '*And all at once I spied . . . a solitary bunch of primroses*.' I decided Wordsworth could keep his daffodils.

'Chop chop! Haven't got all day,' Steve shouted, interrupting my reverie, as he slung an empty milk-crate on the back of the float. I almost jumped out of my skin. One of the bottles slipped from my fingers and shattered on the ice. I knelt on the frozen ground to pick up the shards of broken glass thinking 'Bastard. Who the *fuck* does he think he is, with his chop, chop?'

When I got back to the float I leaned in to the dashboard to get some tissues to blow my nose and I caught sight of myself in the rear-view mirror. I looked a mess. Red-runny nose, panda eyes where my mascara had run—of course it was full-slap as usual despite the early hour—and my hair was wet and flattened to my scalp because it had started to snow. I turned to Steve.

'This is the last time I'll ever come on the round with you.'

It was too.

4

I was at a loss when I jacked in the milk round. Only then did it hit me how much time it had all taken. I'd become used to rising at 2.30 a.m. so I'd have time to put my face on and have a cup of coffee. We'd be leaving the flat at 3.15 to go to the depot to collect the milk float. It would take us twenty minutes to stack the deliveries on the float. The round was finished by around 12.30 or 1.00, when we'd drive the float back to the depot and collect the car. We'd stop off at the shops on the way home. Steve would sit in the car while I went in to get our provisions for the day. He wouldn't put his hand in his pocket for anything of course; not that he ever offered. By 3.00 p.m. I would be so tired that if I made the mistake of sitting down I'd fall asleep in minutes.

Now that I had so much time on my hands I quickly fell apart. I found I had so many thoughts tumbling around in my head I couldn't even settle to reading a book. The nightmares returned. I'd had a few bad ones before Steve moved in, but they'd disappeared. I suppose it was the comfort of human contact which helped. The thoughts were always jumbled up, and didn't make a lot of sense, but they always featured the women from the streets, police, nuns and Dolores, always Dolores.

Dolores started haunting me again. I became afraid to close my eyes at night and lay awake in the moonlight listening to Steve snoring. I wanted to talk to him to make the fear go away but he needed to sleep. As if a veil lifted from my eyes I realised I now resented Steve, but I was afraid to be alone with Dolores. I grew more and more afraid of people, and of going out of the flat to face the world, so I stopped. I locked myself away and refused to see anyone, other than Steve, my buffer from the haunting.

Steve was compelled to shop for groceries, though I paid for them, or we'd have starved. I would go for days and nights without sleep, too scared to close my eyes in case Dolores came to visit. I paced the flat, chain-smoking. I had mysterious aches and pains and illnesses; consulting my medical encyclopaedia I discovered I was suffering everything from yellow jaundice to leprosy. I scrubbed the flat from top to bottom, again and again until it smelled like a hospital, in an effort to wash away the stain of my involvement.

A letter arrived from the Environmental Health Officer addressed to the occupier saying someone would call to discuss a health issue. I was a little perplexed. Sure, I knew Steve had become lazy about cleaning up after the dogs again; I did it mostly, but environmental health? Then I thought it must be the bloody ferret; they probably thought it was cruel to keep a living creature in the shed. I presumed it was the chap who lived in the upstairs flat who'd complained, I'd seen him looking in the shed.

I went in to the garden and put my ear to the shed door and listened but couldn't hear anything. I stood for a while to make sure the ferret wasn't running loose on the floor, and hearing nothing pushed the shed door open half an inch and listened. Still nothing. It must be asleep in its basket. I pushed the door open another couple of inches, getting ready to run if I heard movement. Nothing. I pushed the door a little wider, still keeping my eyes glued to the floor. I was surprised to see the floor was spotless—I'd been expecting it to be covered with droppings from the ferret, knowing Steve's laziness in cleaning up after his animals. The silence struck me. And the stillness. I took a deep breath and opened the door fully. The ferret basket was on the shelf underneath a fishing tackle box and a big bag of dog biscuits. It took a couple of seconds to register what I was seeing, and smelling. The stench of death assailed my nostrils. I put a hand to my mouth to stifle a scream and backed out of the shed hurriedly, pushed the door closed and ran back indoors, my legs shaking.

Three weeks had passed since Steve had put the ferret in the shed, the day Sue had left it in the garden with Lick-Lick. Stacking the fishing basket and dog biscuits on top of its basket meant he obviously hadn't seen it since, hadn't fed the unfortunate creature. How could he? I felt sick to my stomach when I thought of the poor thing imprisoned in the basket, dying from hunger and de-hydration. How could Steve do that? Steve who was forever attending Weight Watchers, who loved food above all else. Why the hell hadn't he just shot the bloody thing?

The death of the ferret pushed me further along the path of total breakdown. It became entangled in the awful events which occupied my thoughts constantly. I was so rattled, just about everything made me jump out of my skin: a car door slamming, voices of people passing my window, a dog barking, even the sound of the letterbox as the postman made a delivery. I was still pacing the floor, chain-smoking, the weight dropping off me. I couldn't force myself to eat. I shrunk away from Steve, hating him for letting the ferret die.

On the rare occasions I closed my eyes and slept I had terrible nightmares: Dolores with a ferret's head, a shrunken Dolores in a ferret's basket, the ferret being buried in a coffin along with Dolores, coffins stacked in a pile of six. The bottom three contained the remains of the Lynches, the three tiny ones on top held a kitten the father of my children had killed years back, my baby sister who'd known nothing but pain in her short life, and the top one the ferret.

I finally accepted that I needed help. Steve called a doctor to the flat to see me. The doctor sent a psychiatrist to assess me. I don't remember much about it. I was hallucinating, due to lack of sleep I suppose, and had difficulty separating fact from fiction. I was given the choice of either being committed, or volunteering to get help as a day patient.

I was in no state to make a sensible decision. In a way I wanted to be committed because there's a certain attraction to just letting go, and mentally and physically I was exhausted. Yet there was a deep fear I couldn't name that stopped me from taking that route. I now realise it was the fear that once admitted as an in-patient I might never see the light of day, might never escape from the asylum.

At 8.00 each morning a mini-bus collected me from the flat and delivered me to the psychiatric day centre, along with another dozen or so patients we picked up on the way. We were given tea and coffee when we arrived and sat around waiting for our daily assessments. During the day we did some occupational therapy, but I must have been quite ill because I can't remember what we actually did. Mostly we seemed to sit around and talk to one another. I didn't notice any particular structure to any of it.

By a strange coincidence I met a woman who'd been a friend of mine twenty years previously. We stared at each other as we worked out why we were so familiar to one another; obviously we'd both changed a lot. Val was being treated for depression. Three months back she'd woken in the early hours of the morning for no apparent reason, full of apprehension. The phone had rung and she'd known before she answered it that it was to tell her that her eldest son was dead. He'd been killed in a road traffic accident. I knew the boy because I had been at his birth. Val had given me her floor to sleep on for a few nights when Craig Nelson had beaten up a friend of his in whose flat we had been staying. Val and I had given birth within a month of each other, both of us doing the right thing by our macho partners in producing sons. I felt guilty that my son was still alive, so didn't mention him, or that he was doing a three-year prison stretch.

Val asked what had happened to me that had brought me to the day centre, but I couldn't bring myself to tell her. We reminisced for an hour or so, then we retreated into our individual shells. I saw her a few times after that, just sitting and staring into space with tears streaming down her face. I turned away each time, not being well enough to help her through her grief.

The food at the day centre was good, something to look forward to as my appetite gradually returned. At lunch one day someone at the table said something—which wasn't meant to be funny—but I laughed because her face reminded me of the skinny one out of Laurel and Hardy. She had that same doleful expression. A woman at our table shook her head in admonishment and said:

'They don't like to hear you laugh.'

'Who?' I asked, mystified.

'The staff,' she replied, shaking her head in reproach. 'They think you're not ill if you laugh,' she added in a whisper.

I found myself looking over my shoulder to see if there were any staff within earshot when I spoke. It didn't make a lot of sense, as I couldn't conceive of any of us being there for any reason other than we needed to be.

Steve did all he could to help me get through my breakdown.

When I arrived home from the day centre he'd have cleaned the flat and cooked dinner. I appreciated it; all the men I'd known hadn't lifted a finger around the house. One day I arrived home to find the table laid as if for a romantic evening. He'd used a frilly bedspread in place of a tablecloth because I didn't have one. I'm a heathen when it comes to food and just shovel it in from a tray on my lap; I hate the social thing of eating in company. He'd bought candles, cooked a roast beef joint and had even picked some flowers from somewhere and put them in a milk-bottle—what else! I was greatly touched. He'd learnt all the words to 'The green fields of France', which he sang to me softly accompanied by his guitar. A song lamenting the lost youth of a whole generation wasn't the wisest of choices given the circumstances, but the fact that Steve had taken the trouble to learn it for me, knowing I loved it, meant so much to me. And I was crying for young Willie McBride, for Dolores, her mother, her aunt, my kitten, my baby sister, the ferret, my children, myself—it was like a tidal wave of grief and I couldn't stop.

I'd been attending the day centre for two weeks when I battened down the hatches and withdrew. I found a quiet spot away from the other patients and sat, brooding about the past, until they called us to do something. Now and again a member of staff would happen by. They never moved you on, merely acknowledged your presence with a nod of the head and an 'All right?' I continued in this vein for another two weeks.

The day came for me to go in front of the 'panel'. I wasn't looking forward to it; the other patients had given it a bad press. As I walked in to the large, bright, airy room six people sat in a semi-circle watching my entrance; I felt as if I was walking in to a courtroom. The doctor in the middle (nicknamed Jekyll by the patients for his moody demeanour), motioned me to a chair and I sat down, shaking all over. No one spoke. They all stared at me. I felt like the Elephant Man. It seemed ages before someone broke the silence, then most of what was said I didn't hear, I was so nervous. I felt I could have reached out and touched the hostility which filled the room; I was in the witness box all over again only this time *I* was on trial, being called to account for being me.

One of the male doctors asked a few questions about the sexual abuse I'd gone through as a child, which made me feel angry. I felt as if I was wearing the Emperor's new clothes. There were too many people in the room for my liking; I felt it a bit too voyeuristic in view of the intimacy of the details he was seeking.

A female nurse asked me what I'd been like as a child.

'Can't remember.'

Had I made friends easily? I'm forty years old, what the hell kind of a question is that? I told her that I'd never liked a lot of people round me and had always limited myself to one friend, be it male or female.

'I can't cope with more than one person at a time,' I added, inadequately.

She asked me to elaborate. Suddenly my heart was pounding, 'I can only cope with one betrayal at a time,' I said defiantly, glaring at her.

The strange thing was they never asked me about the murders. When I'd first got to the day centre I'd given the examining doctor a *Magill* magazine, which had published a detailed account of what had happened in the murder trial, because I couldn't tell him to his face. I thought that he might think I was making it up, that I was really was crazy. Giving him the article was my way of explaining why I was at the hospital. They left me to sweat for a while as they whispered to one another and made notes. I continued staring out of the window because I had cottoned on to the fact that they'd already made up their minds about me. I wouldn't find my salvation there. They said I could go.

They sent for me later in the day. Dr Jekyll told me I wasn't mad. I knew that. He said my problems, the anxiety, the depression and the insomnia were the result of the life I'd led. I knew that too; what I needed was help to teach me how to live with my past. And as to the allegations of sexual abuse:

'I may not have flown in from California but I suggest they were planted in your head in Dublin.'

I could barely speak, a rare phenomenon. I stood up, picking my handbag up off the floor as I pushed my chair back.

'Thanks for your help Doctor,' I said dryly as I walked out the door in a huff.

I couldn't say what I really felt but when I got home from the day centre I wrote Dr Jekyll a letter suggesting he read *Freud: The*

Assault on Truth by Paul Masson. I also told him that he should be aware how harmful his dismissive attitude was to his patients and that he needed to do a little work on his bedside manner. I don't for one minute think that my letter made the slightest impression on him, but it sure as hell made me feel a lot better. Professional arrogance was what ailed Jekyll. Because I'd been treated in Dublin, and the therapy I'd had was quite new and forward thinking, the English doctor looked down his nose at it. He'd asked me about my holistic treatment in great detail and then had proclaimed that it probably had its roots in California. He intimated that the Paddies were a load of idiots when it came to therapy. Arrogant Brit.

What had really hurt was his assertion that my accusations of sexual abuse against my father weren't true. I should have sent him a gynaecological photograph of my mutilated genitalia. Dr Jekyll was simply hostile to me, Ireland and Irish psychiatry. Had he but known it, my Irish doctor was a professor of psychiatry, trained in Dublin, London and a graduate of Harvard University in Boston. I had a lot of anger in me at the time, which probably saved me. I imagined some timid little soul coming up against Dr Jekyll in similar circumstances to mine, and he could have destroyed her.

Before I could leave the day centre the nurse who'd asked about my childhood caught me by the arm and led me to a room where she asked me to sit until I calmed down. I launched a tirade of abuse at her concerning Dr Jekyll. She smiled, and agreed he hadn't much of a bedside manner, but she insisted he had the best interests of the patients at heart. We looked at one another for a few seconds weighing each other up, and then she advised me it was time I learned to trust people. Hah! I laughed bitterly. She studied me in silence, which put me on the defensive.

'Look. I wouldn't give *that* lot the satisfaction of telling them, but have you *any* idea what it's like to grow up without ever meeting a *single* person you can trust?'

A professional listener, she smiled, but didn't reply.

'Well let me just tell you. My father couldn't be trusted with any kid, let alone his own.'

I began counting on my fingers.

'I couldn't trust me mum an inch, she sold me down the river a million times. I got pissed off with her using me for a bloody punch bag so I hitchhiked all the way to London to see Granny. Hah! So what happens? Granny turns me away at the door.' The nurse wore a slightly bored expression that said she'd probably heard it all before, but she obviously decided to let me spit it all out because she didn't comment. The silence stretched out.

'Imagine your own granny turning a thirteen-year-old girl away at 10.00 at night? And before you say anything, yes, I know it was no time of night to call on an old woman. I know that *now*, but I was just a kid then. It wasn't even the fact she wouldn't let me in—it was a bit much to expect—there's not much maternal instinct in our fucking family. It's the way she said it: "Can't come in Lynda. And don't be hanging around in the neighbourhood either; I don't want the neighbours to see you hanging around on the doorstep in the morning." Don't try to tell me about trust.'

My arms were so tightly crossed across my body my breasts were sore. I'm useless with silence when I'm with strangers and the nurse waited me out.

'I pleaded with her to at least let me stay out the back, but oh no, she couldn't even do that. I coulda been murdered!' I added dramatically.

When I'd finished the nurse looked at me as if to say, do you feel better now? But I didn't, I was filled with self-loathing, I hated myself for letting my guard down, for pouring my heart out, for admitting the pain of betrayal I'd felt through the years, but I couldn't take the words back. I got this impulse to scream and claw my face to shreds, my hands were clenched so tight my long nails cut into my skin. What the hell was happening to me?

She said she would come to the flat to see me over the following days, when we would work out a strategy for getting me to face going out. As it happens I thought she was OK, but the fact that she was one of the panel brought out feelings of resentment and mistrust in me and I told her not to bother, I'd sort my own problem.

I realise now that going in front of the panel was part of the therapy, that it forced your grievances against life out in the open, helped lift the lid off all the suppressed anger. The anger had to go somewhere, I guess, which was why the poor nurse had had to listen to a forty-year-old woman complaining that her granny had turned her away. God, I still feel hot when I think of it.

Oddly, as I heard my self-pitying voice going on about the betrayal by the women in my family part of my brain was saying: 'What? I didn't know you thought that!'

It was a revelation to me. I'd wasted all my energies, my intellect, just struggling to stay alive all my life, and had never bothered, or had the time to look too deeply inside myself, to analyse my hang-ups. So I hadn't understood where my deep mistrust of people, women especially, originated. It was a given that no man could be trusted, but I made allowances for them because they knew no better. Women, on the other hand, were supposed to be gentle and caring. Where these ideals sprang from I don't know; probably from my Catholic upbringing and the concept of the Virgin Mary as the perfect woman that I'd had drummed into me. Obviously I hadn't met any women who lived up to the mythology, and so I had judged all women harshly by the standards of my mother, my grandmother and the nuns I'd encountered in Hammersmith House.

Maybe it was just bad luck, but when I left home to get away from my mother and got in trouble and was sent to prison, I met some cruel, spiteful prison officers who compounded what I felt about women. It wasn't until I started mixing with prostitutes that I knew there was such a thing as a soft woman. I suppose it was their vulnerability, as well as lack of self-esteem, which had led them to choose, or be coerced into, a life on the streets in the first place, so it's not that odd an assertion really.

Time has taught me that my beliefs were unfair to both sexes. I can no longer make allowances for the evil that men do because I now know that not all men are bad, and that not all women are made from the same mould as the women who'd influenced my earlier life.

I'd put all my eggs in one basket and had used the day centre as a lifesaver, thinking the answer to my suffering lay there. Of course the answer really lay where the suffering sprang from, in my own thoughts. For three days and nights I still paced the floor smoking roll-up after roll-up as I figured out where to go from there. On the fourth day I slept for ten hours and when I woke I got dressed and went to the corner shop to buy cigarettes. Thus the cycle was broken.

I have never truly recovered from the phobia about leaving the house, but it is better than it was. I coped as best I could at that time.

I found a book called *Self-Help for Your Nerves* by Dr Clair Weeks and took a small measure of comfort from it, feeling the fear, but doing it anyway. Every couple of months or so I got up the courage to travel to the supermarket, as opposed to going fifty yards to the corner shop. Even then it wasn't always a success and I'd have to abandon the shopping trolley half way through my list and hurry to the bus stop, breathing through a brown paper bag.

I was still getting nasty letters from my landlord over the rent I owed. I saw an ad in the evening paper inviting people to apply for re-housing in the roughest area in the city. Single people and couples without children welcome to apply, it stated. I knew of the area's reputation, but I thought Steve and I would give it the once-over because we had to move soon before we came face to face with my landlord.

The neighbourhood was even worse than I'd remembered it from twenty years back. Visually it hadn't been any worse than any other working-class council estate, but it had quickly earned itself a reputation for petty crime and vandalism, and decent people would be reluctant to give it as their address.

It certainly had deteriorated over the past twenty years. There were broken windows everywhere, some boarded up, graffiti-covered walls and doors, hardly a fence left standing on any of the gardens. 'Gardens'—that was a terrible misuse of the English language if ever there was one, they were nothing but rubbish tips. There was more litter on the streets than on the council tip. Scruffy kids and scruffier dogs abounded. The house with 'Beware Guard Dog' written with a paintbrush on the front gate had an ancient washing machine in the front garden, and a tin bath that obviously predated it dumped on top. By the looks of the guy sitting on the doorstep smoking a fag he'd never been acquainted with either. It was all too depressing for words. In *Anna Karenina* Tolstoy wrote: 'There are no conditions to which a man cannot become accustomed, especially if he sees that all around him live in the same way.' I've since discovered this to be true, but as we drove home we decided we didn't wish to become accustomed.

The very next day, fate dealt us a hand in the form of an unsigned letter. The letter read: 'Found you, you bastard. I hear you've found yourself another toy boy. What is it with you? Can't you find a man your own age? Don't think you're safe there. You can't hide. I've already written to Cullen in Portlaoise and given him your address.'

Craig Nelson had found me. I had been half expecting it. He was an arrogant man with a huge ego that had been badly bruised when I'd walked out on him, and he got a kick out of finding me no matter where I lived and sending me threatening letters as proof of his success. He was in touch with our two sons and I knew he was very adept at getting information out of them. I can't begin to explain how terrorised I felt when I opened the letter.

I rang the City Council right away and asked them to send me an application form for housing in the 'Bronx', as the area we'd gone to look at the day before was commonly known. I also rang the local police. To give them credit they sent two plainclothes policemen round to see me within a couple of hours. They turned out to be from the anti-terrorist squad. They had already done their checking into what I'd told them about my links with Ireland and John Cullen. While John Cullen was only beginning his life sentence I was in grave danger from friends of his, or other villains who had grievances; they hate it when you climb out of the lobster pot.

The two cops brought me a panic button, which was linked to the local police station. I always thought of a panic button as a dainty little button like a doorbell. In reality the device was housed in a shoe box and was as heavy as a couple of house bricks, though that was twenty years ago and they're probably very sophisticated now. The thing is neither Steve nor I felt any safer. Having been continually on the receiving end of extreme violence I know that it only takes seconds for a lot of damage to be done and I was mortally afraid of what could happen to Steve and me. Poor old Steve, he was certainly getting more than he bargained for. I can't remember what excuse he gave to Sue but obviously we couldn't have the boys to sleep over, which was a relief to both of us because our nerves were shot.

Now Steve joined me when I paced the floor, scared to speak in case we missed a noise. When we eventually plucked up the courage to go to bed we left the shotgun—loaded and ready to shoot—standing up beside the wall. If the dogs had been there we could at least have gone to bed safe in the knowledge they'd alert us if they heard a noise, but there's never a gundog around when you need them—Steve's father had borrowed Zach for hunting, and when I'd been going to the day centre Steve had lent Lick-Lick to an old lady whose Jack Russell had got run over. The old lady soon fell in love and Lick-Lick was equally smitten, so we hadn't the heart to take her back.

The panic button was sited in the front room so during the day you could forget about the danger for periods of time, but I felt the vulnerable spot were the French windows in the bedroom and we had to go through there to the bathroom. Clever sod Steve rigged up a trap with a tripwire stretched taut between the French windows and the door to the bathroom. If you accidentally touched the tripwire it set off a mini explosion via two shotgun cartridges out of which Steve had taken three-quarters of the ammunition—not wanting to kill either of us—something along the lines of the bird-scarers you hear in the country. When he'd set it up he made me practise stepping over the tripwire and I was under strict instructions not to forget it was there. We slept not too badly that night.

Unfortunately, staggering out to the loo in the moonlight in the middle of the night, half-asleep, your concentration is zero and . . . Bang! Bang! The first time I did it I wet myself with fright. I thought I was being shot at. Well I suppose I was, only it was friendly fire. In the still of the night all sounds are magnified anyway and the two shotgun blasts in such a small space terrified me. Night after night I did it. I figure the reason was the crazy situation. We were so wound up that it took us ages to fall asleep in the first place and when we did we just died. The odd night I made it safely to the bathroom without tripping the wire I sat on the toilet as pleased as punch with myself, only to trip over the bloody thing on the return journey. It was like a sodding French farce. We abandoned the tripwire a week later by which time the skirting boards were destroyed and the carpet and lower wall was blackened from the explosions.

Once more the gods smiled on me because about a month after Craig's unsigned letter the City Council rang to offer us a three-bedroomed house and set up a viewing. Steve and I went to have a look at it. It was in pretty bad shape, but nothing effort and motivation couldn't fix. It was a house. And a new beginning.

5

We didn't have two pennies to rub together moving in, but we were relieved to be away from the flat with its panic button, and panic stations. I love DIY, as did Steve and we both set to decorating, hammering and fixing the place up to make it habitable.

Steve got fed up doing the milk-round not long after I stopped helping him, and went to work for a friend of his who was a plumber. One day I was standing on a ladder in the lounge in my black fur coat—I was as usual frozen to the bone, and we had no fire—helping Steve who was up in the attic feeding new wiring for the light fitting through the ceiling, when there was a knock on the door. I got down off the ladder in annoyance to see who it was. A man with a clipboard stood on the doorstep.

'Mrs Ahmed?' he enquired.

'No, she's moved. I'm the new tenant.'

'Have you got a television?' Who hasn't? What a dumb question.

'Of course, it's on now. Can't you hear it?'

'I can indeed,' he smiled. 'Have you got a television licence for it?'

Shit! I thought he was one of my new neighbours trying to flog me a telly. I had to go to court, and I got fined £75. I was also compelled to buy a TV licence, the first I'd ever had. In my previous existence I'd never lived at any address long enough for any of my bills to catch up with me, but within weeks of moving into the house I had a shoebox full of the sodding things and I was getting a fair idea of why straight people always looked so bloody miserable.

The house was nearer to where Sue and the boys lived and Greg and Glen took to coming round to us after school, which was nice for them and for Steve. Sue hadn't let the grass grow under her feet and had picked up with a Jamaican man. The guy had a little six-year-old boy named Darryl and Steve's kids used to bring him when they came to see us. Darryl was a lovely little lad, very polite; I felt sorry for him, because he was the only black kid in the school and was teased constantly. Steve was miffed that Sue had gotten herself a black boyfriend, but to his credit, he was kind to Darryl.

The only fly in the ointment for me was Glen, Steve's eldest son. Glen was ten years old, going on thirty-five and always at Steve's side. He didn't say a great deal; he didn't have to—his eyes said it all. He made it clear he detested me, so of course I couldn't stand him either. I decorated the toilet and was chuffed with the result; Greg and Darryl thought it looked great and offered to help me clear the painting paraphernalia away, they were very willing kids. I went to use the loo one day and discovered Glen had smeared shit all over the walls. I decorated the small bedroom, my room, and Glen *accidentally* tripped and spilt a bottle of coke all over the wall near the window. As it was wallpaper I had to strip the wall and redo it. Whenever I complained to Steve, Glen always played the innocent. I'm sure Sue was glad, and who could blame her.

Time and distance enables me to say I can understand how hard it must have been for Glen. His dad was gone off with a new woman and a new dad moved into his house, plus he had to accept a new brother. I think Glen hated Darryl even more than he hated me. At the time, of course, I didn't care about Glen's point of view, I only knew he was giving me a hard time. I forgot I was forty years of age and acted like a ten-year-old.

Around that time my first royalty cheque finally arrived from my publishers. On the day it came I was brimming over with excitement. In the bad old days when I walked the streets it would only have amounted to three or four weeks pay, but in my poverty-stricken circumstances it was like manna from heaven. I was brushing my hair, getting ready to go to the bank to lodge it, when Steve said perhaps it would be a good idea to open a joint account with him. I was thunderstruck. I stopped brushing, and looked at him in the mirror: 'What on earth for?'

'Well, Sue and I always had a joint account,' he said reasonably.

Hah!

'Yeah, and look what that got you. You've done nothing but moan about her running your bloody Barclaycard up to the hilt after you left.'

He had the grace to look embarrassed. I continued talking as I resumed brushing my hair.

'I can look after my own money thank you; I don't need you to supervise it.'

I would have thought nothing of giving him half my money, but Steve had proven himself to be tight-fisted, with no generosity of spirit, and there was no way I was going to give him power over my finances. Even at the time I surprised myself by my refusal and was inordinately proud that I'd finally said 'no' to a man.

I left the house at 9.30 a.m. and was still at the bank at 11.15. I hate Barclays Bank. OK, so I hadn't got a bank account, but I'd gone to the bank armed with enough identification to equip six illegal immigrants and still the bank refused to let me open an account, or to let me cash my cheque. I felt like an impostor. Heads were looking out of the office window at me and at one point I wondered if it was a case of mistaken identity. Were they confusing me with someone else, someone who'd managed to put one over on the bank or something? I wondered if the hold-up was a delaying tactic to keep me there until the police came. Then Steve arrived.

My first thought was that Steve must have been worried sick that I'd buggered off with the money, which of course was the reason he'd followed me down. I explained the situation to him and he had a word with the bank manager and offered to give me a reference, as he banked with Barclays himself. Barclays agreed to let me open an account, but first of all the bank manager rang Julian, my agent, who had issued the cheque, to ask him to describe what I looked like. If I won the lottery ten times over I would never put a penny in a Barclays Bank.

As soon as the cheque cleared I gave Steve £500 to buy a car he'd had his eye on. Yeah, I know, but this was my idea. I had been able to say 'No' when I needed to. My next stop was the dry cleaners to collect some curtains I'd left in, but unfortunately they'd been sold to defray the cost of the cleaning because I hadn't collected them in time. I could have cried. They were wall-to-wall, floor-to-ceiling Sanderson print I'd brought with me from Dublin. The cost of the dry-cleaning was £48 back then, and the awful thing is I knew when I was leaving them in I wouldn't be able to afford to get them out, but had been too embarrassed to admit it in the shop. The rest of the money I spent on furnishing the house and within two weeks I was broke again. It was lovely spending the money though.

The last room I decorated was the box-room. It was a very small odd shaped room, and was earmarked as a junk-room, but I didn't want any reminder of previous tenants. It's nice when you get your own smell in a house. When I'd put all the painting gear away and hoovered the new carpet I sat on the floor to have a ciggie and admire my handiwork. As I inhaled I heard an echo to my breathing. I sat motionless and listened. There it was again. The hair on my forearm stood up and I got a shiver down my back. There was this soft rhythmic breathing, rising and falling. I'd been holding my breath so I could listen and I let the air out of my lungs and got up from the floor in a hurry and out of the door faster than a hare.

I always end up having a room to myself when I'm in a relationship, as I really hate sleeping with anyone and when I went to bed that night I lay there pondering exactly what I'd heard in the box-room. I listened intently. There it was again. Only the breathing sounded laboured and quite loud because the rest of the house was asleep. I thought it might have been Steve so I lay perfectly still and concentrated on the sound. It wasn't coming from the other side of the passage where Steve was sleeping. I homed in on Steve's room then discovered that if I held my breath I could hear him snoring faintly. I got out of bed and went to the door and stood stock still listening. In a few seconds I was able to separate the two different breathing patterns. I knew perfectly well that there was no-one else in the house because I'd checked all the rooms—including the wardrobes and under the beds—before retiring for the night as I've always done wherever I live. I wasn't afraid exactly, just slightly spooked.

As it was only a matter of weeks since I'd attended the day centre I hadn't told Steve about the breathing in case he would worry he had indeed taken up with a head-case. I was worried that my anxiety was causing me to hear things that weren't there, or to imagine things.

I'd become quite friend

me and during one of our cha

heard in the box-room.

'Thing is Mandy, I daren't te

I joked.

Mandy turned as white as a she

'If I tell you something it won't ma

I smiled nervously, but assured her

She told me that a little baby girl

She'd been about six months old and

difficulties. Mandy told me I looked as whit

When I got back to the house I told Steve ad told me. I said that I hadn't dared to mention hea reathing in case he thought I was going round the bend. He id solemnly:

'I heard it too Lyn. I thought I was going round the twist myself and I daren't mention it to you in case it pushed you into a breakdown.'

We both saw the humour in that.

That night I went and sat on the floor of the box-room and talked to the little girl before I went to bed. I sat perfectly still until the breathing started and then spoke to her in a low soothing voice until the breathing stopped again. I didn't feel crazy doing it, now I knew I hadn't imagined it. I made her my last port of call for ages afterwards, before climbing into bed at night. I guessed she was lonely and didn't want to be alone. I didn't notice when the breathing ceased, I just sat on the floor to say goodnight to her one evening and realised I hadn't heard her in a while.

Sadly the little girl wasn't the last person to die an untimely death in the box-room, nor even the last child to die in the house. Mandy always said it was an unlucky house. Neither of us knew how prophetic she would be.

Mandy earned a little money on the side to supplement her social security by pairing socks and I used to give her a hand whenever I dropped in. We'd sit with a huge cardboard box on the floor between us containing hundreds of pairs of socks, which we'd examine and pair. You didn't realise you were working at first because you'd be too engrossed in conversation; it was our version of an American quilt. The chats were a tad one-sided because I never did [illegible] Mandy got very bad back pain from [illegible] socks so I did them on my own for two [illegible] sat propped up in an armchair. I figured she'd [illegible] of the money when she got paid for them but she [illegible] she did buy me a packet of cigs), and I hadn't the heart [illegible]ention it. She had three kids to look after.

You'd think I'd have learned my lesson, but no. Mandy, her husband and the kids went to stay with friends for a few days and she left me her house keys to go in to turn the lights on and draw the curtains. I thought it would be a good chance to earn some money for myself so I hefted boxes of socks next door to my house. For four days I worked from 9.00 through to bedtime sorting, pairing, labelling and boxing socks and I worked out I'd earned £37; homework wages have always been scab labour. Mandy was thrilled to bits when she got back and saw the finished quota. I'd already spent the £37 ten times over and could hardly wait for payday. I saw the sock van pull up outside her house the following Thursday so knew she'd been paid. Thank you God, I was dying for a ciggie. I waited for a respectable interval then went next door. Mandy put the kettle on and we chatted for a bit. She got up to make the tea.

'Are you not going to take your money?' she asked, nodding to the mantelpiece, as she left the room.

I stood and stared at the £5 note in disbelief. I wasn't sure if I wanted to laugh or cry. I liked Mandy enormously so I couldn't bring myself to say anything but that was the last of the sock pairing as far as I was concerned. I didn't have the courage to say why I now sat and watched as Mandy worked; it wasn't easy for me to do. Mandy never remarked on it.

I reconciled myself to being skint most of the time. I still got some royalties every six months for a year or two, which staved off the worst of the poverty, so felt rather lucky compared to my neighbours. I was just grateful to have survived. I saw refugees on the news, fleeing drought, famine, guerrillas, floods or persecution, having lost everything. I saw the despair etched on their faces and it hit home just how self-indulgent my fears were; any one of them would have loved the luxury of deciding whether to go out or stay home. I knew how lucky I was, to be living in the affluent west and I thanked God for the roof over my head, the food in my belly.

6

Now that I'd moved from the flat and felt safe—for the time being—I wrote to Craig Nelson just to let him know he wasn't the only one who could play hide-and-seek. I have lost count of the times he's discovered my whereabouts since I left him in 1979. He always followed through with threatening letters and phonecalls, both to me and anyone who knew me. He'd once sent me a bullet through the mail from Israel saying 'This one's got your name on it', when he'd taken my children to live there after I left him.

His taunt about me having a toy-boy was a bit rich seeing as he was living with a girl sixteen years his junior; he hadn't got room to talk about the eight-year age difference between Steve and me. I don't think Craig needed a nubile body as a bit of arm candy so much as a blank canvas to paint his views and overpowering personality on. He always said he hated women of his own age because they were too smart-assed and bitter. For 'smart-assed and bitter' read 'not gullible'.

My heart sank whenever I picked up the mail and saw his handwriting on an envelope. I knew I would have to up sticks yet again. It was a pointless exercise anyway because he always used a mixture of threats and intimidation and the parental fear they felt for him to force one or other of my sons to tell him where I'd moved to.

I left him many times over the fourteen years I lived with him and each time he caught up with me he caused such misery to the people who sheltered me that I would end up totally isolated, leaving me no alternative but to go back to him. I was always reluctant to make a friend of anyone because I knew their lives would not be worth living because he would hound them to death with threats, letters and phone calls as punishment for their involvement with me, long after I'd returned to him.

He is the most tenacious person I have ever known and he would hold a grudge for ever, which is a very effective weapon in his arsenal because the kind of shallow friendships I made in my old life couldn't withstand that kind of pressure. Of course my girlfriends would turn against me; who needed a friend like me? After it happened a second time I gave up on friendships, further isolating myself, and I now realise that by the time I met John Cullen I'd painted myself in to a corner, with no support system.

The kids and I were all scared to death of Craig, especially when he was drunk. He wasn't a monster when he was sober, though he was far more dangerous then because his punches were calculated, measured and accurate, whereas in his cups he often missed.

According to my sons their dad's girl was jealous of me, because Craig was obsessed by my leaving him, even though seven years had passed. I had never met Sara but she once sent me some photographs of her and Craig taken in a photo-booth (she looked like a schoolgirl, pretty little thing, hair in a long pony-tail), along with a letter telling me how much she loved him, and slagging me off for walking out on him. She ended it by telling me that he was unaware she was contacting me. Codswallop, of course. Craig Nelson was a total control freak and it had his hallmark all over it. I've lost track of the letters to people he dictated to me who displeased him and it made me smile to picture him leaning over Sara's shoulder as she wrote.

I knew Sara's dictated letter was intended to make me jealous, but it didn't have the desired effect. Craig didn't know me at all. I wanted to cry for Sara. She appeared to be a nice, friendly, respectable girl with a scar-free face. I bet if I saw an up-to-date photo her face would resemble a jigsaw. She wouldn't have to have done much to earn it either, something as simple as forgetting to salt the potatoes would do it, which was one of my party pieces.

We'd all sit down to the dinner table and Craig would take his first mouthful—no salt! I'd be knocked off my chair with a punch, the table would be up-ended, dinner splattered over all of us and on the floor, the kids cowering, not daring to cry or they'd be in more trouble. Mealtimes became an ordeal for me and the boys; they'd be hovering at the kitchen door, ostensibly tapping a football or some such but really keeping an anxious eye on me as I cooked in case I forgot the salt. I got so scared I often salted the potatoes two or three times, not convinced I'd already done so, thus rendering them inedible and earning another beating. After I left him I couldn't look at a boiled potato for ages. And forget looks, job prospects or even moustaches, spuds became a litmus test in future relationships with men. If they didn't shout the roof off when I forgot the salt I was full of gratitude.

My son Joey told me that he felt sure Sara would not like it if she knew that Craig had written to me because she would view it as a declaration that he still loved me, rather than the outward show of his bruised ego that it actually was. Though Craig always succeeded in frightening me into moving house each time the dreaded letter arrived I don't think he realised that I'd only done so because, frankly, I couldn't stand the nuisance value. That man and his ego were a giant pain in the neck, and I just craved a quiet life. It wasn't that I felt brave enough not to fear him that I state this, but hell, there was the Irish Sea separating us! Now that I was back on British soil though I couldn't afford to be blasé and his saying he'd informed John Cullen of my whereabouts put a new perspective on things. Yet I decided that I was done running.

I carried on decorating the house and going about my daily business, all the while mentally composing various letters to him filled with pages of sarcastic brilliance. In the end I decided that less is more. I wrote: 'Craig, This is tiresome. You have my children. What more do you want? Do what you feel you must. Lyn' I wrote it on a postcard so he wouldn't be able to hide the contents from Sara. He must have got a shock because he never replied. Grammar-school boy he may have been, but it obviously hadn't occurred to him that I could find out where he lived too. I had never asked the kids his address because it would not have been fair on them, not that I was curious but my eldest son told me that his dad had moved into a flat that he moved out of and I remembered the address.

Ann, a friend of mine who recently read *Lyn* commented that Craig Nelson sounded quite *nice*. Huh? 'In comparison', she added, seeing the surprise on my face. I had to re-read the book to see how she reached that conclusion and in doing so saw that the portrait I'd painted of him was way off beam. I'd glossed over what life was like with him for two reasons; firstly, because he was the father of my children and secondly, after life with Dave Black and John Cullen Craig seemed like 'a bit of a pussycat' (Ann's description). It's my belief that John Cullen was a natural born killer, to quote Tarantino; Craig on the other hand was not. He did have scruples and morals, however twisted. Unfortunately, he also had an extremely violent and uncontrollable temper. A very complex man, he's one of only a handful I've met whom I believe could never rape a woman. On the other hand, he almost killed me.

One New Year's Eve I'd left him babysitting while I'd gone to work on the streets, but on my way home I spotted his BMW parked outside a nightclub he frequented with one of his girlfriends. He'd obviously left the kids on their own. I was already feeling sorry for myself because I was frozen to the marrow and envious of the happy people out and about enjoying the night. My spirits sank even further knowing what lay ahead of me when he came in drunk.

When I got home I put two more pairs of socks on underneath my knee length boots because he had a habit of kicking me on the shins to reinforce whatever point he wanted to make when he was on one of his drunken rampages. My legs were constantly covered in bruises. I was so used to it that I laughed with him once when we were in a shop buying him some Oxford brogues, and he jokingly asked me if perhaps he should kick me on the shins to see whether they were up to standard. I also put on another sweater and a cardigan for extra padding hoping they would help lessen the impact of his punches, while knowing they wouldn't. I settled down to wait with every fibre of my being as taut as a violin string.

At 3.30 a.m. I heard him shuffling about on the doorstep. A bad sign, it meant he was too drunk to get his key in the lock, so I stuck a nervous smile on my face and opened the door to him. He stood swaying on the doorstep. I wished him a Happy New Year. He gave me a punch on the jaw that lifted me off my feet and knocked me flat on my back in the hall. What happened next is a blur, but I dimly remember him jumping up and down on me as I lay on the carpet. I suppose I must have lost consciousness, because mercifully that's all I remember.

I woke up on the floor of the lounge the following morning wondering what I was doing there, how I got there. Breathing was extremely painful so I took shallow gasps. My mouth hurt. My right eye was closed, but I could see a little through my left one. As I raised my hands to feel my face, I saw they were bruised and swollen. My face felt enormous. I soon discovered movement was painful so I lay still and surveyed my surroundings through the slit of my good eye. The room looked as if a herd of cattle had passed through. To my right I noticed the coal shovel on the floor covered in jam and feathers. How odd. I stretched for it, held it closer to examine it, and realised that the jam was in fact bloody hair and some type of white sticky matter. What the . . . ? I lay still trying to piece it all together. Judging by the carnage, I gathered I must have put up a struggle, which caused me a miniscule particle of pride. It was to be days later that I began having blurry flashbacks of Craig hitting me on the head with the coal shovel, over and over again, and I had flashes of his arm coming down on my skull repeatedly.

When Craig woke up, he took one look at my face and moved out of the house because he said he couldn't bear to look at me, I repulsed him. I reckon it was the guilt and being confronted by his handiwork that he couldn't face. He refused to believe that he had done the damage and insisted one of my clients must have done it. I know there is such a thing as alcoholic amnesia but in this case, I think it was a load of cobblers.

Before he left he rang Michael, a gay man who used to do the odd bit of babysitting for us, and asked him to come over and clean up the trashed lounge and cook something for the kids. It was obvious I wasn't capable myself. Craig and his current lady-friend checked into Jury's Intercontinental hotel for two weeks, which proved fortuitous for me.

I'd first met Michael when he was hustling for business, dressed as a woman, when I worked the Hagley Road in Birmingham. I realise now he was little more than a kid; I was twenty. I liked him immediately; he had a great sense of humour and we became good mates. He was *my* friend, not Craig's. He was a Dubliner, married to Sadie, a friend of his who knew he was a homosexual. It was he who'd suggested I move to Dublin to work when we'd had to do a runner because Craig was expecting to be arrested for beating a guy up.

Michael was appalled at the extent of my injuries and advised me to get away for my own safety. The thought hadn't entered my head. This was my life. Michael shook his head from side to side.

'He's getting worse Lyn. He's gonna fuckin' kill you one of these days.'

I was in no condition to think about anything at that moment. Michael tidied up a bit and fed the kids. I couldn't eat because my top lip was cut, but I had some soup.

A girlfriend, Stella, came to visit me the next day and I struggled downstairs to the lounge to talk to her, but I had difficulty staying awake. She thought I was dying. She suffered terribly with her nerves and she was so distraught by my appearance she started throwing sleeping tablets down her throat.

'What's that?' she asked suspiciously, pointing to the coal shovel I'd thrown in the hearth.

'Bits of Lyn's grey matter.' I attempted a smile but my face was too swollen.

'Huh?' she frowned.

'Me bloody skull! Bastard hit me on the head with it!'

'The bastard! Tell you one thing Lyn, it wouldn't suit you to be fat!' she said, indicating my swollen face.

She opened the lounge door to go to the kitchen to make me a cup of coffee.

'The house is on fuckin fire!' she shouted, and ran out the front door, screaming hysterically. I rushed into the hall and was stunned to find it full of smoke; thick grey smoke was billowing down the stairs and you couldn't see the landing. It didn't cross my mind to phone the fire brigade and I somehow managed to take the stairs two at a time.

I somehow had the foresight to feel my way to the bathroom where I grabbed a wet nappy, which was soaking in a bucket, and put it over my nose so I could breathe. I felt my way into the kids' bedroom and screamed their names. The smoke was so dense I couldn't see the bed; I had to feel for it. I found Chris straight away, dragged him out, stood him up, and kept a tight grip on him, but I couldn't feel Joey. I roared hysterically, over and over, as I ran my free hand over the length of the bedcovers up and down, up and down, up and down, then patting, feeling, patting, feeling, patting.

Crazy by now I pummelled the bed frantically then felt a little curled up lump under the bedclothes right at the bottom of the bed. I dragged him out by the leg of his pyjamas with one hand, sobbing with relief, and carried him down the stairs, pushing Chris ahead of me as we went.

We ran out of the house and I collapsed, just as the fire brigade pulled onto the kerb. The fire crew took one look at me and presumed whoever had battered me had left me for dead and set fire to the house as a cover-up, so they called the police. I had a job convincing them otherwise.

Stella was hysterical by then. She popped another two sleeping pills. Because of the fire and the state I was in I wasn't aware she was overdosing, I later found out she ended up in Dublin's St Brendan's Mental Hospital and had her stomach pumped out.

I had acted purely on adrenaline, had felt no pain or discomfort whatsoever. But it all kicked back in with a vengeance, only I now had a sore throat, streaming eyes, and a tight chest to add to my injuries. I looked at normally fair-haired Chris, who was shivering uncontrollably, his face and hair filthy. How had I let him go to bed so dirty? I looked down at my nightdress, it was dirty too. Why is . . .? Then it registered that Chris and I were black with smoke. Joey had escaped the smoke thanks to being under the bedclothes fast asleep and didn't know what was going on.

Someone put a blanket round the kids' shoulders; I stared at their bare feet and wondered what to do about their shoes. As I stood in the road in my nightdress, I could hear people discussing the state of my face. It didn't take too long for the fire to be brought under control.

Mrs McHugh, my kindly next-door neighbour with whom I'd previously merely exchanged pleasantries, took the boys to her house and then insisted on driving me to the hospital where they stitched the cuts on my scalp. X-rays showed that I had broken ribs and a fractured skull. My face had swollen up so it looked like a purple pumpkin. My top lip was cut where my teeth had cut through and both my eyes were blackened, one of them completely shut, the other with vampire-like blood vessels. I've looked prettier.

Nature is wonderful because, as I also had concussion, I did a lot of sleeping, and the next few days passed in a haze. Because the upstairs of the house was uninhabitable and my bedroom was totally destroyed, I put the bed-settee down and the kids and I slept there. I suppose I must have managed to look after the kids in a fashion, but it's all a blur. I know Mrs McHugh fed them, and I survived the week on her wonderful homemade chicken soup. I can't even remember if I ever let her know just how much her help and kindness meant.

The insurance people sent someone to see how the fire had started and when they'd gone I noticed Chris was unusually subdued. I asked what the matter was and he asked if the police would come and arrest him. What on earth for? I laughed. Then he told me he'd gotten out of bed while Stella and I were downstairs talking in the lounge. He had starting playing with a box of matches he'd found on my locker and had set fire to my bedroom curtains, just to see what would happen. When he'd seen the flames he'd been scared witless and had run back to bed and hidden under the covers. No wonder he'd lost his appetite, poor little sod; what a big secret and a heavy burden for a five-year-old to carry. At last I knew how the fire had started.

A week later Michael called to see me and said he'd arranged for me to stay with Sadie, in Birmingham. I didn't take much persuading. Craig had only been back to the house once, and that only in response to Mrs McHugh phoning him after the fire. Even then he'd only come—accompanied by his blonde, bejewelled, fur-clad, upper-class girlfriend—to check for smoke damage to his Chester Barrie suits.

'What about you, Michael? No point me leaving. You know he'll come looking for you to find out where I've gone.'

Michael's eyes widened. 'You must be fuckin' joking! I'm going meself!' He shook his head and rolled his eyes theatrically. 'I'm not hanging around waiting for that psycho.'

I sent Michael to buy two suitcases and fetch the kid's clothes from the launderette, and mine from the dry-cleaners. While he was gone I started throwing stuff together. The kids asked if we were going on a holiday, I said we were. Michael took the ferry that night. I followed the next night.

Luckily Craig was still holed up with the girlfriend at Jury's but it was still nerve-wracking waiting for the taxi to pick me and the kids up to drive us to the ferry. I daren't even tell Mrs McHugh we were leaving.

The ferry crossing was horrendous. Our clothes still reeked of smoke from the fire in spite of having them cleaned, and the stench filled the cabin. Movement was painful due my broken ribs, and a three-year-old Joey, so traumatised by the recent events, vomited through the entire crossing. I thought it was forever, but, as usual, Craig found me, after kidnapping poor Michael from a gay nightclub and putting the fear of God into him, so that he had to tell him where I was staying. I'd had five weeks of freedom. At least it was long enough to recuperate in peace.

Chris recently told me that while he'd grown up thinking domestic violence was a normal way of life and, sadly, had himself hit women a couple of times as a consequence, he'd lost respect for his father because, as he said in disgust. 'Dad was a professional boxer Mum, and he used to hit you as if you were a man. Real men don't do that.'

Sometimes I felt Craig saw me as his opponent in the ring because I would see him mentally sizing me up and picking his punches, like when I dared to answer him back once and he gave me a classic punch in the solar plexus which doubled me over. I sank to my knees with every ounce of breath knocked out of me. I was heavily pregnant with Joey at the time. I think Joey was born depressed. He's always been sad and when I think of what he suffered in my womb, I suppose it's not surprising.

Life with Craig wasn't all doom and gloom. We had tranquil spells when we got along fine and behaved as a family should. It was he who bathed the kids and washed their hair, taught them the clock, how to tie their shoelaces and their school ties. They learnt quickly, thanks to their dad's short fuse. He wouldn't let me teach them anything because they played me up. Craig was a reader, but he drew the line at teaching them to read—he lost his rag too easily—so he left it to me.

I felt warm inside as I witnessed the kids pleasure when the letters began making sense. I watched excitedly as they experienced the euphoria I'd felt when I'd first learnt to read. It was *the* most truly happy time for me and the boys. They were both good readers by the time they started school.

However, it was I who struck the first blow in our relationship by going on the streets behind Craig's back, giving him cause to hate me. It embarrasses me to say that at the time I didn't view what I'd done as a big deal and couldn't understand what all the fuss was about. We'd only been together about three weeks and it was my body. I was only renting it out occasionally when I was desperate for money for essentials, like food and heating, not making a life choice. Sandra, the girl who got me started on the game, only did it for a couple of months before getting a job and never looked back. Had we still been hanging out together I'd have followed suit, as always, and how different my life might have turned out.

Craig should have left me when he discovered I had a self-destructive streak. However, his principles weren't so lofty that he didn't capitalise on my betrayal by making me walk the streets full time and pimping off me for years. If it was my betrayal which turned Craig into a bad guy as he claims, I wonder how he accounts for all the other women he's hospitalised (including his first wife, long before we got together). No matter who started it, the fact is that the violence intensified the longer we lived together, and the good times were just a memory; even if a good time dared to surface I barely recognised it, I knew a bad one was a micro second away. I refuse to accept that my betrayal of him was responsible for him battering our two sons. He didn't hit either of them when they were really small, but when they reached that age when kids are waking up to the fact that their parents aren't omnipotent, in this case around seven or eight, he began treating them as if they were his worst enemy.

Up to then they thought he was God. He told tall tales of his army days as the boys sat rapt in hero worship. The nearest he ever got to an army uniform was when he failed a medical at the Army Recruitment Office because of an ear problem. He had tried to enlist to escape a prison sentence. I didn't tell the boys about his army career until years after I left him, and they were grown up, because I didn't want to belittle him in their eyes.

I was shocked the first time he battered Chris. The child had done no more than fail to look suitably impressed by some stupid joke his dad had told him. I happened to be looking at his dad and I knew by his face he was angry and that he was going to start shouting at him, but the next thing he was, literally, frothing at the mouth with temper.

'When I was in the army we'd be down the glasshouse for

insubordination to an officer if we dared to smirk at him like that. March! On the double! Get your feet up laddie!'

He roared, punched and slapped Chris as he marched him up and down on the spot by the scruff of his neck. It's always shamed me deeply that I'd lived in fear of his dad for so long I made no attempt to intervene, just stood with my arm round Joey in a futile attempt at shielding him from the horror unfolding before us as we trembled in fear. That was the start of the beatings for the kids. Joey started copping it about a year later when he too reached the stage when he no longer believed everything his dad said and unfortunately for him he also looks very like me.

'You're just like your fucking mother. You've got the same stubborn, fuckin' Paddy look in your eyes. Don't you *dare* look at me like I'm a fucking idiot!' was the refrain every time he punched Joey round the room. Joey told me he got pasted on a regular basis after I left because of his resemblance to me.

'Did you hate me for it?' I asked sadly.

He nodded. He tries to pass it off with a joke today by saying he's glad he's as good-looking, but I understand the resentment and bewilderment he must have suffered. The odd thing is my mum used to batter me because *I* looked like my dad.

It wasn't just the odd slap the boys got, sometimes matters got badly out of control. I recall one particular episode when one minute the family were all having a good time horsing around then something triggered Craig into losing it and he threw Joey from the top of the stairs. Joey landed badly on his back on the half-landing where he lay in excruciating pain, crying. I knew the pain was bad because it was the one and only time he ever let his dad see him cry. I took a step forward.

'Don't even *think* about it! I'll break your fuckin legs!'

I had a flash of the coal shovel descending. I froze. He then started on poor Chris who hadn't opened his mouth. He rained punches down on him, then picked him up by his jumper and hung him on a coat-hook in the hall, and left him dangling.

So there's Joey on the half-landing on his back crying silently. Chris hanging on the coat-hook in the hall, crying and three-year-old Fiona screaming hysterically: 'Stop it daddy!' 'Naughty daddy!' Stormy, the Doberman, was lifted in the air with a kick that sent him flying into the kitchen because he dared to growl, and useless me pinned against the wall with Craig's hands round my throat almost crushing the life out of me. Happy families. It wasn't the worst beating they had by a long shot but one that sticks in my mind. That one person can have, own, so much power and total control over so many—one person who is but (when you think about it) an insignificant speck in the universe—angered me. I decided the time had come to take the kids to a safe place and I did a runner, taking Joey and Fiona with me.

I'd told Craig I was taking the kids off his hands for a bit to give him a break; at the time I was commuting to Dublin weekly. Craig grew suspicious at the last minute and scuppered my plans by refusing to let me take Chris. I was in a quandary. I didn't want to leave Chris behind but I couldn't make an issue of it or Craig would have known what I was up to. As we sat on the plane I felt weighed down by what I was intending to do but the kids were excited as hell. It was the start of a big adventure and they were unaware of the turmoil I was in. By the time the plane landed I knew I couldn't go through with it; without Chris I was leaving a part of myself behind. I knew I had no alternative but to go back at the end of the week.

Fate took a hand when Craig rang me in the early hours of the morning two days later.

'Is that you slag?' that was his usually friendly greeting when he was pissed, which always made me seethe, but I never dared react. I was dog-tired, just on the point of putting my book down ready for sleep. Bleary-eyed I looked at Fiona sleeping peacefully beside me in the bed, and at Joey who was now rousing from sleep on the settee.

'Yes it is. Pimp!'

There was a split-second stunned silence, then all hell broke loose. He screeched like a fish wife, threatening death and destruction. I put the phone down on him, signing my death warrant. I went into hiding in Dublin. Craig came over from England a few months down the line, drugged me, and forced me to go back with him to his parents' house. When they left for work early the next morning he kicked me out of bed to make breakfast for Fiona. He started shouting down the stairs for me to get a move on. He was waiting to torture me, was going to learn what I'd been up to in the time I'd been apart from him. Propelled by fear I reacted by doing a runner out the kitchen door, up the lane, across the park and on to a Midland red bus. I didn't know it when I ran, but it was to be the last time we lived as a family.

I was so brainwashed by Craig that I believed absolutely that everything that happened to the kids was my fault; that it was his anger at me that caused him to lash out at the boys. When I think of the grievous injuries he inflicted on them, long after I was just a memory to him, I find it hard to forgive him for making me believe that.

Twenty-six years have passed since I left Craig Nelson and I don't wish to turn this into a vendetta; spite and revenge are anathema to me. However, were I to omit the facts of my children's upbringing it wouldn't fully explain how and why all their lives were destroyed. I also failed the kids, over and over, by getting mixed up in bad situations, which affected their lives and I'm haunted by this. I have apologised to them numerous times, but it doesn't make it better.

One thing I can't forgive Craig is his lack of conscience about the way he treated the kids, his total denial concerning the level of violence he used. Joey had a big row with him recently when he'd bumped into him while Craig was drunk as a skunk. There's no talking to him when he's like that so Joey made the excuse that he was in a hurry because he was meeting a pal. His dad went ballistic: Joey's friends were more important than him, he, the selfless man who'd done his best for his kids, only to be treated as if he was of no account.

Joey may always have been scared to death of his dad, but a lifetime's resentment erupted and he gave vent to his own anger: a father doesn't beat his kids to within an inch of their life, does he? Craig had the gall to say he didn't know what Joey was talking about, that he may have given them the odd slap but that was all, as any good father would. Good father? Had he forgotten he attacked Chris with a machete one drunken night, slicing his arm to the bone as Chris tried to protect himself, then left him to make his own way to casualty? He attacked him with a bottle another night, just two examples of many other such incidents. Craig denied it point blank; accused Joey of fabricating, Chris too. Joey told him he'd witnessed it himself, had gone to the hospital with his brother, watched as the doctor sewed him up, twenty-seven stitches. Anyway, what about the time he attacked him, Joey, with an iron bar? Or the night he'd used a Bullworker as a weapon, or anything else that happened to be near to hand, on too many other nights to remember. Joey offered to show him the scars to help jog his memory. Craig was shaking his head, muttering 'That's not the way I remember it. Not the way I remember it at all'. He wouldn't make eye contact. He must have been astonished that the worm had finally turned. Joey ended up telling him to fuck off. So much for truth and reconciliation.

I was nineteen years old when Craig and I met and I have learned a little along the way. At sixty-two I no longer take all the blame for his mistreatment of our children. I also no longer take his violence towards me personally; he went on to treat Sara the same way, breaking her arm one drunken night.

Of all the beatings I ever had the New Year's Eve one is super-glued in my brain; it still bugs the hell out of me why the mere sight of my face filled him with so much anger. It's one thing for an argument to get out of hand, and a man who has difficulty controlling his temper lashing out in frustration, but drink or no drink I reckon you'd have to feel a whole lot of hate towards someone to unleash that level of violence. It still gives me the shivers to think someone despised me so much. Possibly, because he hated her so much—even refusing to go to her funeral because she battered him as a child—all women represented his mother. Maybe women frightened him subconsciously.

In spite of all our negative history, I thought I knew Craig Nelson well enough to know that he wouldn't actually write to John Cullen informing him where I was. As an intelligent man he would be aware of the consequences were I to be found. No, Craig's kick was keeping me on my toes, proving his superior intellect, his powers of detection, making sure that I'd never be able to forget him. As if. I'd only to look in the mirror at my scarred face. Knowing all this didn't help lesseon the fear too much though, but I made the decision to stay put and tough it out because I just couldn't face moving on before I'd even finished decorating the house.

My son Joey and his girlfriend Linda came to stay with me and Steve for a few days. Joey was nearly seventeen at the time and Linda was fourteen years older, and she mothered him. Lord knows he needed mothering. I liked Linda, she was an easy-going person and she looked after Joey very well. Joey wasn't working at the time, just getting by. I'm sure he was doing a bit of thieving too, but I didn't ask because I didn't want to hear the truth. I had enough guilt to cope with. I was disappointed when I saw that he'd started smoking as he'd always been so anti. As an adolescent he used to hang out of the kitchen window breathing theatrically when I lit a fag, and refused point blank to go to the shops for me to buy smokes no matter how much I offered as an inducement. I once tried to bribe him with a tenner if he'd fetch me a pack from the grocery van parked outside our flat in Ballymun because I'd just washed my hair when I realised I was out of them, and I was gagging, but he still refused. He's always been a stubborn sod. Still at least he had no truck with drugs, which was a small miracle in the circles he mixed in and I thanked God.

I told Joey about his dad writing to me and my reply. He said he occasionally bumped into him in Liverpool; his dad was always drunk and causing trouble with passers-by and trying to goad him to fight with them. Then he'd buttonhole him while he ranted and raved about me and the past. He always hashed up the same old gripe; Joey was a traitor to him by being in contact with me. After a few hours of this Joey would lose his temper himself and storm off. Poor Joey, all he wanted was a mum and dad, not to have to choose. Joey and I were just getting used to each other again and I was really upset when he and Linda had to go home. The emptiness I felt seemed more pronounced when I saw Steve interacting with his kids. I envied him.

In the hour before the dawn, without the alcohol dulling his brain, I wonder if Craig ever asks himself why none of our kids are still on speaking terms with him. Perhaps he wasn't too pushed about it anyway because he went on to have three more children with Sara, and then he didn't want to know our three, just as he totally blanked the two daughters he had when I met him. Some men seem to find it really easy to do that.

My eldest son Chris was doing a three-year prison stretch for grievous bodily harm. He was only seventeen at the start of the sentence and by the time I went to live in England he was coming to the end of it. It saddened me deeply that he was already on his way to being a recidivist, though it was probably inevitable with his background.

I sat across the table from Chris in the prison visiting room and watched his eyes as he filled me in on the details. He'd been badly beaten up by a gang after a football match, and a few weeks later, at an away match, he came across one of the gang, who, unfortunately for him, had become separated from his mates. Chris attacked him, leaving him in a bad state. How could you? I asked, sick to my stomach. Why so much violence? He hung his head and studied his hands for a while as the question hovered. Then admitted he felt sick when he thought of what he'd done. He hadn't set out looking for trouble that day, he told me, hadn't noticed the chap who'd been part of the gang who'd beaten him up. Chris's mate had spotted him and pushed Chris in the direction of the helpless quarry, and he'd felt pressured not to back down.

Oh how wonderful! Some poor bastard had his features rearranged because he didn't want to look a fool in front of his mates. 'You're like a load of Apaches, hunting for scalps! Who were you meant to be? Geronimo?' I still feel sick twenty years on when I think of what he did to that man.

I couldn't turn my back on him no matter what he'd done, but I had bad dreams that one day he could kill someone. If I thought his three-year jail term an arrow to my heart I was glad I had no idea what was on the horizon, because he went on to serve an eight-year term, followed immediately by a ten-year stretch. Thank God we can't see into the future. I only saw him once a month for a couple of hours for the full three years because, of course, he lost all his remission for minor infringements of prison rules, as he would insist on playing to the gallery. After the first couple of visits we didn't talk much about the reason he was in, it didn't seem right for me to keep harping on about it, so I tried to keep the visits light and neutral because prison life is pretty hard to deal with anyway.

My sons are like chalk and cheese. Joey is quiet, serious, intense and very shy. Chris is outgoing, gregarious and full of bluff and banter and it was he who cheered *me* up on the visits. I don't know how he kept his spirits up really, even allowing for the front that most prisoners feel obliged to put on.

Prison must have been hard for Chris because he's always been a bundle of nervous energy who couldn't sit still for two seconds, always had to be up and doing. If you went to a pub with him he'd be like a blur going one from one table to another chatting to people.

Within two minutes of visiting me at home the place would look as if a German Panzer division had just rolled through, pictures on the walls up the staircase at half-mast, rugs curled, ornaments flying and ashtrays overturned. When he was a child every ornament I owned was glued together. I bought him a bicycle when he was ten and he landed back at the house carrying a wheel in each hand. When he came home from school he'd throw his satchel in the back door and run off to play with his mates without as much as a slice of bread.

Unlike Joey, who'd shadow me for a while before quietly going to his room to do his homework, which he loved. As Chris grew old enough for me to laugh at his jokes he never failed to bring a smile to my face no matter what mood I'd be in and he always had loads of people around him, drawn by his good humour and personality.

My role of a mother ended forever, as it turned out, when the Lynches were murdered and I'd had to send Joey to England at the tender age of fifteen (a very naive fifteen at that), so he'd be safe. I was living with round-the-clock police protection, but it was hard on Joey not being able to go out on his own through fear of being attacked. Then word reached me that John Cullen had put the word out that Joey was to be kidnapped, perhaps killed, to frighten me off going to court.

It ripped me apart to send Joey away with no one to welcome him on the other side, no home to go to. It was too much for one so young, but I couldn't risk his life. My police escort dropped him to the ferry where I gave him £200, with instructions to distribute it inside his clothing and watched him as he walked up the gangplank, with a rock in my throat the size of Gibraltar He's not even fully grown, I kept saying to myself, he's not even fully grown.

Eventually he wrote to tell me he'd found a derelict house to stay in, along with a young drug addict, and two old alcoholics. He slept in the bath with newspapers underneath him, listening to the mice, but at least it was dry, he wrote. He went back to the house to sleep one night only to discover it had been boarded up again, with all his worldly goods inside, so had to sleep in the park. The pain I felt on reading his letters is indescribable. Poor Joey. We have parents we expect to care for and nurture us but he had to have us.

The angels must have been watching over him because he met Joanne who was a year younger than himself, fell in love, got engaged, and was welcomed into the family by her parents. They took pity on him, gave him a roof over his head and a loving home. As they were only kids the engagement was soon off. He then got engaged to the next sister up the age ladder, seventeen-year-old Vivian, who before too long decided he was too young. He then moved on to Linda, the eldest sister and fourteen years his senior, who was in the process of leaving her violent husband. What the sisters' parents made of all this I can only imagine, but Sally, the matriarch and absolute ruler of the family, joked that at least the family jewels were safe, with 'the engagement ring' staying in the family. I shall always be grateful for the love and care the whole family showed to Joey.

I took the ferry to Liverpool to visit Joey and booked myself in to the Adelphi, but Sally wouldn't hear of me staying there when there was a perfectly good bed going at hers. I was looked after as well as at a four star hotel with one of the daughters giving up her bed for me as she bunked in with her sister. Sally even had one of the girls lend me her dressing gown because their routine was to get ready as if for bed as soon as it got dark. I suppose it was a girly thing to do and I felt surrounded by love in that house. Sally was so thin she looked ready to snap. I knew she was ill, she couldn't sleep, she was in too much pain. As I was leaving I handed her an envelope but she wouldn't take it from me. I told her it was only a thank you card and left it on the settee. I'd put money in it of course, I couldn't take what little they had; but when it came to love the family was as wealthy as royalty.

Sally said she looked on Joey as the son she never had, and when she knew she was dying of cancer and was arranging her funeral she said to the priest: 'I want me daughters and me son to carry the coffin', pointing to Joey. Joey being Joey didn't bother telling me Sally was dead and I sent her a Christmas card. I was so upset when I heard about Joey carrying the coffin; he said Sally was as light as a feather. He was broken-hearted. He thought I was crying because Sally was dead. I couldn't explain that I was crying for his loss, because he'd had so little stability in his life. Sally was his family. The Goulding family probably saved his life.

7

The next four years flew so quickly I felt as if I'd been beamed there down from the future from the star ship Enterprise. I was relatively content, provided I stayed at home. Steve still played guitar, sang me songs and called me lovely lady. I was warm, well fed, and had somewhere to live. There were bad days, like the day I was skinning a chicken and it turned into a baby; I threw it on the floor and ran crying out of the kitchen in a panic. And the night I was babysitting for Mandy when a male friend of theirs knocked on the door, and I fled the house, leaving the kids, with the stranger sitting in the lounge. The guy was a friend they'd been out with, they were going to play cards, he said. The irony is it was the combination of the darkness, the night, the close proximity of a male in such a small space and the smell of alcohol wafting from him that had made me dizzy with fear. Me, who'd, spent a lifetime around men!

I still suffered panic attacks when I left the house, so I only went once a fortnight to buy groceries. It was not strictly a fear of being away from the house, but a fear of people, that I still could not overcome. On the rare occasion I was compelled to talk to a complete stranger I hurried home as if I was being chased by a bull; then stood inside the front door shaking like a leaf. The whole thing was stupid really because I can remember being like that as a child, and it made me feel as if I was regressing instead of moving forward. On particularly bad days I felt as if I was carrying my clothes instead of wearing them; my coat, especially, was as heavy as a block of concrete.

The Lynches still occupied permanent residence in my head, but the nightmares were fewer. My social circle consisted of Mandy, her husband and kids, and Karen who lived next door to them. I used to chat over the fence to the family who lived on the other side of me; they were no threat because they had four daughters, no sons. I surveyed my self-imposed boundaries through my front window one morning, fifty yards either side of me. I saw how minute my universe actually was and I knew the way I was living was unhealthy for my emotional well-being, but I still wasn't ready to join the rest of society.

I thought about the ferret a lot too. For me, the rot set in in my relationship with Steve when he let the ferret die. Sometimes we'd be in the middle of a conversation and an image of the basket on the shelf would jump into my head, and I'd turn away from him. I never told him how I felt; I've always been useless with recriminations. I had let the good things sway me. Steve always treated me with respect. He never threw my past in my face. He was kind, he marked out and dug a Star of David in the front garden and planted it up with polyanthus for me, and him a Polish Catholic. But the death of the ferret still festered.

Steve's attraction was fading for me, but I've always been a thicko when it comes to men and what's staring me in the face. I hated his laziness. I hated his gluttony. I hated the fact that he never finished any DIY job he started. And I hated when he looked down his arrogant Polish nose at me, which he did occasionally.

I had been cited as the scarlet woman when Sue filed for divorce. I'd even signed the papers when Steve asked me to. Not that we'd ever discussed marriage, it just seemed churlish not to sign. The divorce was now finalised. Steve's mother said how great it was that we were now free to marry. Steve replied with a shake of the head and a roll of the eyes.

'I don't think so!' but copped on to himself when he saw the look I shot him.

He added defensively: 'I don't want to marry anyone.'

His mother was embarrassed, I'd always got on very well with her. The speed of his response was was a revelation. After four years living with the idle sod, marriage to Steve was the last thing I wanted, but I would have *loved* the chance of refusing him! I laughed at his obvious discomfort as he sat in the chair looking down at his feet. I woke up the next morning and decided that Steve was a total waste of make-up. It was time to move on.

When you share a house and neither of you has anywhere else to go you have no choice but to make the best of it. As there was no animosity between us it wasn't as difficult as it would have been had we hated each other. So we just drifted along, while going our separate ways. I still sat in every night, but Steve took to going to pubs, on the lookout for a bit of skirt. I got myself a cleaning job for an Irish couple with three children. They'd lived in England for years so their accents were a bit diluted and it was only when I met the family that I discovered they were Irish. I would not have taken the post had I known; it was a bit too close to home in view of the fact that I was undercover. I started off doing two mornings a week. The pay was crap but it kept the wolf from the door.

I was used to going to bed at 6 p.m. because we couldn't afford to run the gas fire. Steve would watch TV while I read; somehow it wasn't the same on my own. I still read voraciously out of habit, but most of what I read went right over my head. My thoughts kept wandering to Dolores and John Cullen. I saw how Steve's company had helped shield me from the fallout from the past.

Within no time Steve met a woman he liked well enough to move in with. (She was a great kisser, he said.) I packed all his belongings, making sure there was nothing in the house he'd paid for. We wanted to part as friends, it wasn't that we'd hurt one another, we'd just drifted apart. We packed the car with all his belongings then we had a sort of last supper together. We chatted as we ate. We agreed that our break-up was sad, and neither of us could really pinpoint what had driven us apart. Though Steve did say he didn't like the way I kissed! I laughed and made light of it saying:

'Sorry! I grew up on early Hollywood kisses . . . no tongues and all that yackymatut . . . uh!

Steve shook his head sadly and said: 'Mmm. I never could understand why you couldn't have been a bit more adventurous with sex, what with you being on the game an' all.'

Bastard. 'The price wasn't high enough!' I shot back, accompanied by a phoney smile. It had taken him four years to show himself.

A few weeks after he left, his mother came to see me. She was a very devout (convert) Catholic, and while she disagreed with Steve leaving Sue she had taken a great liking to me and had prayed for the divorce to come through so that we would get married. (Mind you, I don't think Steve had told her about my past.) I made us a cup of tea and we sat making chitchat. She looked rather uncomfortable, but I presumed it was because her son had, in her eyes, all but abandoned me. She said she was really sorry it hadn't worked out with me and Steve; she'd been looking forward to having me for a daughter-in-law.

'I'm sorry if this pains you Lynda, but I have something to tell you,' she said, in obvious distress. 'Steve and Angela are getting married.'

Well, you could have knocked me down with a feather, I was so shocked. I wasn't jealous, but I was miffed and insulted that I hadn't been good enough to ask. I thought of what my sister had said when I'd asked her what possessed her to marry for the second time and she'd shrugged and said: 'Why not? We were living together anyway, if I'm good enough to live with I'm good enough to marry.'

Months passed. It was nice to have the place to myself. I cleaned and cleaned excessively, there wasn't a speck of dust in the house. I then went over to my sister's house to clean hers, it was a proper paid job. She is almost crippled with the pain of arthritis and has always employed a cleaner so it seemed the logical solution to offer me the job after she sacked a woman. My sister kept lodgers and the kitchen was like a tip—not one of them cleaned up after themselves—so I earned my £3 an hour.

Samantha, my sister, is a big softie, a bleeding heart for the whole of humanity who always tries to help people. She never sees the bad in people. One of her lodgers was a man who was a depressive with a severe drink problem and Samantha asked me to talk to him and see if I could help him. She'd tried, but hadn't got anywhere.

'Will you try Lynda? You're good with people. People know you're kind and sympathetic, people listen to you because they know you care.'

Gosh! Sam is not daft, she knew such flattery would appeal to my vanity; how could I resist? I took over her missionary work.

His name was Jeff. He was forty years old, tall, dark and handsome, a Brian Ferry lookalike. He wore a look of perpetual sadness; a lethal cocktail for my sister to foist on me, in retrospect.

But Sam didn't really know me at all. We'd been separated when she'd emigrated to Australia when she was fourteen, she was six years younger, and I left home at seventeen. We hadn't spent much time together prior to that either as we'd both spent years in children's homes.

I would chat to Jeff in the kitchen when I'd finished my cleaning; we got along well. Sam used to poke her head round the door, a benevolent smile on her face, to see how we were progressing. I don't think I was much use to him, his depression and his drinking habits were too deep-seated. It was a case of the blind leading the blind anyway, I was still trying to get my own act together. One of us should have thought of that.

Sam rang me late one night to say Jeff was threatening to harm himself and would I take a taxi over and try and calm him down. He was asking for me. Say no more. I set off on my white charger with my 'Male in Distress' signal flashing and raced to the rescue.

'What kept you?' Jeff asked, plaintively, as I rushed through to the kitchen.

'I'm here now,' I soothed.

'I know. But I needed you earlier,' he said petulantly. 'I'm ok when you're here.'

I was hooked instantaneously, like a trout: that knew the fishhook held a maggot—not a tasty sprat—but ignored what it knew. Fool. Fool. Fool! Jeff's eyes were full of pain and suffering, as if he'd just returned from the Somme. It was to be four years before I discovered where this well of suffering sprang from. I wish he'd had enough trust in me to share it with me.

Jeff maintained that he was ultra sensitive, as indeed he was, but I think it was Oscar Wilde who said a sensitive person is one who because he has corns himself always treads on other people's toes. Jeff sure as hell trod on mine. He was scrupulously honest in his dealings with me. He insulted me on a daily basis and never bothered to pretend he even liked me. And of course I loved him for it. I was on call whenever he needed me. I took his washing back to my house and did it for him. I mended his clothes, attended to his affairs, and I looked after his son when he had visiting rights. I listened to his problems. I shared bottles of wine with him while I let him unload the burden of all injustices done to him. I tried to look intelligent as he waffled on about the Rosicrucians' science fiction, scientology, space, the planet Sirius, Ron Hubbard, religious fundamentalism, and whatever else he was interested in. I also sat and let him insult me to the hilt. It was no big deal; I was used to men abusing me. Would I have done all that had he been five-foot-four and as ugly as sin? Don't be daft.

On the days Jeff got his giro, Sam asked me to accompany him to make sure she got her rent before he spent it in the pub. I knew before I met him I'd only end up tagging along with him to the pub until he coughed it up, but by that stage I didn't care. When we were in the pub, a novelty for me, he would tell anyone within earshot that I was his best buddy and as such was to be shown respect. Then he proceeded to tear me to shreds in front of them. When Jeff arrived home drunk at my sister's house he caused uproar, shouting and arguing with the other lodgers, kicking doors and cursing. One night he yanked my sister across the room by her poor arthritic wrists, making her cry. One of the lodgers and I tried to calm him. Sam begged and pleaded for me to get him out of the house and take him to live at mine.

I'd only just got my life back after Steve. I was attracted to Jeff, but bring him to my house? No way.

'Please Lynda! You can handle him,' she begged.

That clinched it. I still said no, but the seed had been planted and began to germinate. First though, my sister took him to the YMCA and paid for two weeks' lodgings, just to get him away from the house. It would have ended there—I wasn't in touch with him—but Sam's caring nature was our undoing. She went to see how he was getting on and she ended up feeling sorry for him all over again, told him to pack his bags, and took him back to her house. And yes, Sam would have done the same for a five-foot-four-inch ugly git. Within a week he was up to his old tricks, causing mayhem after the pub. Sam pleaded with me again to take him to my house. I'll pay you, she said desperately. Once again I refused.

Jeff had a bit of the wanderlust about him, and the answer to my sister's predicament was solved when he sold his house. He'd always been fascinated with Iceland and Sam managed to plant the idea in his head that it would be a good place for him to go to live, to settle down. I helped him pack his suitcase, after making sure all his clothes were laundered. He bought me some cigarettes to thank me for taking care of him. He bought my sister a ship in a bottle; men haven't a clue. Sam drove him to the airport and he apologised for having been such a pain in the neck.

'I felt ever so sorry for him, Lynda. He looked like a little kid.' I wasn't the only one with a blind spot, it's a family trait; my mother's had some right tosspots too.

I can't remember how long Jeff was in Iceland, probably only weeks, before he began phoning my sister all the time saying how miserable he was. It was winter time, with only two hours of daylight per day. Though the atmosphere was good in the pubs (there are more alcoholics there than almost anywhere else in the world it seems, so he was in good company), the cost of living was sky high. The only work was in the fish factories and he'd been unable to get a job; his money was running out. Sam told him to come home. When he got back she let him stay for a few days as promised then asked me to take him in. As he was technically homeless I felt sorry for him and home he came with me. Sam drove us.

When we arrived, he inspected the house from top to bottom, silently, then went out to the garden and gave it the once over before delivering his verdict.

'Nice house. Needs a bit doing to it. Didn't Steve finish anything?'

He was looking at the unfinished fishpond, and the just-started garden path. No, not too often. To decorate a room would have taken him weeks, with a pit stop for a couple of fags and something to stuff his face with after every strip of wallpaper. The fishpond had been under construction for three-and-a-half years.

Jeff stayed true to himself and didn't offer to help when I said I'd sort it myself. I thought he had a cheek really, insulting Steve's DIY. Then again, he was only a lodger; we hadn't got round to the naughty bit yet.

The Irish lady I cleaned for gave me another job so it brought my illegal earnings up to £30 a week. She had a house let out in bed-sits. I only had to do the hall, stairs and landing, the bathroom and the kitchen. I didn't realise I was overcoming my fear of going out and talking to strangers, I was just making a buck. When I got my first week's wages I ordered some sand, ballast and a bag of cement and set about finishing the fishpond. I had watched Steve when he started on the pond so I had a fair idea what to do. I asked the builders merchant what the ratio was for the mix, and had all the supplies delivered to the front garden because there was no direct access to the back. Steve had fenced it all in when we moved in.

I set to and broke slabs with a lump-hammer. I mixed sand, ballast and cement with ever increasing confidence until I got the mix just right. I loved the work. I made a run with a plank up the step to the gate and wheel-barrowed my supplies up to the back garden as I needed them. 'What are you doing?' people kept asking, it was that kind of neighbourhood.

One day I barrowed a load to the back and started to mix it when a guy knocked on the open gate and stood trying to see over my shoulder. I asked could I help him. He said he was overcome with curiosity, he'd been watching me for weeks and wondered what I was doing. Did I mind if he took a look? I shrugged. Help yourself. He stood for a while, raking his eyes over the pond.

'Fuckin' 'ell! 'ave you done all this yourself?' he asked, in amazement.

'Yeah.'

'Fuckin' great job you done, man,' he said. 'Fuckin ace.' He had a last look. 'You can come and do mine next,' he joked, as he left.

I finished the pond and surrounding area with crazy paving and I put coping-stones round the periphery, then continued all the way up to the gate, my spirit level and plank of wood at the ready. I ploughed all the money I earned at my cleaning jobs into my project, for weeks. I developed stomach muscles the like of which I hadn't had since I was a teenager and calf and thigh muscles I didn't know existed, from all the cement mixing. Jeff would come home each day and survey the site, then give his opinion with a solemn air.

'Ya doing a good job, pork-pie.'

Jeff and I settled down together and were happy enough in our own way. He never paid his way mind, though unlike Steve he wasn't mean, but he was irresponsible. He only had his dole money and he needed what little he had for booze. The odd time he had a few bob he wined and dined me and he always bought me presents for Christmas and birthdays if he was in funds.

Whereas Steve had played guitar, sung me songs and called me lovely lady, Jeff sat with his headphones on, listening to his own music and said I was unattractive. When we went out for a drink he would look at me over the rim of his glass and tell me how badly in need of a facelift I was and so on. The pub would then turn on him, the men in my defence, the women on me, demanding to know why I put up with him. These 'new' young women were a shock to me; I'd been submerged in my own subculture so long I didn't know such women existed. I put up with Jeff for many reasons. I saw through his charade and forgave the insults because I knew he didn't mean what he said. Abuse was my familiar, was where I belonged. I also liked Jeff when he was sober; he was nice to be around. The main reason I put up with his insults was because I viewed it as a punishment from God. Intellectually I knew it sucked, nevertheless, that was how I felt. The more he insulted me, the worse he treated me, the more I accepted it as penance, and I was making reparation for my sins, like a good Catholic.

Jeff fell in love with a puppy that lived next door and persuaded me to buy it. The puppy was a Staffordshire bull terrier with a beautiful red coat, like desert sand, so I named him Monty, after Field Marshall Montgomery, who was known as 'The Desert Fox'. I fell in love with Monty in an instant. He was a real character; everywhere we went he had admirers. He changed my life when I think about it. I now had a real reason to wake up the next morning; I had something to lavish love and care on. Jeff and I walked miles every day with Monty, over the fields and far away. Sometimes Jeff took Monty to the pub with him when he was on one of his benders. He would keep him out all day and night while he was on his pub crawl, and I sat at home worrying over both of them. Jeff adored Monty, he wasn't being cruel to him; he was just irresponsible, about everything. He still kept going over to see my sister and mithering her, we were like his security blankets; he wanted to keep us both.

We spent Christmas day with Jeff's family. They were very kind, lovely people; his mum in particular was really sweet to me. Jeff bought me a present! (Craig Nelson had always been generous—with money I gave him—but apart from that I hadn't had a man buy me a present since I was sixteen.) I burst out laughing when I unwrapped it. He'd given me a gift set of face cream etc., which stated it was a miracle in a jar in the fight against wrinkles. I loved him for it. He hadn't a clue it was an insult.

I loved going for a drink with Jeff in the early days. At the start of the night he became happy and alive with the first few drinks, sort of manic and bright-eyed and could entertain the whole pub with his wit and conversation. People would be smiling in our direction as if his joy was contagious. He made me feel carefree, nothing mattered but the elation he was experiencing. He would promise that if he ever got the chance of some money he would pay for a face lift for me.

'I bet you were beautiful. What a shame you had to age. Ah, poor Pud,' he'd say as he held my hand and scrutinised me with his happy, shiny eyes.

He told the whole pub that I had a heart of gold and that it didn't matter that I was over the hill in the looks department.

'She's got heart, has Pud,' he'd declare fondly. As I was only forty-four and, having never sunbathed, I didn't have that many wrinkles anyway, I didn't pay any heed to the insults. I knew it wasn't normal behaviour, but I'd never lived a normal life.

I don't think Jeff himself realised there was a method to the hurt he threw at me. I may have done some stupid things in my life, but I'm not thick. I'm a past master at sniffing out people's true colours and I knew Jeff loved me in his own peculiar way. He was as jealous as sin when other men tried to chat me up when we were out, which happened frequently, mainly because they couldn't understand why I was with Jeff, owing to the way he treated me in public. When one guy told Jeff that, contrary to needing a facelift, in his opinion I was the most attractive woman in the room, Jeff offered to buy him a pair of spectacles. He held on to my hand so tightly I thought he'd crush my fingers; and never left my side the whole night.

There were other nights when being his drinking buddy wasn't a good move; nights when the manic side of Jeff never surfaced. I would sit beside him in the pub without him uttering a word, and the vibes he gave off would have felled a Roman Legion. I soon came to suss when he was in one of those moods and thought it wiser if he went alone. I would lie awake in anticipation and, sure enough, the whole neighbourhood would hear him, shouting abuse at the world in general and knocking all the copingstones off the walls along the street as he staggered home. When sober he laid the blame firmly on the electric shock treatment he'd had. Perhaps he was right.

Steve arrived unexpectedly one day to fetch a ball of string he'd left in the shed. He couldn't stay long, he said, he had his new step-daughter in the car. Hmm. Obviously the new missus didn't trust him to come alone. He was gobsmacked when he saw the fishpond and the building work I had done. Who did it? How much did you have to pay? I pointed to my chest.

'You don't need a man at all, do you?'

It wasn't a question, but a statement. He looked quite sad. I guess he wanted to feel that I missed him, or at least needed him for DIY. He asked me if I was happy, I said I was doing OK. He looked at me sideways and said:

'How could you go with Jeff? You know he's a racist and how sexist he is.'

'You're wrong you know. He's not racist at all, he just hates everybody. He married a woman with a mixed race kid, adopted her, and loved her as if she were his own. You couldn't have done that when Sue had Darryl.' He admitted it was true.

'As for being a sexist . . . aren't you all?'

I felt bad about that. But his parting comment when we split up, about my lack of sexual adventure, still rang in my ears. When he got to the gate he said softly:

'If you ever need me ring me Mum and I'll be straight round.'

I didn't ask if *he* was happy. I was more miffed that he'd relieved me of a ball of string, petty sod. Why couldn't he have just gone and bought a new one? Typical tightwad.

I was still signing on the dole and they began giving me grief because I hadn't got a job. My panic attacks were getting fewer and I was quite well as long as I stuck to my small circle, my sister's house and my two cleaning jobs. I was still scared to death of going into the grown-up world though, where I'd meet real people. But I couldn't covey that in a two-minute job interview. One snotty middle-aged interviewer asked me what I did all day. I couldn't very well say I had a couple of little cleaning jobs on the side, so I told her I cleaned the house.

'You must have a clean house!' she said sarcastically.

'I have!' I replied defensively. I didn't tell a lie. I was still at the scouring, bleaching, polishing and dusting. I carried the obsession out to the garden where I dug and cultivated, cut and trimmed, raked and hoed, and mowed the lawn into submission. I suppose I've always been that way inclined anyway, only the obsession had worsened since the murders.

I remember once when I went to see Róisín when I lived in Dublin, I flopped on her settee and asked her if there was any chance of a cuppa. I was knackered after a shopping trip. I could hear her and Alice giggling helplessly in the kitchen and shouted through: 'What are you two up to in there?' Róisín came in carrying two cups of coffee still giggling.

'Will you take a look around ye. I just said to Alice before ye came "this'll be the very time Lyn will pick to visit us," then ye rang the bell.'

I looked around me. Sure enough it was spectacularly untidy.

'Ah c'mon Róisín. I'm not that bad!' I protested.

'Sure ye are. Sure Terry was just saying the other day, when he leaves your flat he always has a pocket full of ash.'

'What do you mean?'

'He's scared to use the feckin ashtray! He gives one flick and you take it away to wash it.'

If they could only see the way I live today, cloudy windows, dust on every surface, though I do still vacuum every day. It's not the cleanliness that has always obsessed me, it's the order. I feel that my surroundings are all I can control, and if the place is in a mess I get tearful. I'm quite happy sitting in someone else's untidy home. It's not a clean house I need, it's control of my life.

To get the dole off my back I signed up for a five-week word-processing course. The classes were held at the local senior school on our estate, so I didn't have to worry about having a panic attack to travel there. There were ten of us on the course, all women. Jeff felt threatened right away, though of course he wouldn't admit to it. He took to walking Monty past the school as I was leaving in the evening. Pure coincidence, he said. Pure spying. The fact that there was also a carpentry-training workshop on campus didn't help matters, even though all the guys were young and wouldn't have been interested in me anyway.

Jeff did his best to sabotage my efforts. He'd cause arguments late at night so I'd be knackered in the morning, or try delaying tactics—where's this or that—so I'd be late arriving at the school. But I was on to him. He started a massive row one night, just as I was going to bed. I lost my rag and told him to fuck off. He left. He owed me money, but was due to be paid next day and we'd eaten all the food, but I didn't care, I got a good night's sleep.

The good thing about the course was we got a free lunch, which was always tasty, with good, fresh ingredients, things that I couldn't afford on my meagre budget and I used to look forward to it. Unfortunately, kicking Jeff out coincided with a bank holiday so I had no food on Saturday, Sunday or Monday, apart from two spuds, a pound of carrots and half a swede I found in the pantry. I knew I wasn't in danger of starving, but poor Monty was out of food too and he wasn't too happy with my vegetarian offerings, though he wolfed down the carrot peelings. When I got home from school on the Tuesday there was a ten pack of cigs, small tin of rice, two large tins of dog food and six eggs on the back doorstep, obviously left there by Jeff. It made me smile and my anger dissipated at once.

I didn't enjoy the course for the first few days. I was the oldest, apart from Kath who was of similar age and the rest were all very young. I hadn't done anything school-wise since I was fifteen and I found the discipline of sitting at a desk all day onerous. I kept losing the menu and had trouble with the new terminology. Mouses . . . mice? Floppy disks, menus, DOS, etc. Kath had trouble too. All those brain cells dying! But by the second week I was fine. I completed the course, got my certificate and life went on as it had done before. I was at a loss. While I'd been doing the course I hadn't had any nightmares because my mind was otherwise occupied. Within a week they were back. After a particularly bad one, where John Cullen had me tied to a chair and was tearing flesh off my legs in two-inch strips, I had to start sleeping with the light on in the hall. John Cullen once told me his fantasy was to carve up his enemies like a kebab, just a little piece at a time, not enough for them to lose consciousness, so he'd have the pleasure of hearing them scream and beg.

As luck would have it, I had made friends with a woman who was considering doing one of the adult education classes, which were also held at the local school. Rita was too shy to go on her own so she asked if I'd go with her. We went along on a fact finding tour, then we opted to study for our GCSE in English Literature, which was right up my street. Both of us had left school without any qualifications. O-levels hadn't been around in my day, I was so ancient. Needless to say Jeff did his best to belittle me. Why on earth did I want to go back to school at my age ? What was I going to do with an O-level? What good was it? It wasn't gonna make me any richer was it? And so on.

The day before we were due to enrol Rita arrived to say she wouldn't be coming to the school with me, her husband was ill. I told her I was sorry, she looked so disappointed. What's wrong with him? She looked evasive, studied the carpet for a second then said she didn't really know. She knew alright, we both knew. Sabotage. I'd seen the relief on Jeff's face while Rita was talking. He put his arm round my shoulders.

'Never mind Pudding. We'll go for nice long walks in the fields now the weather's turning fine. Monty will love it.' He kissed me on the top of my head in commiseration.

'I'm afraid you'll be on your own love. I'm still going.' That shook him.

I went to the front garden and began digging over the soil in my Star of David; I wanted a nice tilth to the soil in readiness for some bedding plants and was soon happily engrossed in the task. Jeff announced he was off to the shops with Monty to buy some lager. Time passed, I stopped for a minute to stretch my back and spotted Monty, then Jeff, turning the corner, so I went back to digging. I didn't want him to see how tired I was. He shut the gate after him, took the lead off Monty, then came and forcibly took the spade off me and took over the digging.

'Can't you just *once* in your bloody life ask for help!'

As it happens I'd been quite content with what I was doing—I certainly didn't need any help—but I was so shocked to see him actually working that I was rendered speechless. Jeff was such a strong man with a beautiful physique, his body in motion was a fine sight and I just stood and watched him in action for a while. It was to be the only finger he ever lifted round the place; in fairness perhaps he saw it as Steve's house, though he never said so.

Because Jeff's money was earmarked for booze he would spend hours making things, improvising if anything needed mending that would normally cost money. When my boots needed heeling and we were skint, he fixed them with some steel bolts which made a racket when I walked, and I tried my damndest to wear them out for that reason. Years later I threw them out when the leather was too worn and they still had those bloody bolts in. When my shoes had holes in the soles he fashioned some soles from a rubber car mat then glued them on. I was in town one day and on the spur of the moment I decided to have the heels done, the cobbler laughed his head off when he saw the soles. I told him my partner had repaired them.

'Stands for Wally does it?' he asked, pointing to the 'W' on the right hand sole.

'Actually,' I said frostily, 'It's the W off BMW.' I then saw the funny side of it and we both laughed. The bloody soles refused to wear out.

So at the age of forty-five off to school I went. I loved it right from the start. I love the English language, even though I don't think I speak it and wouldn't know an aitch if it came up and slapped me round the face. As you would expect in a greatly deprived area such as ours, my new fellow pupils were all females. I wonder why it's us who always look for more. Its probably because men get out and about, unfettered by kids and hearth. Even the ones on our estate who didn't work—which were the vast majority—always seemed to be on the move. Whereas if women wanted to go somewhere they had to take the kids with them, and they'd need feeding, nappies changed, toilets located. Two years or so ago *The Times* published a league table of the roughest estates in Britain, which I read with great interest. Sure enough my old homestead was right up there. Things couldn't have improved much in the twenty years since I left it.

We were a mixed bunch of varying ages, though only one was older than me—she'd gone along with her daughter as a bit of moral support—and we all had children. One girl was Spanish. She wanted to be able to read and write in English, though she spoke it perfectly, better than me, or I? I don't think most of us were there because we had a thirst for knowledge, at least not at the outset. No *Educating Rita* there.

It was in the tea breaks that an undercurrent of excitement could be felt, when we'd all be trying to talk at once. Our class teacher was brilliant. She calmed us down and showed us how to order our thoughts, how to discuss, to debate issues properly, to wait our turn, which was all new to us. Now we tried to voice the stirrings of excitement we were feeling, which might sound crazy or pathetic even, but it sure as hell wasn't.

One woman said she was there because she was sick of the sight of the four walls. Another said drolly that she was sick of the sight of the kids and the budgie. Another agreed, and then said she was sick of the sight of her old man and we all laughed. We knew where she was coming from. One said she didn't want to stagnate. When it came to my turn I shrugged.

'Dunno really. I just feel like I've never done anything with my life.'

As I listened I could see one common denominator; they all had spirit. I only spent a few hours a week there, but looking back they were happy days.

Jeff was still trying to sabotage things for me, but I would not let him. He wasn't alone. Three or four of the other women fell by the wayside as their partners placed obstacles in their paths. Why the men felt so threatened God only knows, the women were hardly going to go out and get a high-flying jobs. Two women had to drop out when they couldn't get anyone to look after the kids. None of us had two pennies to rub together; money for paid childcare wasn't an option since we were all on benefits.

The day I was to take my oral examination I woke up violently sick and full of nervous tension. I couldn't leave the house. I had no phone so I couldn't phone the school. The next day I got a grip on myself and went over to the school to apologise, even though I knew I was too late for the exam. I was secretly glad I wouldn't have to sit the exams, but I owed it to my teacher. She was kindness itself; she knew how nervous I was. She said she wouldn't be able to get the examiner back, but to leave it with her and she'd see what she could do. She fixed a time for us to meet later that week.

On the day, she produced a tape recorder and said she'd managed to get a special dispensation from the exam board for her to take my oral examination. She was to record it and then send it to the examiners. I hate anything that captures the human voice—phones, video, tapes—so I immediately tensed when I saw the tape recorder. I told my tutor I was so nervous that I'd give an arm for a ciggie.

'How many do you smoke a day?'

'Too many,' I admitted. I started telling her about all the different aids I'd tried in the battle with the evil weed. I had one eye on the dreaded recorder as I spoke, anything to delay the bloody thing being switched on. I rabbitted on as if I was on speed for about ten minutes. She was smiling all the time. I stopped suddenly and said: 'Sorry. I do go on don't I?'

She grinned. I shifted about to make myself comfortable, and then said 'Right. I'm ready to start now.'

'Don't! Please!' she laughed, holding a hand up in a stop sign. 'I've got it all on tape.'

I couldn't believe it. I felt like hugging her, I told her so.

'*I'm* glad that the board let me tape it, too. I couldn't believe it when you hadn't arrived the day they were here. I said to myself 'Please come Lyn. You're my best pupil.'

I was walking on air when I left.

The elation didn't last long. Two days later, the day the written examination was to take place, I knew as soon as I opened my eyes that it wasn't a good day; my euphoria had vanished in the night. I sat at the desk looking at the paper in front of me and my mind went blank. Everything I do, I do quickly. In the normal run of things I'd have had the pen in my hand in a flash and been scribbling furiously, finishing well ahead of the rest of the class. The test paper was written in Sanskrit, the words indecipherable. Latin would have seemed more approachable. Daily mass in the convent, year after year, making the responses in Latin—sheer repetitiveness ensuring the language stays in the memory. My mouth was dry, I popped a mint in to activate some saliva as I took a look round the room. Everybody was busy writing. We had to draft a letter to Kent Council objecting to the Channel Tunnel being built, listing various endangered botanical species that would suffer if the project went ahead. I can't recall a word of what I wrote but it was crap and I knew it. The next paper was to be an advertising blurb for a computer; they gave us the choice of three different computers. I find it funny now, but all I will say is Saatchi and Saatchi had no need to look to their laurels.

I trudged home. I wished that I had some money for once and could afford a bottle of wine, because I really wanted to get maggoty drunk. Jeff cradled me and said comfortingly:

'Never mind Pud, it's not the end of the world'. Of course it wasn't. It just felt like it.

'You know why you failed don't you?'

'No. I'm just thick I guess.' I gave a little sniffle. I felt as if I was five years old.

'Nah. Its because your teacher said you were her star pupil.'

He kissed the top of my head again and dried my eyes with his fingers.

'Puts pressure on you, does something like that,' he added, with rare insight.

I knew I'd failed the exam so didn't bother going to the school on the day the results were to be displayed on the board. I was busy cleaning, scouring, bleaching, polishing, dusting, battering the garden and taking Monty for long walks. I bumped into Eileen, one of my fellow students in the park and she asked why I hadn't gone to the little celebratory party they'd held when the pass certificates were handed out. The teacher had been disappointed I hadn't showed and was worried I was ill.

I congratulated Eileen on her pass, she'd gotten a B. I confessed that I hadn't gone to the school to check my results as I knew I'd failed, so I knew nothing about the party.

'You didn't fail, you daft bugger. Your name was called out.' She laughed excitedly and threw her arms around me.

'Congratulations Lyn! We're not so dumb after all, are we?' We held hands at arm's length grinning like fools. 'Next time that bastard of mine calls me a stupid cow I'm gonna stuff me bloody O-level down his throat!'

She told me my certificate was waiting for me to collect. I did not want the actual certificate because it was in the name Madden, a name I no longer used, but I was curious to learn what marks the exam board had given me so I went along to collect it. When I was at school years ago there were only A, B or C classes. I'd always managed to scrape by in an A class because I loved English. I loved my English teacher too because she took an interest in me, a rarity in my life. My admiration for her paled a bit though when she would read my essays out to the class.

'This is how as essay *should* be written. Make me *interested* in what you have to say.'

Mortifying for a teenager in an under achieving school. On the other hand I hated maths and was always near the bottom of the class. I never saw the point of maths, being earmarked to work in a factory for £7 a week when I left school. I could count to seven, still have thirteen digits left to play with, or use an abacus. I once dated an accountant, before I chose criminals for my peer group, who told me mathematics were exciting. I thought he was nuts. I wish I'd paid more attention.

I saw I had only got a C in the written. Dunce, I thought, but hadn't expected any higher. The exam board had given me a grade one in Oral Communication! I stared at the certificate in disbelief. Me, who says innit instead of isn't it, me instead of I, and has never sounded an aitch in my entire life. I was still staring at the piece of paper when a teacher happened by. She congratulated me and wished me good luck for the future.

'There must be some mistake,' I pointed to the oral grade. 'I never even sound me aitches.' She explained that when it came to the oral examination the board made allowances for regional differences and dialect. Detractors will say it validates their claims that standards have dropped. I ain't gonna argue the toss because I ain't gonna be offered a job with the BBC anyway.

'Well done Pud,' said Jeff, patting me on the head, just as he did with Monty. In his own way, he meant it. I was forty-six years old or I would have skipped.

8

Jeff and I were watching telly late one night when someone rang the bell. He went to answer it and came back.

'Someone's saying something about your daughter, couldn't hear properly.'

I got up off the settee and went to see for myself. Steve had fenced all the back off for obvious security reasons and the front door, which in actual fact was now a side door, was hidden from view so I shouted over the fence, asking whoever it was what they wanted.

'It's your daughter, Fiona,' a man's voice said.

'You don't sound like a Fiona to me,' I shouted back, trying to give myself time to think.

'I'm her boyfriend. She's here now, Fiona.'

I shouted back that I wanted to hear a female voice.

'It's me, Fiona.'

I almost fainted. As I reached to turn the key in the gate my legs turned to jelly and my heart was thumping. A couple stood before me. I couldn't look at the girl—my daughter. I ushered the two of them into the house and asked them to sit down. Monty was excited and went from one to another wagging his tail in greeting.

Fiona screeched: 'Get him away from me!' The boyfriend ignored him.

Jeff looked uncomfortable, he didn't speak. Neither did I. I stood, sat, stood, sat and looked around the room, desperately trying to think of something to say, something adequate to the situation. Inspirationally, I asked would they like a cup of tea or coffee. Mercifully they said yes. I had to force myself not to *run* out of the room. Jeff followed me; he didn't know what to say either. My hands shook as I made tea and coffee, buttered bread, the first slice landed on the floor, and sliced cheese. Not a single word passed between Jeff and me.

I hadn't seen Fiona since the time I'd prised her three-year-old fingers from my legs on the day I did a runner from her father. She'd be fifteen now. Would she remember it? Three years old, now here she is, fifteen, with a boyfriend in tow. I felt a panic attack coming on, and fought against it. I overfilled the mugs as a million thoughts crashed through my head like a bulldozer. I took as long as I could making the sandwiches. I was walking in the door when it struck me that she probably knew I'd been a prostitute too. Oh God! I kept my eyes downcast as I handed her the sandwiches. They should run 'How-To' classes for this kind of situation; it's not at all like you see in the movies.

As it was, I played it pretty badly and did all the wrong things. I acted as if my daughter and her boyfriend were strangers at a bus stop. I small-talked about the motorways and the weather, Liverpool, and her brothers. It was Chris who had given her my address. Fiona hardly spoke. I took it as a sign of condemnation. Her boyfriend Colin did all the talking, he wasn't a bit shy. He gabbed away to Jeff as if he'd known him years. I hardly dared look at Fiona; I was scared to meet her eyes. I wondered if she knew I'd been with John Cullen the night he set fire to the Lynches' house. She must have been ashamed I was her mother. She seemed cold and aloof; I had an unpleasant feeling that she had come to exact some terrible revenge on me, to get even with me for walking out on her. Then again, she could just have wanted a mother.

We were all tired, but it was ages before I plucked up the courage to ask if she and Colin slept together. She laughed and said of course. I gave them my room and I climbed into bed with Jeff. I couldn't sleep. It's a peculiar feeling to lie awake knowing your little girl is in bed with a man in the room next to you. For me Fiona was frozen in time, an intense little three-year-old girl in a pretty dress. Who was at that moment engaged in rather noisy sex with her boyfriend. Please God, I beseeched, please God, help me get through this. I was consumed by guilt of what I'd done to her; if she cast judgement I hadn't a single word in my defence. It would not have been any use slagging her dad off, or explaining how terrified I'd been of him. She wouldn't have cared, she'd have only known I betrayed her, I abandoned her.

Fiona and Colin stayed for a few days and even looking back I can't find anything good to say about that time. If Fiona and I had a conversation I missed it, but Colin could waffle enough for all of us. I didn't like him, in fact I think I detested him on sight, with his whiny Scouse accent. Isn't it odd how a Scouse accent can seem quite cute on someone who is cute themselves, but sucks when they are not? Fiona and him were living with his grandmother in Liverpool, and she was quite strict so they began yo-yoing between her house and mine, a week at the grandmother's, a week at mine. It sounds petty, but the truth was I could not afford to feed us all, so I asked Fiona to come on her own the next time.

When she came I took her to town and bought her a winter coat and we had lunch together, and tried to get to know each other. I noticed she wasn't wearing a ring I'd sent for her birthday a couple of years back. I have very small fingers, and I'd bought her a sapphire and diamond ring and had it cut to fit my pinkie, thinking it would fit her second finger. I asked her if she still had the ring. She said she had not received it. I knew she didn't believe I'd sent it. Craig still being spiteful, I guess. On the day I did my cleaning job I came home to find she'd vacuumed everywhere, which I thought was a nice daughterly thing to do. I still hadn't broached the subject of the past, I just couldn't do it, and I don't think the week we spent on our own was a resounding success. The odd time I dared to look her full in the face I felt as if I'd been struck; it was her father's dark brown eyes that stared back at me and they were full of contempt, just as his had been. I couldn't even begin to guess at the dark tales he'd told about me. The boys said that Craig initially told her I was dead. The stark truth was I could tell Fiona did not like me. After that visit Colin always came too.

Perhaps we could have found a way of building a relationship if she'd come on her own that very first night. If she'd left Colin behind until she and I had got to know each other things may have worked out. As it was he ruined everything. He spent every waking moment scheming and plotting and scrounging. Everybody on the planet had been put there for his amusement, to be taken for a ride.

He boasted about the people he'd outwitted, and fleeced. The stings, the strokes, the scams, the frauds, the swindles. As he neared the end of whatever tale he was spinning about some poor sucker he'd conned, he'd be laughing, and shaking his head in awe of his own genius. He mistook my silence for admiration. What could I say? He was my daughter's boyfriend, a guest in my home. I wouldn't have granted him breathing space had it been otherwise. I have a video of him, when he was a guest on a daytime TV programme, being given a rough ride by the studio audience. He's bragging about how he could milk the system, and would never do a day's work 'till the day he died. I also have a newspaper clipping with a photograph of him, under the heading, 'Is This Britain's Biggest Scrounger?'

Whenever they came to stay Fiona mostly stayed up in the bedroom; which meant it fell to me to entertain Colin. Jeff of course used to stay out all day sooner than have to deal with the situation in the house. Colin would give me Fiona's menu order for the day, which I'd cook, and then he'd take it up to her on a tray. Therefore, instead of gaining a daughter I felt I had gained two scroungers.

Colin and Fiona were having a big bust-up in the bedroom one day and began throwing things around so I stormed upstairs and threw the door open without knocking, just as she was throwing her make-up bag at Colin.

'I fucking hate you, you bastard!' she screamed as she threw it. It hit me instead.

'Do you mind?' I said, through gritted teeth. 'You're not at home now!'

I closed the door and stormed downstairs. Ouch! No sooner were the words out than I knew I should have gone straight back up to apologise. Instead I stood seething with anger in the kitchen. I wasn't going to put up with that in my own home. I can still see the look Fiona gave me when I uttered those ill-fated words.

Colin came down a few hours later to ask for food for Fiona. 'What would the princess in the tower like?' I asked dryly, compounding the damage I'd done, but I was still fuming. Fiona didn't show her face over the next two days. Colin carried on as if nothing had happened. He sat around like a useless lump, chatting as I cleaned or whatever. Occasionally he spent a bit of time upstairs with Fiona. On the third day I never set eyes on either of them, but

I wouldn't give in, so I refused to knock to enquire how they were. With the benefit of hindsight I'd do it all differently if I could.

I was reading in the lounge when I suddenly heard a lot of activity in the hall and went to investigate. I saw Fiona scurrying out of the front door with a package under her arm. I realised she was leaving and panicked.

'Please. Don't go Fiona!'

She actually *ran* down the garden path as if someone was chasing her, and was gone. Colin came hurrying down the stairs with two bulging black bags.

'See you', he muttered, pushing past me.

I followed them out to the car to ask them to come back. Fiona turned her head to the side when she saw me coming down the path and said something to Colin. He started the car with a crunching of gears and took off in a hurry.

I sat on the back doorstep and burst into tears. Why hadn't I apologised? She was only fifteen after all. I'd let my dislike of her boyfriend over-ride my feelings for her. I'd found her difficult, and downright miserable to be around, not once did I see a smile on her face, but what did she have to smile about? I'd also let Jeff influence me. He'd whittled away at me constantly, pointing out that Fiona wasn't there because she wanted a mother, but was using my house as a doss house. She and Colin were saving their benefits while they ate all 'our' food.

I loved the *our* bit. He'd give me money towards the food on a Tuesday, and be borrowing it back by Thursday. I'd had a second chance with my daughter, and blown it.

I went indoors and upstairs to the bedroom. I stood still, soaking up the atmosphere, as if to conjure Fiona back again. Eyes circling the room, I saw all my satin cushions were gone off the bed. I had a sinking feeling as I went next door to the box-room, opened the wardrobe, and found some of my clothes and my towels were gone too. The bulging black bin-bags!

I rushed downstairs to the hall where I kept my handbag hanging on a coat-hook. My bank book was missing. I felt ill. I only had £130 in it, but it had taken me a year of scrimping to save it. My disappearing money I called it. I never knew when John Cullen would catch up with me, and I needed money to run.

I hurried to the local bank to report the book lost and the manager told me that a young woman had gone in to the main branch in town to draw on the account. She had produced a utility bill as proof of address, but the staff had become suspicious and asked her to wait while they checked it out and she'd left the bank in a hurry. The bank manager asked if I wanted to press charges. Of course I declined.

Poor Fiona, how she must have hated me. I didn't blame her. I knew her reasons. It was Colin I blamed, and I didn't owe him. Years later I discovered the theft had in fact been Fiona's idea, not Colin's.

'Told you so,' Jeff crowed.

*

Now that my O-level was out of the way, I was once more at a loss. It was all a bit of an anti-climax. The house could have done with re-decorating, the wallpaper was nicotine stained thanks to all the roll-ups Jeff and I smoked, but I couldn't afford to do it. I'd tried to give up smoking for years; acupuncture twice, hypnosis twice, herbal cigarettes, nicotine gum and patches.

Jeff and I tried giving up together but only succeeded in getting ratty with one another and eating like pigs, sitting in our chairs with swollen bellies, like a couple of stuffed Christmas turkeys.

On one of our joint attempts I rushed to the shops to buy a pack of fags as soon as Jeff left the house, then got on a bus and sat on the top deck puffing to my heart's content. I passed Jeff walking along the street puffing his head off too; we saw each other at the exact same moment and waved our cigarettes in salutation.

Luckily, Jeff was a reader too and we spent many a companionable hour quietly reading. We played Scrabble a lot, but Jeff cheated terribly; he was dead childish like that. I did a lot of jigsaw puzzles and knitted jumpers and cardigans for myself to save money. Jeff asked me to knit one for him, but I said no because his arms were too long and I would have been fed up looking at the same colour wool by the time I finished it. I was learning! I had knitted one for Steve, which had taken me ages because I could not keep pace with his weight gain.

I became a grandmother. Chris was out of prison and had met a lovely girl, Gill. They all came to stay with me. I liked Gill from the start. I was smitten with Adam, my first grandchild.

'Please God, let this be *good*,' I asked, as I held the defenceless little bundle in my arms. A new life. New beginnings.

I was amazed at all the stuff babies have these days, the house was awash with *things*. The proud new parents and I, the ecstatic grandmother, walked round with huge grins on our faces the whole week, none of us could leave poor baby in peace. Chris did all the nappy changing and made all the formulas, as Gill and I looked on, full of love and maternal pride for our sons. Chris has always been a natural with kids, I don't know where he gets it from. As a child he always offered to feed my friends' babies when we called to see them.

I spent hours lying on my back on the floor with Adam on my chest fast asleep, listening to his little baby heart beating next to mine; my first-born's first-born. It was the most unbelievably awesome, beautiful feeling I have ever experienced. If I die tomorrow, at least I will have had that.

When Adam cried in the night I got up and took him downstairs with me, I warmed his bottle and fed him, changed him and put him back in his cot. Gill was so proud that he had slept through the night. She laughed when I told her he had not. Gill was fragile, warm, friendly, beautiful and charming. She was a hairdresser, had her own business, a brand new car. Why she picked up with an ex-prisoner heaven knows, she could have done so much better. Chris must have laid the charm on thickly, because she came from a good family. It was obvious they loved each other, but life is so much more than that. As they were leaving I put my arms round Chris.

'Stay out of trouble Chris, make sure he has *good* life.' I said softly. We both had tears in our eyes. We stood with our arms round each other, locked in the sorrow of the moment. He was still dabbing at his eyes as he walked out of the door.

Inevitably, as this is not a fairy story, when they turned up unannounced two months later their circumstances had altered. Chris was on the run from the police after a robbery he had committed. Gill's hairdressing business had gone down the drain, her new car had been repossessed by the finance company because she had failed to keep up the repayments and she was now driving a ten-year-old model. She is a skinny little thing at the best of times, but I could still tell she had lost a fair bit of weight; she looked dreadful.

The enchantment of a new life in the family had vanished in the mists and we all moved about the house quietly, avoiding eye contact. Tempting fate, we had dared to hope; how the gods must have laughed. When Adam cried we looked expectantly at one another to see who would go to him, it was as if we were all afraid of him; of the burden of his need.

Just as it had been with Fiona and the boyfriend, lack of money was to prove a curse once again. I couldn't feed us all on my dole money, though they got free milk formula for the baby so it was one less thing to worry about. We managed for a few weeks by using my disappearing money, when it had gone I told Chris he'd have to think of something soon. He responded he'd thought of nothing else since he arrived, he needed cash to do his own disappearing act. He wanted to take Gill and the baby to live in Israel, where he'd lived briefly when I'd left his father. All pie in the sky of course, but you can't say that to someone who's so naively optimistic. It just makes you sound like a cynical old bugger.

Gill, placid by nature, didn't nag or make demands on Chris, but her disappointment in him was evident, as was mine, which, combined with Adam's very existence put him under pressure from all sides. He'd effectively deceived Gill (into thinking she had a normal happy life ahead of her), Adam (who hadn't asked to be brought into the world) and me, because he'd failed them both. We were waiting for him to solve the problem. I blamed myself; I'd made him what he was. He knew nothing of responsibility, or accountability. Where would he have learnt it?

I had gotten over the initial shock of the change in circumstances and was once more pretending to play happy families. Chris said he was off to rob a bank. Gill and I laughed and put it down to attention seeking, he'd been feeling a bit neglected since the baby arrived. Had we known he'd set off with an imitation handgun Jeff had given him we might have paid a little more attention. As it was we were too busy cooing over Adam to pay him much heed. When he returned a few hours later and said something about not getting any money, Gill shrugged as if to say what's new, but didn't say anything. I kept out of it, not wanting to be the interfering mother-in-law. I noticed he was a bit distracted as he sat playing with Monty's ears but put it down to the problems we were having.

I don't think I've listened to local radio in over twenty years, but by some kind of fluke I was in the kitchen washing up when the newscaster giving a roundup announced that a man with a handgun had attempted to rob a certain bank, but had left empty-handed when a cashier had raised the alarm. He ended the bulletin by giving a description of the would-be robber.

I stared at the sudsy water in shock, as if someone had cast a spell on me. I know a description of my own son when I hear it. I walked to the open door drying my hands in a daze. I locked eyes with Chris; wordlessly we turned to look at Adam in his cot. We sat beside one another and watched him in silence for a while, overwhelmed by the spectre of his future.

I took Jeff to task concerning the replica gun. He pointed out that he wasn't to know Chris would actually have the bottle to rob a bank. I suppose he had a point; it's the kind of thing most people joke about—I've done it myself when my credit card bill has arrived. When Jeff read about the raid in the local paper he got paranoid about the police finding his fingerprints on the gun so he wiped it all down. Still not satisfied, he dismantled it and threw the parts away.

Being on the run meant Chris couldn't sign on the dole, or claim benefits so pressure was still mounting on him to do something about his family's situation; we had no money at all. Only people who have never been in prison would see it as the obvious solution but I did half-heartedly suggest he give himself up to the police, but he couldn't face it. We couldn't just sit around and slowly starve to death. In the end desperation forced Chris to siphon some petrol from a parked car and he Gill and the baby got in their car and drove down to London, where they went to stay in a hostel. Once there Chris did a bit of shoplifting to get by. Realising it wasn't going to get them very far he ended up robbing a couple of banks.

Needless to say, any thought of escaping to Israel vanished and it was a case of let the good times roll. He couldn't wait to get rid of his haul—Robin Hood the Younger. He dropped £100 in a beggar's hand, £50 in a busker's hat and it was drinks all round in the pub—he was always the generous type. I know it's easy to be generous with someone else's money, but he was the same with his own. Which was why he was in the predicament he was—he gave whatever he had in his pocket to any Tom, Dick or Harry. He'd gone through Gill's hairdressing takings like a dose of salts. He knew no better, he was a casualty of his upbringing. He had no idea what it was like to work for a living. His father had always had wads of dough, without working for it, so for Chris money had no true value, it was worthless. When we lived in Dublin Chris would land on the doorstep with some complete stranger he'd picked up off the street, who was down on his luck, needed a train ticket home, a new pair of shoes, or money for food.

'Me Mum'll help you out,' he'd say. I always did; it's my fault he has no concept of money.

He was the same with animals. Every stray dog in the neighbourhood ended up at our house when he was a kid. He once brought this mangy, scabby dog home and sneaked it into his bed for the night, and caught ringworm off it. His dad had a cruel streak with animals so keeping it wasn't an option. Chris was heartbroken; he couldn't eat or sleep, so we went scouting for the dog on the sly and I paid a vet to treat it. The vet took a shine to Chris and used to let him help feed the animals and clean out after them, when they were recovering from surgery. He even let him attend operations once or twice; he called him 'my apprentice'. From vet to bankrobber, what a difference a decade can make.

Gill and Adam were back at the hostel one day, waiting for Daddy to bring home the bacon, when the police arrived to say they had him under arrest. They searched the room while they were there, taking Adam out of his carry cot and lifting the mattress too. Gill was in floods of tears. Chris was kept in custody until the trial and sentenced to eight years. Gill and the baby stayed on at the hostel for a few weeks (it was by all accounts a dump). We wrote each other long letters and I sent a bit of money to help her get by, though it wasn't enough. Eventually, Gill swallowed her pride and contacted her mother, who'd more or less fallen out with her over her involvement with Chris, and asked if she could come home. When she arrived home, she was carrying some extra baggage. Gill was pregnant again.

*

I visited Chris in every young offender's institution in the land when he was doing his three years; now I had to do it all over again in adult jails. It was one way to see the whole of England, I suppose. At the outset, Gill got a lift from Liverpool to visit him wherever he happened to be, but she eventually got fed up. I think they argued a lot on the visits, which dwindled eventually. He thought he'd only to ask for something and she'd get it, or do it. He mistook her for a mother. Prisoners can be quite selfish; they think nothing exists outside of their insular little world. The fact that he was, as usual, doing his Cool Hand Luke bit couldn't have helped matters either. Paul Newman's role in the film could have been modelled on Chris: Jack the lad, treat it all as a joke, act the clown, don't let them see you're beaten. He even looked like a young Paul Newman, the same smiley blue eyes.

After a couple of years there were times I just could not face seeing him, knowing the mess Gill was in. I dreaded the long journeys too: trains, buses, coach stations, travelling home late at night. Jeff used to go in my place. Not that he was keen to visit Chris, he just loved to travel and to see new places. Prisoners are such a drain financially as well. Every penny I earned on the side now went to him—postal orders to buy things from the canteen, clothes, a radio—anything he needed I got for him. When I thought I'd been struggling before, I'd been kidding myself. He complained that Gill had 'gone a bit mean'. I set about him; I tried my best to make him understand how hard it was for Gill with now two children to bring up on her own.

'She's got her mum,' he replied.

'Jesus,' I said, 'her mother needs a life too!'

9

Jeff threw my family in my face all the time: my son was a convicted bank robber, and my daughter a thief, a leech, a parasite. Look who's talking. This was on top of the usual insults concerning my appearance, which I'd listened to for three years.

I knew I was starting to show my age. Lines were appearing around my lips and eyes, my skin didn't appear to be as firm, the skin on my hands didn't spring back as quickly when I pinched it: it was all rather depressing. Considering it was the natural ageing process (and being no vainer than the next woman), I'd have learnt to live with it, but thanks to the endless barbs and insults I had come to look on it as a major crisis. And it came to pass that I awoke one morning unfair of countenance, the ugliest in all the land. It's what men like Jeff excel at it, chipping away relentlessly—a little bit here, a little bit there—like a demented sculptor. You grow smaller and smaller while waiting for the final tap of the chisel and ultimate disintegration. Years of chipping away will do that to a person.

I decided I needed a facelift. I felt I was so ugly I walked with my head down when I was out; anyone who gazed upon me would surely keel over, struck down with fright. I hurried past shop windows in case I accidentally caught sight of myself. It became an obsession. I bought a book on cosmetic surgery. I sent off for brochures. I bought any women's magazines that listed anything pertaining to it and watched, with longing, anything showing plastic surgery on TV. I hadn't a penny to pay for a facelift, but I could dream. Then a strange thing happened. The moment I conceded to Jeff he'd been right in saying I needed a facelift, he stopped!

'Don't be daft, Pud. You're alright.'

He had to have something to taunt me with now my looks were no longer an issue, so when he drank he brought up my past instead. I worried about it a lot because I never knew who his drinking buddies would be. The pub could be full of Irish for all he'd notice, he was very indiscreet when under the influence. We had an argument one night when he arrived home, pissed as a newt, and started going on about me being on the game. I didn't need him to flog me with my past—I did a pretty good job of it myself—so I asked him to leave. He got nasty, so I rang the police to remove him from the house. They asked what the problem was and I explained quietly.

'Listen officer, let me tell you about this *lady*,' said Jeff, trying to stand upright and stroke Monty at the same time.

He gave them a condensed history of my life—and more—John Cullen, Dublin, the murders, he even threw in the IRA just for good measure—all of it at full throttle. My neighbours couldn't fail to hear it. The police calmed him down and escorted him out the back gate; he went peacefully enough. I had to hold Monty's collar because he was all for following him, thinking he had a good pub crawl ahead of him.

Jeff had been trying to persuade me to move away from the city for months. He was nervous word of my whereabouts might have filtered back to Dublin. Well, that was the argument he used; he just had itchy feet. After the episode with the police, and mortified that my neighbours probably heard every word of the commotion and that my cover was blown, I decided he was right. It was time to make a new start. I was very scared; I was discovering I didn't like change. But more importantly, I had lived at the house for five years, an all-time record for me. It is not easy for someone who has a phobia about leaving home to actually leave home.

Jeff had always had a hankering to live at the seaside so we decided on the east coast because my mother had moved down there two years before. What a mistake that turned out to be—it was bloody freezing nine-tenths of the year. I had one major reservation against moving that I set out to Jeff and I *warned* him. He'd earned a reputation as the drunk of the neighbourhood, but was accepted as such because it was a rough area. I didn't want the embarrassment of hearing him before I saw him when we moved, because where we were going was more up-market. He promised, solemnly, that he would mend his ways when we were there. According to him the only reason he drank to excess was the worry of living with me, waiting for the axe to fall, for John Cullen to find us. I didn't believe him for a minute and was moving against my better judgement. In spite of it, I told Monty we were going to the seaside and began packing.

I had kept Koi carp in the fishpond but sold them to a garden centre to raise the money for the move. I was sad to see them go, having raised them from young; they used to eat out of my hand. There were some fine specimens among them; one had a perfect orange spot on its head like the Rising Sun, much prized in Japan.

I was more or less all packed, ready for the off when who turns up on the doorstep only the bold Steve. He was shocked to hear I was moving. He didn't say what he'd called for. I sat on the back doorstep and smoked a cigarette with him while we talked. His marriage was in trouble, he told me. The wife worked as a PA for some bigwig and had to spend a lot of time away from home in the course of her work, and when she got home she took Steve to task for not doing anything around the house and nagged continuously about all the unfinished DIY projects.

'Yeah well,' I said, waving a hand around the garden, taking in the finished pond and the completed garden path. 'We're supposed to learn from our mistakes. Don't forget Sue was left with a house falling round her too.' I couldn't resist.

'I know,' he said wearily, running his fingers through his hair distractedly. Jeff came out and asked if we would like a cup of coffee. We declined and he went back indoors.

Steve turned to look at the house and said 'You know Lyn, I felt like I was coming home.'

I didn't respond.

'I should have married you,' he nodded, looking straight ahead.

I shrugged, 'Yeah well'.

I felt a smidgeon of sympathy for him, just as I would for anyone who had fucked up. I walked him down the garden to the front gate when he was leaving. He leaned close and said 'May I?' I offered him my cheek to kiss; I wasn't about to get a gobful of saliva! As I turned towards the house, I caught Jeff trying to straighten the corner of the net curtains.

I went to say goodbye to Mandy and the kids. We were all crying when I left. Next I called on Karen and there were more tears. I took Monty for his last walk over the fields and we stayed out for hours; I couldn't stop crying the whole time. Monty wasn't bothered—he was too busy sniffing out rabbit holes.

The removal van had taken everything so we slept on the floor. It's only as we were bedding down on it that it dawned on me we'd forgotten all about the carpet. We needed it when we moved. I rang the van driver and he was rather snotty about it, said he couldn't fit it on the van. I went next door and told Mandy to help herself to the carpet after we left and gave her the keys to the house. Mandy was chuffed. At 6.00 a.m. we helped load the van up and while Jeff and Monty were clambering in, I stood and looked at the house for a few seconds before saying goodbye to it. I wasn't to know I'd be seeing it again, on national TV news. I turned and walked towards the van, choking with emotion. We sat up front with the driver and set off for pastures new. New beginnings.

*

My mother had bought a holiday chalet not far from her bungalow and I was to rent it from her. I hadn't actually seen it, but she'd warned me not to bring too much stuff, so I'd given a lot away. As soon as I set eyes on the chalet I knew we'd still overdone it. I made a quick decision and told the men to leave most of the stuff on the front lawn; we'd have no room to shift it once it was in-situ. I stood in the empty chalet for a few minutes looking around, trying to decide how to set it all out, while Jeff stood outside smoking a fag. After the van driver had gone Jeff and I lugged the bed in, then the settee, the cooker, some pots and pans, bits and pieces. We kept bumping in to each other in the small space. After a couple of hours Jeff said he needed a breather. I don't know why: he hadn't done a great deal. He said he would take Monty for a walk and a quick look at the town. It's all right for men, I thought, but was soon engrossed in the task.

I was at my wits end trying to fit all we had in such a small space. I decided the sideboard and an armchair would have to stay on the lawn for the time being. It looked like rain so I ripped open plastic bags trying to find a sheet or something to cover them. I could hear shouting far off as I knelt on the lawn to open another bag. Monty came charging down the avenue and knocked me flying as he ran a circle round me and took off back the way he came. I shouted at him angrily while I followed him with my eyes and saw Jeff staggering down the road, swaying from side to side and yelling at the world. Monty greeted Jeff as if he hadn't seen him for years, jumping up excitedly, wagging his tail, which caused Jeff to lose his balance and fall over in the road. Oh no! I shot a look at the nearest chalets and people were pulling their curtains back and peering out, and opening doors for a better look at the spectacle. I sank back on my heels, lowered my head and covered my face with my hands. We had been there a grand total of six hours.

In defiance of the inauspicious start to our new life we settled into the chalet as best we could. It was hard to make it look anything because it was so cramped and it was terribly damp and smelt of mould. I set about decorating, hanging wallpaper, and it was starting to look a lot better. However, by the time I'd moved on to the next wall the paper was coming down, in slow motion, off the one I'd just finished. It was like a sketch from *Some Mothers Do Have 'Em*, with Jeff trying to hold the top of the wallpaper flat to the wall and me brushing away furiously, trying to re-paste the bottom. We ended up in a heap on the floor, along with the wallpaper, and got stitches from laughing so much.

I asked for advice at the DIY store, they said it was a common problem with the chalets owing to the damp, and sold me some special paste. It was like superglue; they could have used a mould and made tanks out of it. If you didn't position the wallpaper exactly on the first go, you couldn't slide it. Jeff surprised me by artexing the ceilings. Perhaps I'd been right in assuming he'd had no interest in the last house because he thought of it as Steve's. Bit by bit, it all came together.

I was up at daybreak every morning and took Monty for his walk on the beach, leaving Jeff sleeping off his regular hangover. There were donkeys kept in a field around the corner from the chalet and Monty used to go crazy each time we passed. He hated them, his hackles would rise as soon as we turned the corner and when we were abreast of them he'd make a lunge, barking like a Baskerville. Though he had short legs he was as strong as an ox and I had trouble controlling him. A few such episodes later, I started going the long way round to avoid the donkeys.

If Jeff hadn't taken a drink the previous night, he came on the early morning walks. We also went to the beach in the afternoons, come rain or shine. We'd walk for miles along the coastline. Jeff would throw a bit of driftwood in the sea and Monty would chase after it. He'd forget he was supposed to retrieve it and swim about like a happy little water baby. Suddenly he'd raise his head, searching, locate the piece of wood and then swim back to shore. He'd come bounding up and drop it at Jeff's feet, wagging his tail as if to say 'More!' They were lovely days.

I made friends with a German woman, Ilse, or rather, she commandeered me. She lived in a chalet directly facing mine and was dead bossy. She'd married a Brit, long dead and spent the summers in her chalet but also had a huge gothic house back in Nottingham. Ilse had her five-year-old grandson, Charles, staying with her while his mother was at work back in Nottingham. I don't know why she picked on me, apart from the fact I was too passive to tell her to get lost; no one in the chalets gave her the time of day. She was kind to me, cooking little treats for me because she insisted I didn't eat enough, but she was so damn overpowering, a caricature of the German who grabs the deckchair.

Her kindness did not extend to her grandson, however and she treated Charles abominably; she was so strict with him. She had a battle of wits with him over the slightest thing and made him stand to attention in front of her, his little legs buckling, until he saw things her way. He wasn't allowed to leave a morsel of food; he'd be made to sit for hours while he finished what was on his plate. If he didn't it would be served up to him for breakfast. I once dared to ask her if it really mattered if he didn't eat it, and got a lecture about the way the Brits brought up their children. She'd knock late at night and ask me to come over for a coffee, but I'd try to make excuses. I guess she was lonely for some adult company but I couldn't cope with her for long periods. I finally resorted to sneaking out the back way to avoid her.

Monty and I set off for the beach as usual one morning; Jeff declined the invitation. When we got there I looked around for a bit of driftwood and not finding any I picked up an empty plastic bottle, put some sand in to add a bit of weight and threw it in the sea for

Monty. I threw it a few times and he brought it back, after the usual swim. We walked along the coastline for an hour or so, kicking over the sand, picking seashells. 'This is as good as it gets', I sighed contentedly, turning for home. The sun was coming up. When the sun comes out, I go indoors. I hate it.

On the return, Monty found the bottle and lobbed it at my feet. I threw it in the waves, he watched it land, bounded to the edge of the sea and suddenly stopped dead in his tracks, his body rigid, listening. He raised his head in the air, looked to his right, and took off up the beach like a streak of lightening. What the . . . ? I followed his progress with my eyes. Shit! Shit! Shit! The donkeys were coming towards us, a long way in the distance. Monty must have heard the bells they wore round their necks. He was a blur of red fur as he raced to intercept them; I set off running, screaming, 'Monty! No! No! No!' I ran and ran, shouting his name at the top of my voice. I thought my lungs would explode. Monty raced like a greyhound, with me in hot pursuit, sand sucking at my feet, my screams carried in the wind. As I drew closer, I saw one of the donkeys carried a small child on its back. No . . . Please God, no . . .

Monty was straight in there, going at the donkey's throat, the child, a little girl, screaming. The donkey reared up, then galloped off in panic, Monty with it every inch of the way, underneath it, jumping up to rip at its throat, the screaming child hanging on for dear life. Someone, must be the father of the child, was streaking after the donkey, all of them heading my way. I'm running towards them, slower now, breathing raggedly. The father caught up with the donkey and dragged the hysterical little girl from the saddle. The donkey was coming towards me still, Monty, even now, snapping at its throat. Suddenly, the donkey changed direction and veered off to the left where the beach huts were, Monty glued to it like a shadow. I followed, by now staggering, rather than running, my forty-nine years telling on me. I caught up with the little girl and her father; she was bawling her little socks off. 'I'm *so, so* sorry,' I managed to sob.

'You're sorry?' the father said incredulously.

'Oh God. So sorry,' I said, tears streaming down my face, the sand slowing me down as I lurched past.

'You're sorry?' he repeated in disbelief, shaking his head in disgust.

Up ahead, people had come from nowhere and were doing all they could to get Monty away from the donkey—kicking him, hitting him with a deckchair, one man lashing him with a long chain—all to no avail. The poor donkey was cornered because he'd backed himself into a recess between one of the beach huts and the wall, Monty still grabbing at his throat. I could barely see for tears. By now I was walking, the only pace I could muster, gasping for breath, chest heaving. Damn cigarettes. As suddenly as the horror had begun, it ended. Monty stood still, raised his head, sniffed the air, turned, looked in my direction and came bounding towards me. He jumped up to greet me, wagging his tail. I was in so much shock I did not attempt to chastise him. Acting instinctively, my hands shaking, I put his lead on. He was trying to lick me but I couldn't look at his face. Struggling to get my breath back, I stumbled up the beach crying my heart out.

A man stopped me and said 'You needn't think you're leaving the beach. We know you live local; you've been seen here every morning.'

'I don't know what to do,' I cried helplessly.

'Go see Dallas, who owns the donkeys,' he said, pointing up the beach.

I trudged up the beach with Monty trotting beside me as happy as a sandboy. I must have looked like a puppet, my limbs were shaking and I had trouble coordinating. When I got to where the donkeys were tethered I tied Monty to the leg of a table, well away from them, and went in search of Dallas. I told him who I was and what had happened, but he knew nothing about it. The injured donkey was nowhere in sight. I was so disorientated I wasn't aware of what I was doing, or my surroundings. Strangely, Dallas didn't seem to be too concerned about the plight of the donkey. I gave him my address and phone number and he said he'd contact me if there were any vet's bills incurred. The walk home was one of the longest of my life, Monty led me as usual; I was so blinded by tears I could barely see.

As soon as we got back to the chalet Monty went straight in the bathroom, something he'd never done before, and lay on the floor trembling. I don't know whether it was because of the beating he'd suffered, or whether he knew he'd done wrong. I couldn't look at him, let alone stroke or comfort him. The bathroom was so small you couldn't swing a cat in it and I had to step over him to use the loo, but he wouldn't come out. I kept replaying it all in my head repeatedly, the little girl screaming, the poor donkey rearing back trying to escape, the eyes on the child's father, the people beating Monty. I tried closing my eyes to rid myself of the images, but they wouldn't go away. The day had begun with warm expectation; it had ended in blood, savagery, mutilation and grief.

My mother rang to tell me Monty's attack on the donkey was on the local television news and in the evening paper. The paper asked people to come forward with information. Jeff and I went to the police station to ask if they wanted to see us, but the cop on the desk told us they hadn't had a complaint. The cop suggested muzzling Monty when we took him out, but it wouldn't have worked. I had tried to get him used to a Halti to stop him pulling on the lead but he hated it, ran round in circles clawing at it, trying to get it off. He had such energy and enthusiasm he still barged ahead determinedly and ended up with deep cuts to his muzzle.

I knew I'd never dare to take Monty out again because I patently could not control him. Our garden wasn't fenced in so we couldn't have kept him in, and after some soul-searching, I agreed with Jeff we had no alternative but to have him put to sleep. Destroyed. What a dreadful word that is. Because we'd decided Monty was condemned to die neither of us could bring ourselves to stroke him, or baby talk him as we usually did. We'd have felt like Judas. I sobbed when I placed his dinner before him, knowing it was to be his last.

He wasn't himself at all that night. He kept looking at us in a pitiful way. Each time I looked at him I saw the terrified donkey, the hysterical child and the tears kept coming. I know from bitter experience how trauma suffered in childhood can taint your whole life; I was responsible for the little girl's future memories. She was about five years old. How could she ever think of a holiday again without fear? Beaches, holidays, sand, beach huts, donkeys, to say nothing of dogs, would forever hold fearful connotations for her.

Monty was up early next morning, hanging around me, looking at his lead on the back of the door, then at me. I couldn't do it; it seemed too hypocritical, knowing it would be his last walk. I tried to busy myself cleaning, but kept bursting into tears. I gave up and sat on the settee chain-smoking, trying to avoid looking at him. He laid his paw on my knee, whimpering. I thought I would choke, tears, mascara and snot running down my face.

I couldn't even touch Monty to say goodbye before he left. I was too broken-hearted. I took the coward's way out and let Jeff take him to the vet to be put down. I sat there as if carved in stone. And believed I heard Monty yelp, saw the surprise on his face when the tranquillising needle was put in his paw as we'd arranged; we couldn't bear for him to be given the 'Big One' without it. I was still sitting like a statue when Jeff came back. As soon as I saw him without Monty, I burst into tears. So did Jeff. The vet had been upset too, she hated to put a young, healthy dog down.

We both cried for most of the day. I couldn't cook, not that we had an appetite, but we couldn't bear sitting in the chalet; Monty was everywhere. I rang my mum and we met her at the café. As soon as we set eyes on each other she burst into tears, she'd loved Monty too. That started Jeff and me off all over again. We must have looked a sorry trio. People probably though we'd just come from a funeral. Our food went uneaten. We bought a bottle of wine and mourned the passing of Monty that night. We wept and wept, the chalet was so empty without him curled up beside us. The next morning Jeff got up very early, for once, and took Monty's bed and all his toys up to the charity shop so we wouldn't have to look at them. We both felt as if we'd lost a child.

*

Everything seemed to fall apart once Monty was dead. Though I still got up early, the joy was gone out of the day. It's amazing just how much presence a dog has; the chalet now seemed a bleak, lonely place. Every time I looked at the empty space where Monty's bed had been I burst into tears all over again. I moved the furniture to cover the gap but it didn't work; I could still see it in my head.

Logic told me Monty was a dog, only doing what dogs do; dogs bite other animals if given half a chance. I couldn't have foreseen the donkeys would be working earlier than usual. However, when you're traumatised, logic doesn't enter into the equation and because of the past, I endowed myself with supernatural powers. Death had come again and I had somehow made it happen. It seemed everything I touched turned to dust. The bad dreams returned. They must have been lurking, lying in wait. Monty, Dolores, the child on the donkey, the ferret, the donkey, my kitten, my baby sister, the blood, all ravelled up in juxtaposition.

Jeff was suffering too; he'd lost his best buddy. No matter what faults he had, he'd loved Monty to bits, they'd gone everywhere together. We were like parents who discovered their dead child had been the glue that held them together. I turned my hurt inwards—my duodenal ulcer gnawing away, migraines, raging eczema—whereas Jeff turned his outwards and propelled it at me. Though he'd never quit drinking he'd been in happy, manic mode since we moved, had even stopped the verbal attacks. Now he went on binges and returned home full of aggression, slagging me off unmercifully. The same old fodder: my criminal offspring, my looks, my age. One night he crossed the line.

He had been going at it for over an hour when he got carried away with himself, saying I was a destroyer, a seducer of men. I smiled at the description. I thought he was referring to my old profession. Actually, they came looking for me. I didn't need to seduce them, I thought, but didn't voice. He called me a Lolita. I spluttered with laughter.

'Think you'll find she was a teensy-weeny bit younger than me, actually.'

'You know what I mean,' he said. 'I'm talking about when you were a kid, I bet you wanted it really.'

I threw the cushion at him and jumped to my feet.

'Little girls do have sexual feelings you know', he proclaimed.

It hit me in the face like a fist.

'How the fuck would you know?'

I stood over him, white-faced with fury. I felt the rage slowly rising from the centre of me, up through my heart, my lungs, my windpipe, before erupting through my lips. I leaned over him in slow motion, retrieved the cushion and hit him across the face with it, slowly.

'How dare you! Don't you *dare* tell me I wanted it.'

I hit him twice more with the cushion, slowly.

'I was three years old when it started. I wasn't old enough to be a Lolita. You drunken, good-for-nothing bastard you!'

He laughed at me. I was crying and hitting him with the cushion, left, right, slowly, left, right. He fended me off, laughing, told me to stop over-reacting.

'No! I won't put up with it,' I cried, still whacking away at him.

'You can slag me all you want for my past and what I've done. But don't you dare negate what was done to the child.'

He took the cushion from me and pushed me away.

'Don't you dare deny me,' I wept, falling back on the chair in exhaustion.

He sobered up rapidly, surprised by my outburst. He started to talk quietly, asked me to try to see the bigger picture. I wasn't the only person in the world it had ever happened to. Things had happened to him too, he knew what he was talking about.

'Oh right. What? What things? Tales of mystery and imagination I suppose,' I wept, 'as usual.'

For a second there was an air of hesitancy about him.

'Ah forget it,' he said.

He shook his head, sighed, reached for a cigarette, lit it, inhaled deeply, leaned back on the chair and closed his eyes, shutting me out. I could have sworn I'd seen a fleeting, naked vulnerability in his eyes, yet it vanished so quickly I thought I'd imagined it.

'I'll never forgive you for tonight Jeff. I swear I will never, ever forgive you for what you just said.'

I left him sitting and went to run myself a bath. Instead of the usual sheep dip, I lay there mulling things over until the water was cold. I asked myself why, four years on, we were no nearer to some sort of peaceful co-existence. I thought long and hard about what exactly it was I wanted, or needed from Jeff.

I hadn't been in a pub since the first couple of months we were together. I never went night-clubbing. I never went out on my own. I sat in every night. I had never been unfaithful. I never became argumentative. When he did, I didn't scream and shout; the most he'd get in the way of retaliation would be sarcasm or caustic retorts. I kept house and looked after him well. I made no demands on him.

I reflected on a Freudian slip Jeff had made in the early days, that was always at the back of my mind and which I took out to examine from time to time. He was mending a chair in my sister's kitchen, with his headphones on as usual listening to his music, as Sam and

I sat having a cuppa. She asked him what was taking him so long. He pretended not to hear. He didn't know we knew he had no batteries in his headset—Sam had removed them as a joke when he'd gone to the toilet—so he was earwigging on our conversation. Sam tapped him on the shoulder, he pushed the head phones back on his head and lifted his chin in query. We were in stitches by this stage. She repeated the question.

'I have to get the sluts in first—if you think it's that easy do it yourself, or get someone else to do it,' he responded angrily, thinking we were laughing at his slowness.

Sluts. How telling. Sam didn't notice it. I didn't enlighten her. I should have listened to my heart then.

I couldn't expect him to respect me; he knew too much about me. He did not glean my resume from me, I had nothing to brag about. I only discovered he'd read a copy of *Lyn*—my sister had it in her house—when he threw all the facts at me one night when he was drunk. He'd already made his mind up about me and came equipped with his own ammunition.

I chewed over what I had actually achieved regarding the way I lived my life since I left the streets. I had so much more insight into the power of the subconscious: hidden agendas, wishes, desires, the power of the past. I'd finally got the fatal attraction for dangerous men out of my system, yet I was still in an abusive relationship. The only difference was that Jeff didn't physically beat me. There's none so blind as those who will not see. I couldn't call it a moment of crystal clarity, seeing as it had taken me so long, but the Lolita business was like a light bulb going on. It illuminated where I'd been, and shone a ray of light on the way forward.

It's hard to stifle one's natural personality over a long period and in the ten years since the murders there were short periods of time when I forgot and thought I was your average citizen. Cheerful and irreverent by nature, I'd be with a girl friend, laughing at some silly thing. I'd catch sight of myself in a window or a mirror and the reflection would show me, white-faced, hanging on the chicken wire while John Cullen set fire to the house. I could be anywhere—walking down a street, waiting at a bus-stop, window shopping, walking around the supermarket preoccupied with a shopping list—and I'd see a woman with a head of curls, like Dolores. I'd have to find a seat until the dizziness passed. 'So-and-so got on like a house on fire', someone might say and I would start to stutter. I could be in a shop holding my hand out for change and as the assistant looked in my eyes I would think 'she knows'. I never knew when these feelings would surface; I had no control over them, they were floating around in my subconscious, as much a part of me as the blood in my veins. But some things I could control. I found ways of ensuring life was not too rosy and steered clear of anything that smacked of self-indulgence. I abolished birthdays, never had a party in my life. Under no circumstances would I have a facial, a manicure, a massage, go to the hairdresser's, however much my sister—a great believer in pampering oneself—tried to coax me. There was to be no relaxing in the bath with scented candles when a sheep dip would suffice. I put off taking painkillers for migraine or arthritis as long as possible, refused to take a taxi, a cold remedy, corn plasters, lip salve, all stupid little gestures.

Once, my sister and I were in a top department store checking out shoes for her when she decided we should get our hair done. I was appalled. 'No way', I said. She blackmailed me by refusing to go on her own. She paid almost £100 to have my hair totally restyled. It did look fantastic. She spent the rest of the day grinning at me, as if to say 'Told you, no harm treating yourself.' Conscious of her feelings, I grinned back in acceptance. As soon as I got home I mussed it all up, biting back tears. Sam sat and watched in silence.

'It doesn't match the inside.' I spoke to her through the mirror.

She rolled her eyes and said, 'For goodness sake Lynda. Don't be so theatrical!'

She did not understand. There was no-one I could discuss my feelings with who could have understood; only someone who had been there at the scene of a murder, who had experienced the same emotions, could tell me how they dealt with them. Being a Catholic (lapsed or not) is no help;, making penance is ingrained in us, looked upon as the solution to everything. It isn't. I never bought into the cleansing through confession either, even as a child. You came out of the box and you still knew you'd nicked a penny from your mum, told a lie, pinched your baby sister. It would take a lot more than a man in a cassock to absolve me of my sins, he'd more than likely turn out to be a client of mine anyway.

No matter. I still had an ace up my sleeve. People who hated the way Jeff treated me, like Ilse, would not have known he was as much a victim in the relationship. I may not have made a conscious decision to do so, but I used him. I'd put up with his insults for almost four years, even welcomed them. If I had to live, so be it, so long as the living was not too pleasurable. Too cowardly to do it myself, I knew enough to recognise that I saw in Jeff an ideal candidate, the instrument with which to torture myself. I had given him too much power and I realised, for the first time, that he was not worthy of it.

As I towelled myself dry, my mind was already made up. By attacking the child in me Jeff had trespassed into forbidden territory. Staying with him would be as good as compounding and condoning the original abuse. I didn't want to leave, yet I knew I couldn't stay.

*

I wasn't dishonest. I told him I was going to leave him. He didn't believe me, I hardly need add, men never do. He thought we'd just carry on as if nothing had happened. I had nowhere to go, so I couldn't just up sticks there and then. I had a lot of thinking and planning to do first. I must be thicker than I like to think I am because it took me a while to figure out that the only way out of the prison I'd made for myself was to go out and find a proper job. A job would get me out of the chalet, which had become a morgue without Monty. It would give me space from Jeff, and provide me with some money so I could save up for a move.

Just because one's circumstances change, it does not follow that their personalities do too. Oh, I'd become a dab hand at arguing, shouting and swearing at men when they put me down, pretending to stand up for myself, but it was all hot air. It was my home, but I was still too passive to kick Jeff out. I knew it wasn't going to be easy overcoming the phobia I had regarding strangers, but I owed it to the child I'd once been.

I called in at the job centre a few times but saw nothing I was qualified for on the boards. Then I spotted an ad in the post office window looking for packers in a factory. No qualifications needed, no questions asked, sounded right up my street. I rang and got the job over the phone. The guy explained it was cash-in-hand, working in a fruit-packing factory, a one-and-a-half-hour drive away. He, Derek, picked up in the town centre at 6.00 a.m. 'It's cold, so dress warmly', he advised.

Jeff sneered when I told him I'd gotten a job. 'You won't go. You're just being a drama queen, trying to prove a point.'

I set the clock for 4.30 to give me plenty of time. I hate rushing. A couple of cups of coffee, three or four cigs, listen to the news, put my war paint on, I was going to work! I was elated and scared at the same time. I dressed in a wool twin set, a woollen knee length skirt, tights, socks and a pair of knee length boots. I was too early at the pick-up point. I'm always the same, I have a dread of being late for anything. There were six other workers in the van, apart from Derek, the boss. They were all young guys, nice open faces, clean cut, half asleep. I felt no fear, only friendly vibes. We stopped off at a town on the way; we all climbed out and stocked up on fags, sandwiches, newspapers, drinks etc. When we got to the factory, we had coffee from a vending machine and a quick ciggie, and hit the factory floor at 8.00 on the dot.

As soon as I walked in the door, a blast of icy air hit me. Christ, and it was only summertime. The floor area was enormous and all around the walls were stainless steel tables, empty wooden pallets beside them. Apart from that, the place was empty. The room was windowless. What lighting there was came from strip-lights that flickered now and then. Great for migraine, I thought. I began shivering right away. Men and women were already taking their places at the tables. I was wearing the wrong clothes; everyone was wearing jeans or tracky bottoms and trainers. They all wore blue over-alls and matching hats, their hair tucked under. They'd travelled all the way from Skegness in another van, even further than me.

Derek told me to wait for Fina, the supervisor; she'd show me what to do. I stood there like a fool, in the wrong clothes. Jesus. It's so cold. How will I cope?

'You there! Who you are?'

I turned toward the voice. A woman in a white coat and hat stood with her hands on her hips as she addressed me. The Spanish lady, Fina the supervisor, I realised.

'Eh, Lynda. I came in Derek's van.' I noticed I could see my breath in the cold air.

'You come with me. You no work with the men,' she said, looking me up and down. 'You work there with women.'

She strode ahead of me, high heels tapping on the concrete, a real sexy walk. She pointed to an empty table.

'You no here to have a good time. You here to work. You no talk,' she informed me. I wouldn't have been surprised if she'd done a little click of the heels.

To say I was furious is an understatement, but I kept it buttoned. Fina was around the same age as me, an attractive woman with brown eyes, blonde streaked hair, voluptuous lips and a nice figure. One guy on the line said he bet she was a passionate woman. A nice description, I thought.

She went off to get me some overalls. I already had a drip on my nose. The woman at the next table said hello. I looked around for Fina before I dared to answer.

'Don't worry. You're all right. She's gone upstairs for your overalls,' the woman said.

'What's she like?' I whispered, like a schoolgirl.

'A bit of a battle-axe. You'll be all right as long as you don't answer her back. She's got a wicked temper.'

'Christ. It's like being in a bloody Gulag!'

We smiled at one another. I asked if she had a tissue for my nose. I walked to her table just as Fina showed up. I stiffened, waiting for her to start yelling at me, but she handed me the cap and overall and stood watching as I put them on. The overall buried me. I didn't know they made them so big. I was only eight stone six at the time; you could have got a twenty-stoner in with me. I kept a smile on my face, rolling the sleeves over and over to shorten them. Her eyes dared me to protest. The woman at the table winked, gave me the thumbs up and mimed 'suits you' behind Fina's back. By then I was fighting a fit of the giggles.

'Thank you,' a giggle escaped, like a snort. 'Just what I needed, nice and roomy, I hate anything constricting.' Fina's eyes told me she hated me.

When she'd gone, Derek sidled by my table pushing a stack of pallets and whispered, 'The lads told me to tell you, you look dead sexy.' I let out a peal of laughter. The ice was broken.

I worked alone at the table packing kiwi fruit the first day. Nice and easy, two, four, six to a pack, you got a rhythm going and could let your mind drift. I wasted half the day rolling my sleeves back, and shoving my voluminous overall out of the way of the table. We got a ten-minute break in the morning, half-an-hour for lunch, and then worked through until 4.30 p.m. An hour-and-a-half for the drive home took us to sixish. I staggered out of the van, cramped up from the journey. After the twelve-hour day, I just sat in the chair exhausted, too tired to cook.

'Told you. You're too old for that crap,' said Jeff. 'They're all kids. Its not for the likes of an old gal like you.'

For the first few days I was knackered when I got home. Well, I was knocking on a bit. I had to work the rest of the week in the wrong clothes. I'd never owned a pair of trainers in my life, let alone tracky bottoms. I usually dress as if going to an office, or wear long hippy style skirts. I have a major hang-up about my chunky thighs so wouldn't be seen dead in jeans outside the house.

On the Saturday, I invested in long johns, thermal vests, roll neck sweaters, tracksuit bottoms, and some hiking boots. I was glad of the roomy overall, I wore most of the gear in layers and looked like a sumo wrestler on the Monday.

Our wages were confusing. I'm confused even thinking about it. All I know is Derek (our gang boss) and Derek's gang boss both took a cut out of our wages and we ended up with £2.50 per hour. We couldn't complain; we were working in the black economy.

We packed kiwis, apples, oranges, grapes, blueberries, cherries, peaches, plums, limes, sugar snap peas, mange tout and syphilis, as the women called Physalis, the Cape gooseberry! The work was gruelling due to the pace and the cold, but I quite liked it really, I was a fast packer. We liked to chat while we worked, which made the day go by quicker; we didn't stop work to talk—Fina was unfair in that respect. We stood on flattened cardboard boxes to stop the cold penetrating and I was still freezing.

It was odd to get out of the van on a summer's evening in my work clothes and to see people dressed in T-shirts, shorts and dresses. I got some strange looks when I went to the co-op for supplies. The sunlight hurt our eyes too: we hardly saw daylight with the factory having no windows and there were none in the back of the van either. I ordered a mini-trampoline from a catalogue, and took to doing between twenty and thirty minutes rebounding every day, to raise my fitness levels, and it seemed to work. I had to keep the pace up. I couldn't let Fina beat me. Or Jeff.

Fina was down on Debbie, the first woman I'd talked to, and had exiled her to Siberia, the other end of the factory. On the second day I was sent to join her. Debbie called it 'the naughty corner', because she wore mascara, as did I. The Skegness gang consisted of young women, mainly, who rolled out of the van at 5.30 a.m., yawning, their hair uncombed, sleep in their eyes, pyjamas peeping out from under their long johns. They couldn't be bothered at such an ungodly hour, probably after a hot night too. They still looked fine, that's youth for you.

Debbie and I worked at separate tables but we perfected our own sign language. If that failed, or if Fina was around, we would spell out words on our tables with blueberries, strawberries, or grapes, though the latter were a bit harder to read from a distance. Debbie became very inventive, the letter 'F' got a lot of usage. It was a bit like being at boarding school (in the Antarctic), and the days passed happily enough. Debbie became a good mate. She lived locally and only worked from 8.00 until 1.00, so Fina suddenly decided she wasn't allowed a coffee break with us, which I thought was a bit mean seeing as she'd worked there three years. I used to run to the canteen, have a quick couple of puffs of a cig, grab two cups of coffee from the vending machine and take it back to Debbie. We'd work through the break, slowly, on a matter of principle. We didn't always work because when Fina left the floor we leaned on the table yakking for ten minutes.

She hated the English, did Fina (though she was married to a Brit), and said they were an idle race.

'They buncha lazy pigs! They no know how to work. In Spain we show them.'

She probably had a point, but as she spent most of the day upstairs in a warm office, no dripping nose or frozen fingers, it was all right for her to talk. I didn't take her comments personally; I'm conscientious no matter what I do. She reluctantly gave me a grudging respect, eventually.

It was rare to see Fina in the staff canteen. Now and again, she'd stroll in and plonk herself down at the dinner table uninvited, nylon-clad legs crossed, while she ate an apple. A hush would fall over the room, everyone suddenly very interested in their sandwiches, apart from the man who thought she was a passionate woman. He'd be salivating, watching every bite of the apple. When Fina swallowed so did he, little beads of sweat on his upper lip. She'd chatter away, oblivious to the silence, without expecting an answer. When she left a collective exhalation of breath could be heard, then we'd all start talking at once.

I got on great with the lads in our gang, which was just as well, seeing as we were compelled to spend three hours a day sitting scrunched up in the back of the van. Being the only female they looked on me as their mascot and treated me with the utmost respect. I was old enough to be their mother. Sarah sometimes came to work with us but they discounted her; she was Derek's wife and sat up front. Their acceptance, and Debbie's friendship, acted like a catalyst and served to make the treatment meted out back home all the more unpalatable.

Jeff felt severely threatened by my working near men and escalated the verbal attacks with ferocity. He'd come in drunk and make lots of noise, knowing I had to get up at 4.30. I tried to pretend I couldn't hear him to begin with but when I did complain he'd fire off a verbal onslaught. I reached the stage where I had visions of hitting him over the head with a hammer just to shut him up. I fully understand women who suddenly snap one day. I informed him that no matter what he said or did, nothing would prevent me from going to work. I had an unopened pay packet put by in the drawer and he stole it, went walkabout and booked himself into a hotel. I was furious with him, but glad of the bit of peace.

*

'Everybody: oranges!' Fina shouted. Debbie and I waited for Martin, one of our gang, to drop a pallet between us. I saw the top two boxes were full of mouldy, rotten oranges. I made an executive decision and told Martin to take them back.

'Martin! Where you go with those oranges?' Fina shouted.

'Lynda doesn't want them.'

Fina was on me like a ton of bricks. 'You think you in charge?'

'No. They're all mouldy.'

'They no mouldy!' They use for orange juice. You don't say take away, or make decision!' Spanish eyes flashing, Spanish arms going like windmills.

I felt sick as a parrot as I packed, fingers disappearing in the rotten flesh. Alexander Fleming would have had a field day; there was enough mould in a single box to find a cure for every disease on the globe. The bottom oranges were so mushy they looked like swede and broccoli mash. I tell people to ignore the 'fresh' on a carton of orange juice. I've never drunk any since.

Summer passed, not that I saw much of it. I was working Saturday mornings too. We would go to the supermarket when the shift ended; we knew we'd be too tired to shop when we got home. We were all single, apart from Derek and Sarah, with no responsibilities, so we took our time. We stopped off in Boston for a McDonalds on the way back. Sometimes Sarah would want to visit a garden centre and we'd all troop in, spend an hour or so looking around, savouring the warmth, freedom from the cold factory, celebrating the end of the working week, the sheer joy of being alive. Martin worked as a club bouncer Friday nights; after staying up all night he tended to fall asleep in the back of the van. The two Andys, both teenagers, were always horsing around, pouncing on him, arm wrestling, lots of testosterone, headlocks.

'Watch Lynda!'

'Be careful, you almost hit Lynda!'

'Lynda's behind you!' They made me feel like a piece of Dresden china. They were decent human beings, every one of them was kind, nice, ordinary, good humoured. Not a woman abuser among them. I loved Saturdays.

Thanks to the long van journeys, a bond existed among the gang, and they socialised after work. On a Saturday night they all (accompanied by their girlfriends or partners), met up with Derek and Sarah in the pub, then went on to a restaurant. They gave up inviting me after a while. I was too embarrassed to admit my partner wasn't fit to be around when he was drunk. I admit to feeling rather wistful in the van on Mondays.

'You shoulda been there Lynda. We had a great night.'

I was the only one in our gang not to go. The places they frequented were not exactly my cup of tea, but I enjoyed their company so much I would not have minded. Being a seaside resort, families, singles, and all age groups mixed in the pubs and clubs, like a Butlin's holiday camp I imagine, though I've never been to one. Age was no barrier.

I stayed away because I did not want to fight with Jeff; I no longer had the stomach for it. He was deeply unhappy already and I was changing, becoming more confident, less dependent on his approval. Our life together had changed out of all recognition. The message was finally getting through to him; I would leave. His life was about to change.

Sundays were spent washing, ironing, cleaning and getting ready for Monday. I had joined the rest of society, and the transition had been painless.

10

The Cranberries were coming—the turkey accompaniment, not the group. It's all anyone at the factory talked about for weeks; it was seen as the major event in the working year. It meant lots of overtime leading up to Christmas, so our jobs would be safe for a while. Being casual we never knew when Fina would decide she did not need us for a few days. We were already doing twelve-hour days, including travelling time and I could not imagine how we were meant to fit it all in. A lot of extra staff were to start on the Monday so we worked all day Saturday preparing the factory, fetching extra tables from the storeroom, carrying them in to the work area and setting them up in long lines. When we had finished Fina told us to give everywhere a real good clean as we would not have time once the cranberries arrived. That should have told me something. I missed the usual Saturday afternoon trip to McDonalds and the garden centre, the highlight of my week

Derek bought another van for the new recruits, and one of the new guys was paid to drive it. We had to take extra workers in our van, so space was at a premium: no stretching your legs over two seats to relax. The atmosphere in the van changed. There were too many people to be intimate, no more joking and winding each other up. It was like sitting next to a stranger on a coach trip, though as we got to know them the new guys blended in quite well. We started working an extra two hours per day, finishing at 6.30, arriving home at 8.00. We worked all day Saturdays too, so we were all knackered, even the two Andys. It was doubly hard for Martin; he was still working the doors Fridays and Saturdays.

Everyone smoked, apart from Martin, and one new guy. Martin was used to us smoking, but I felt terribly sorry for the new chap. We kept the windows closed for the first half of the journey because we were all freezing after coming out of the cold and the heater didn't work. I watched him wiping his eyes with the bottom of his jumper; then he covered his face with it. He was only a kid of around eighteen, too shy to complain. In the end, I could stand it no longer. I tapped him on the shoulder and whispered that I would change places with him. I had a seat on my own next to a small side window at the back. Being polite, he said he was fine. He sat up looking straight ahead for a while afterwards, until the smoke got to him again and it was up with the jumper. Even the smokers were forced to capitulate eventually, no one smoked for the last leg of the journey.

Now that it was winter, all the fruit we packed was very cold to the touch, but at least we only had to pick it up with our fingers. The cranberries were something else; they were bloody freezing. They came in a big blue plastic bath and they were a bit soggy. You had to sift through them with both hands; it was like sinking your hands into a bath of crushed ice. From handling the plastic punnets we all had little cuts on our hands and the fruit acid ate into them. You worked through the pain barrier. The nail varnish stripped from our fingers in minutes and our hands were stained bluish-black permanently. I'd always been vain about my hands and would never leave the house without my nails perfectly manicured. One of the women brought in an industrial size packet of rubber gloves but they hindered the work due to the loss of sensation in our fingertips; we gave up wearing them. We were all in the same boat but it was embarrassing to go to the shop after work with hands like a coal miner's. I discovered that a good five-minute soak in bleach when you got home did the trick, but our nails were a lost cause. Working in the food industry has been a real eye-opener. I don't particularly like turkey and have never eaten a cranberry in my life, now I never would. We all had a steady drip on our noses as we worked, drip, drip, drip, straight into the baths. We had no time to stop and blow our noses; production would have ground to a halt. It was better if you didn't look at each other.

There was a lot of chatter among the new recruits on the factory floor and a holiday atmosphere prevailed because they didn't know

Fina's reputation. Someone said something at one of the lines, which was passed along like Chinese whispers to our line, then down the line to the woman on my left. She muttered something to me. Being slightly deaf due to a perforated ear-drum (old war wound), I leaned towards her.

'Sorry, I didn't catch what you said'.

Fina roared across the factory floor: 'You there!'

You could have heard a pin drop. The whole factory looked at her.

'Yes you . . . Lynda. How come every time you always talking?' she shouted.

I took a deep, angry breath, but before I could open my mouth to protest every single person in the gang and quite a few of the others sprang to my defence. It sounded like a rumble of thunder.

'I asked her a question.'

'We were all talking'. 'It's not her fault.' 'Oh, bloody leave her alone!' 'She's not the only person in the factory.'

'Why are you always picking on her?'

Everybody waited with bated breath, especially me.

A lone voice muttered into the silence: 'Pick on someone else for a change.' It sounded quite loud.

Fina stood with her hands on her hips staring at me for a few seconds, one stiletto-clad foot tapping angrily; even at a distance, you could see the red gash of her mouth working furiously. Thick-skinned as she was, even she knew she'd gone too far. Either that or the mutiny had caught her off balance, because she opted to let it pass. With the whole floor watching I was mortified, but when I thought about it later, I was glad; it proved I wasn't imagining things.

Fina sacked three or four people for not working hard enough.

'You! I no want you. You go.'

Nice and brief, no explanations given. Poor bastards had to sit in the van all day waiting for us to finish the shift. Two older men walked off the factory floor because they couldn't bear being talked down to. Or, as one of them said as he took off his overall and threw his blue hat on the floor in a temper, 'I've got a wife, three kids, a mortgage, a dog and a bowl of fucking goldfish, and I've managed to look after all of them without being told how by some Spanish trollop.'

As it got nearer to Christmas, even more staff was taken on. Jeff got to hear about it and said he wanted a job with us. I knew it would end in disaster and did my best to dissuade him.

'Last time I looked it was a free country. You can't stop me getting the job. Why should you have the right to make some money, and not me?' he griped.

I said I wasn't prepared to be humiliated in front of my friends and work colleagues. He swore on his mother's life he wouldn't. As he'd stated, I had no right to stop him, so against my better judgement I asked Derek to give him a job. Well, it was more a case of feeling fatalistic about the consequences, but resigned to them. What the hell. At least if he had to get up early himself I stood a chance of getting a decent night's sleep. I must have been crazy.

Derek took one of the new guys off our van to make way for Jeff. I climbed up and went right to the back to my usual place. Jeff gave me a filthy look because I chose not to sit with him, but he didn't say anything, he was on his best behaviour. He put a dampener on things from the start. He was smiling, pretending to participate in the light-hearted banter while scowling back at me. Gradually the conversation ground to a halt, the first time it had ever happened. We were all glad when the journey was over.

Fina must have liked the look of Jeff because she gave him the cushiest job in the factory, delivering the plastic punnets, light as a feather, to the packers. She stood with her hand on his shoulder as she explained things, all teeth, red lips smiling. I was relieved he would not be packing on the line—we all were—not that it made much difference because he still watched every move I made. The canteen could not accommodate us all at once so the lunch breaks were staggered. Jeff had to take a different one to me. Sarah looked at me, rolled her eyes and said, 'Thank God for that!' proving how quickly she'd found the measure of him. 'Is he always like that?' she asked, shaking her head.

'Fraid so.'

'No wonder you didn't want to bring him out!'

His status had been sealed on the van journey.

Even then, he came in the canteen on a pretext and had a look to see who I sat with. Derek, Sarah, Martin and the two Andys as it happened. After all we were the A team! Providentially, I was bent towards Sarah as she whispered in my ear (someone she fancied had a nice bum), when Jeff showed up. When we got home, he moaned how shattered he was after such a gruelling day. Speed was not his forte. At least he was too knackered to go to the pub. He was comatose by 9.00. And he was the rest of the week. It was an odd week in other respects. He was quiet and pensive, he obviously had something on his mind, but he wasn't about to share it with me.

He watched me like a hawk the whole time, which I found suffocating. It's hard to be natural when you're under the microscope. Natural to me is good humoured, but by the time Friday arrived I'd reached the stage where I was scared to death to smile at anyone, let alone engage in conversation. Jeff was upsetting the other workers in to the bargain, with his beady eyes on them. It was very disquieting, for all of us, to look up and see his brooding presence hovering in the vicinity.

On the Friday, when we arrived home I told Jeff that I'd had enough. He heard me out in silence for once. When he did speak, the response was not what I expected.

'I think we should get married. Marry me Lyn.'

I stood up straight and turned to look at him in amazement.

'Marry!

'What on earth for?'

He looked at me in silence for a few moments.

'You're too friendly,' he replied.

'What's that got to do with it?' I asked, perplexed.

He didn't respond.

'What's wrong with being friendly? What . . . I should be a miserable sod like you?' He looked hurt.

'You can kill a room stone dead in thirty seconds with your aura. You want me to be like you?' I huffed, throwing the makings of a sandwich on the cutting board. Peeling spuds or cooking dinners were things of the past since I'd been working overtime. He stood with his back to the freezer watching me work, but did not answer. 'And anyway, I'm not too friendly, it's just the way I am. Have you ever known me to be unfriendly?'

He shook his head. I was so used to him talking over me I took my chance while I had it.

'Haven't I always been friendly towards you . . . good natured?' He nodded his head again.

'Depressed, yes,' I went on. 'How could I not be, but not unfriendly. I don't do miserable, there are too many miserable sods in the world,' I said tiredly, smearing butter on bread. 'Pass me the ham out the fridge, please.'

I jumped back in alarm when he leaned over and grabbed my hands, thinking he was going to strike me. I was startled to see his eyes were moist. He grasped both hands in his and said:

'But I thought you only treated me like that. I didn't know, I thought it was because you loved me, that I was special to you.' Oh, bloody hell, now I'd gone and done it. Normally I'd have said something along the lines of being too ugly to marry, asked whether bridal shops carried a range of fancy paperbags to wear over my head on the day, but a look at his face told me it wasn't the time for sarcasm.

All evening he pleaded with me: 'Marry me.' I wondered how the hell I was going to get out of that one. To him it was such a big deal that he had asked me. I knew he didn't really want to marry me; he just didn't want to lose me. I knew the way his mind worked. He thought if he staked his claim on me, the guys I worked with would not be so friendly towards me. Bullshit, it was just the way the gang operated. Sarah was one of the guys and Derek took the banter in his stride; in fact he was one of the worst offenders for winding the women up, whether Sarah was with him or not. Factory life, I should think, though I'm no expert. While I knew all that, I wasn't callous enough to hurt Jeff's feelings by throwing what he saw as a grand gesture back in his face. So though I didn't actually say the word 'yes', I didn't say 'no', merely acted as if the topic had never arisen. I presumed he'd have forgotten about it by morning and I needed to get some shut-eye. No such luck.

I had an emerald eternity ring Jeff had bought for my birthday a while back and he now insisted I wear it as an engagement ring, to prove his ownership, though he couched it in different terms. He had completely blotted out the fact that I had said I intended leaving when I had enough money. He took me to the little jewellers in the town on Sunday to buy me a wedding ring. I bet there never was a more unenthusiastic fiancée. I was playing for time, waiting for inspiration, because I knew the marriage was never going to happen.

Jeff had his manic head on, shiny-eyed with happiness, as I tried on the ring he'd chosen. It was £42. The elderly chap who served us was filling in for the owner; he read the price tag upside down and sold it to us for £24. I didn't like to say anything in the shop, not wanting to embarrass Jeff when he paid. As soon as we got outside Jeff insisted I put it on my finger. I said I would when we got home. No, now, he insisted. He pushed it on the second finger of my left hand then smiled at me affectionately. My eyes watered, I stood looking at my hand in despair. Jeff asked if I had noticed the jeweller's mistake on the price. I nodded, sorry for the old man.

'Y'know Jeff, we won't have any luck if we get married on a ring that's as good as stolen.'

He frowned. He stood looking at me for a few moments, weighing up a few pints of beer against good luck in our marriage. The would be marriage won out and we went back to the shop and paid the difference.

He held my hand in a vice-like grip all the way home, not wanting to let go of me. I had an idea how women entering into an arranged marriage must feel as I trudged alongside with a heavy heart; I felt I was going to the guillotine. That night he pulled the two single mattresses from our rooms and made up a bed on the living room floor. We lay there side by side in silence, he holding my hand so tightly I thought my fingers would splinter. I had to tell him to let go, he was hurting me. Another fine mess you got yourself into, Lynda, I thought. I knew I wouldn't actually marry Jeff, just as I'd known I wouldn't get round to marrying Dave Black when he'd made me an offer I couldn't refuse years ago. I just didn't know how to go about getting out of it. I didn't hate Jeff, I just did not love him. Lolita had put paid to that.

As I stood on the line on the Monday after the engagement I felt different. Fina had put me on the conveyor belt labelling melons, which required considerable speed and I kept catching fleeting glimpses of emerald green as my ring-clad fingers flew from side to side along the belt. I felt frightened and vulnerable, just as I had when I'd had my coil removed when John Cullen had wanted me to have his child. The usual banter was going the rounds but I did not enter into it, I didn't feel light-hearted enough. I was too embarrassed to tell any of our gang about the betrothal for fear they'd laugh; I was old enough to be mother to them all. Sarah would have thought I was out of my mind; they all would, come to think of it. My spirits didn't improve as the week wore on. I kept wondering how I was going to extricate myself from the engagement. I didn't want it to reach the stage where I'd be praying for a file in the wedding cake. Jeff still watched me like a hawk, though now he had a goofy smile on his face whenever I looked at him.

Four more men and a woman walked off the floor in response to Fina's histrionics that week. In fairness to Fina it should be said she was under a lot of pressure from suppliers. We'd lost Marks & Spencer's contract the week before, thanks to the temporary workers who did not seem to understand that while speed was of the essence you couldn't just pack any old rubbish.

The following Monday five new recruits were put to work on the melons, three of whom proved to be useless. The melons were stacking up, falling on the floor the other end of the conveyor belt. Fina shouted at me to leave the cranberries and help sort it out. Within no time the situation was under control. We were going great guns until some silly bugger hit the button that controls the speed of the belt and the melons started flashing by like an express train. We were trying to stick the labels on as they passed, like one of those speeded up old black and white movies. It only lasted for a few moments but we were all laughing like school kids. Suddenly, I was pushed forward onto the conveyor belt by a hard slap on the back. I staggered back, shocked to my hiking boots.

'Old habits die hard don't they Lyn?' Jeff snarled.

I straightened up, threw the roll of labels on the floor and said angrily, 'What the fuck are you on about?'

He spat in my face, unbuttoned his overalls, took his blue hat off, threw them both on the conveyor belt and walked off the floor. I wanted to die. The new guys put their heads down and carried on labelling. Derek came over, put his arm round me, asked if I was OK. I nodded and said I was fine, though I was a little tearful. Derek said he would go and talk to Jeff, but returned shortly and said he must have left the factory; he was nowhere to be found. I wondered how he'd get home, we were fifty miles away and the bus connection was almost non-existent. I knew he'd head straight for the bottle, which was how he dealt with everything. I was rattling. The gang kept an eye on the door as they worked in case Jeff came back. Each of them found an excuse to come by the belt and say a few kind words.

A Skegness girl came over and said, 'What's his problem?'

I told her he was jealous. She laughed. 'What . . . of this lot?' she inclined her head at the men. 'Surely he doesn't think you're that desperate!'

I smiled weakly.

'Not exactly George Clooney are they?' she said.

She put her arms round me and gave me a hug. I carried on working but my hands were shaking pretty badly. Normally I had five labels on the tips of my fingers at a time, feeding the roll with my other hand, but I got so clumsy they were all sticking to each other. Just as well the shift was almost over.

Jeff was totally out of order. Working the melons meant that nobody had time to stop and look at each other, the melons came along too fast. It was eye and hand coordination. It's not as if I was cosying up to a guy. There was one other woman from the Skeggy gang working the belt whose boyfriend was on the cranberry line. He may have been little more than a kid yet he managed to act like a grown-up. Somehow, I got through the afternoon. There was only twenty minutes to go when one of the women told me I was wanted on the phone. My blood ran cold.

'Phone? Where?'

'On Fina's phone.'

Jesus. I crossed the floor to the inner sanctum and picked up the receiver with a shaking hand.

'Hello?'

'Is that you . . . bastard? I'm gonna fucking kill you! You think Cullen was bad, I'll show you bad.'

I thought the receiver would melt in my hand with the heat from the vitriol my fiancé spewed out in a long endless stream.

Fina came round the corner, a woman on a mission. How dare I use her phone. She stood with her hands on her hips glowering right at me.

'I'll go to the police.' I glanced at Fina. 'You won't kill me. I'll have you arrested. I'll go to the police if you come anywhere near me.'

Fina blinked a few times, turned, walked a little distance away and waited with her back to me. Jeff was still screaming abuse as I put the phone down on him. I don't think I'd have found the courage had Fina not been listening to my end.

'You OK?' she asked, as I walked past.

I nodded. The tears were starting.

'You stand for his shit?'

I put a hand over my mouth to stop myself crying.

'You do better, you good-looking woman,' she nodded decisively, both hands palm up as if she was holding a couple of dinner plates. Well!

The van was downbeat all the way home. I couldn't exactly bed down at the factory overnight, I had to get in the van, but I had no plan of action. I sat slumped on the back seat, resigned to my fate. The lads were embarrassed, what little conversation there was sounded stilted and phoney. I was too scared to talk much, but the worst part was the shame and humiliation.

'Old habits die hard.' Four little words had smashed everything to smithereens. The past six months, during which I had earned the acceptance and respect of the gang; the self-respect and self-confidence I'd gradually, painstakingly built up were wiped out in a flash with those four little words. The workers on the melons wouldn't have known what Jeff meant, but I knew. I wasn't Lynda, part of the A team sitting on the back seat; I was 'Lyn' the prostitute, who had deceived them all.

Derek dropped the gang off individually, as usual, and each of them urged me to be careful as they alighted. We dropped little Andy off and were pulling away from the kerb when Jeff loomed up out of the darkness in front of the van and put a hand up for us to stop. Derek was about to wind his window down to speak when Jeff pulled a hammer out of his coat and came towards the driver's door.

'Drive off!' I screamed.

Derek didn't need telling, he already had his foot on the accelerator. Unfortunately, some idiot in front of us decided to pull out at the same time. The back door opened and Jeff lunged at me with the hammer. I screamed, stood up and made for the front of the van, clambering over the seats. I looked back; Jeff was climbing up the back step.

'Derek!' I shouted, just as he put his foot down.

Jeff fell out of the back door and Derek sped off, doors swinging open. I looked back through the open doors. Jeff was picking himself up off the road. He began running, futilely, in pursuit of us, with long lumbering strides. Even in the darkness I could see the malevolence in his eyes. Derek drove like the clappers, both back doors wide open. He stopped at a phone box and rang the two Andys to go to his house and sit with Sarah and the kids in case Jeff showed up there.

Derek drove me to the police station and waited while I went in to lodge a complaint. The police went scouting for Jeff but there were no sightings, which meant he was still on the prowl. I didn't know what to do. No way was I going within a mile of the chalet. I didn't want to go to my mum's in case Jeff showed up; it wasn't fair on her and her husband. I told Derek to go, and went back to the police station to ask their advice. One of the cops had a brother who ran a guesthouse; he rang and arranged for me to have bed and breakfast. I was paying, but I thought it an incredibly kind act. Being out of season the place was officially closed.

I crawled into bed, too weary to wash. I wasn't expecting to sleep a wink with all that had happened, but was asleep within minutes. I'd also been up since 4.30 a.m.

Not knowing what lay ahead, I had to give work a miss the following day. That upset me a lot as I hate letting people down. I felt dread as I walked up the path to the chalet, yet I had to go home sometime. I prayed Jeff would be sober by then, I had done nothing to feel guilty about anyway. Jeff opened the front door as I went to put my key in the lock. My mother was sitting in the chair; she lit into me, demanding to know what the hell was going on. Jeff had rung her the night before asking where I was. The police had called to her house looking for Jeff and she was furious about that too. It hadn't occurred to me that the police would do that or I would have rung and warned her to expect them. My mum always takes the man's side in everything.

I ignored Jeff completely. I spoke to my mother as if he didn't exist. I gave her the complete A–Z of the day before. I must have won her round as she asked what my intentions were. I told her I was leaving the chalet. 'You're coming with me,' she replied.

In an attempt at humour Jeff said, 'I suppose the engagement's off then.'

For once I did not laugh. I set about pulling a few articles of clothing together but he kept taking them from me, trying to prevent me from leaving, not aggressively, but like a child. Don't go Mummy. He looked lost. I gave up the struggle and just grabbed my briefcase containing personal papers, family photographs, and left. He stood crying on the doorstep, begging me not to go.

*

I went to see a solicitor to try to obtain an injunction restraining Jeff from harassing me. The solicitor's fees were £80 per hour. She tried, but failed with the injunction. I can't remember why. She did pro bono work for battered women and was upset the court turned me down. She also wrote an official letter to Jeff asking for possession of the chalet and declined to submit the bill to me.

I stayed away from work for a few days, recovering at my mum's. I'd been more shaken by the experience than I realised. 'Too old for that kind of crap,' as Jeff would say. A nurse from Chapel St Leonard's Hospital rang to tell me Jeff had been admitted. He'd tried to kill himself with an overdose of something or other and was asking for me. I asked her if he was dying and she assured me he wasn't, but he was in a very emotional state. The oldest trick in the book. I stayed well away. My mum told me I was cruel.

I took the opportunity to fetch some clean clothes from the chalet. The place was awash with empty lager cans. Ilse came flying across the avenue the moment my mum's car pulled up outside. She gave me a lecture about staying away from my own home and letting Jeff stay there. She said she'd have kicked him out like a shot had she been in my place. She could see she was getting nowhere so she started on my mum.

'If Lynda *my* daughter, I kill the bastard. You tell him he don't go you cut his balls off!'

Jeff had threatened to tell social security I was working so I signed off the dole and went back to work. The hours had been extended yet again. Now we worked the cranberries until 8.00 p.m., when you add the journey you're talking fifteen or sixteen hours. It was crazy; by the time I arrived home at 10.00 I was that exhausted I felt nauseous, too tired to eat the dinners my mum cooked. I sat staring at the plate as if she'd dished me up a whole cow, uncooked.

One or two nights I fell asleep on top of the bed covers in my full arctic clobber, hiking boots and all, waking a couple of hours later sweating like a pig. There was only another week to Christmas, thank goodness; I was on the point of collapse. I left my mum's bungalow at 5.45 one morning to meet the van. As I was walking up the road Jeff's head suddenly appeared over the top of a low privet hedge of a front garden.

I was so terrified I started shouting.

'Hush! he said, looking about him.

I carried on shouting, backing away.

'Shhh,' he whispered, looking around at the bungalows.

'Don't you dare come near me!' I shouted, as I started running to the corner. I was too scared to look back. As I got to the corner I saw the van coming down the road. I ran towards it in the middle of the road. Derek took in the situation in a flash and opened the front passenger door and I climbed up rapidly. Jeff stood on the corner looking after us with his hurt little boy look as we gathered speed and drove off.

Jeff wrote me long letters every single day, extolling my virtues. I was the most decent woman he'd ever known, I had an enormous heart. I shouldn't tell anyone about my past, they did not have the right to know, they would only judge me on it. I was a wonderful person. He knew I hadn't been flirting on the melons, he'd got jealous when he saw me happy without him. He would never hurt me, I should never allow anyone else to do so, I was worth so much more. Hah! It would have been funny were it not so pathetic. He kept sending me flowers. Thinking he had an ally in my mother, he pestered her with phone calls, begging her to make me see him. My mum was on my case constantly. In the end, I agreed to meet him.

My mum came with me to the hotel so I would be safe. She sat in the lounge while I talked to Jeff in the bar. He had bought me what must have been the biggest bouquet of flowers on the planet. I felt a right prat sitting with them on my lap. In spite of the fact he'd been hitting the bottle since I left he looked beguilingly young, fresh and handsome. His portrait in the attic must have looked wrecked. He held my hand and cried. He begged me to take him back. He apologised for all the hurtful things he'd ever said, he hadn't meant any of it. I wept too. All I could manage in answer to his entreaties was 'It's too late. I'm sorry Jeff. I'm so sorry, but it's all just too late.'

He said he couldn't believe I'd had the hardness of heart not to visit him in the hospital.

'My heart wasn't hard Jeff. You shouldn't have tried to blackmail me. If you'd been truly ill I'd have been there like a shot.' He wouldn't have it that that was what his overdose amounted to. It was like sitting through an old movie you've seen a million times: the words, the tears, the pain, the emotion; I could have superimposed any man from my past on Jeff and not been able to tell the difference. I'd heard all the promises too, could have written the script. Looking at Jeff's grief stricken face I knew he meant what he said one hundred per cent; I also knew it would be back to the same old shit when the pain faded from his memory. You can't leave the past behind. I'd always known Jeff loved me, but he couldn't respect me. I'd always be 'Lyn'.

'You're beautiful Lyn. I only said those things so you wouldn't leave me.'

I sat silently. He was obviously getting desperate.

'Lyn, look at me.'

I couldn't, my heart was breaking. He tugged my hand as if to say 'Look at me.'

'You're beautiful Lyn . . . for your age.'

Quit while you're ahead Jeff.

Even when my mum showed up I still had trouble getting away from him. He was tugging at my sleeve, tears rolling down his cheeks. My heart was gripped in a vice; I could feel myself starting to weaken. 'You're a Lolita.'

'I have to go,' I said, crying, my throat painful.

The child was done paying. He followed me out to the car, still pleading; it really was heartbreaking. I didn't know what to do with the flowers, it seemed cruel to give them back to him. I put them on my lap as I got in the car. I looked at him one more time, we were both crying, both raw with grief. I could hear my mother sniffling as we drove home.

I sat in the conservatory with the flowers on my lap for a long time, dissecting the four years I'd spent with Jeff. When I stopped crying I gave the flowers to Roland, my stepfather, and he took them over to the Catholic church where he worshipped.

11

Derek hired a hall and threw a party for us all on the last working day before Christmas. Everyone looked forward to it, especially me; it would be my first time out with the gang socially. With only one day to go, if people hadn't bought their cranberries by then, tough. Fina gave us permission to knock off at 4.30; we would be home by 6.00, plenty of time to clean away the grime, bleach our hands, and get our glad rags on. The best laid plans of mice and men: a last-minute order came through from Safeway's. Fina seemed genuinely sorry to break the news, but what could we do, we were the A Team, the temps had already left for home, everyone groaned. Our gang had taken first lunch (12.30 to 1.00) so we worked through until 8.45 without a break. Not strictly legal but none of us complained; we just wanted out of there. Fina's husband came to the factory to lend a hand and the two of them kept us supplied with tea or coffee as we worked. No one had time to drink it, full plastic beakers stood everywhere. It was hard on the smokers; we were all gagging.

Fina was in great form, laughing and joking. We all were, we wouldn't have to see another bloody cranberry. Even the four pallets of prickly pears failed to burst our bubble! How humans ever discovered they were edible I'd like to know—they're lethal. In spite of wearing thick rubber gloves yelps of Ow! Fuck! Ouch! Bastard! rent the air, surely the most hostile fruit on the planet. By the time the shift ended, we were moving like automatons; I was so exhausted I could barely stand. Cinderella would not be going to the ball.

The lads tried to coax me to the 'do' all the way home. I kept nodding off. They were discussing how long it would take them to get ready when they got home.

'Half hour max,' little Andy said.

We'd been working flat out for six weeks. The sixteen-hour days had taken its toll on all of us, but as the oldest, I was hardest hit.

'It'd take me a week,' I yawned from the back seat.

'You'll be right. Just throw some cold water on your face,' said Martin, who obviously hadn't a clue about women. The way I looked, a team of Hollywood's finest make-up artists would have had their work cut out to make me fit for the ball.

I was last out of the van. Derek opened the back doors and raised his hand to help me down the step.

'C'mon Granny,' he said affectionately, grinning at my slowness as I tried to straighten up.

'We're all gonna miss you tonight.'

I barely managed a tired smile. 'I know. I wanted to go myself. I'm just too shattered.' The ground looked a long way off.

'Martin will miss you especially.'

'Oh yeah, I promised him a dance.' I yawned. 'Hah. Only dancing I'll be doing is a very slow waltz. . . . in the bath. See you Tuesday.' I stood swaying on my feet as Derek slammed the doors.

'On second thoughts . . . sod the bath. Gimme a push Derek.' He turned me to face the bungalow and gave me a gentle shove forward.

'Merry Christmas.'

'Mum, don't be offended, but please don't put my dinner up. I just couldn't.' I fell asleep in my clothes, my rucksack beside me on the bed.

I found out later that Jeff haunted the party, waiting for me to turn up. Just as well I gave it a miss. I spent a peaceful Christmas with my mum and Roland, but shuddered when Roland asked me to pass the cranberry sauce! I vetoed the traditional after-dinner walk on the beach; I never once set foot on it after Monty died. And I did a lot of sleeping over the two days.

*

I was glad to be back at work, two whole days with Roland and my mother was as much as I could cope with. The frenetic pace of the cranberries was over so it was back to the usual . . . slave labour for a pittance. Debbie decided she was moving on, she'd had enough of Fina and the cold. She went back to her old job as a typist; her youngest was starting school, and she could work a full day. She sneaked round the back of the canteen one lunchtime to say hello. She looked like a bird of paradise in her long flowing skirt, pretty shoes, white blouse and pale blue cardigan. A hint of lilac shadowed her eyes and she wore pink lipstick, pearl studs in her ears, her hair loose on her shoulders. She fluttered her long nails in front of my face saying 'Eat your heart out!' It wasn't the same without her; it was just a gruelling job in a freezing factory without her friendship, wit, and laughter.

January came, freezing cold, and with it the dark despair that always accompanied it but it didn't crush me as much as it usually did. February was almost at an end when Jeff finally complied with my solicitor's request to leave the chalet. My mum met him to get the keys from him. They'd become very chummy, she used to meet him for lunch once a week. Their birthdays were two days apart and they met up and went to the pub for a couple of drinks. He told her he was moving away from the area. I was still relatively wary about moving back to the chalet having seen that, contrary to what I thought, Jeff did indeed have a violent side. But I don't do well living under someone else's roof, so I was glad to go home.

I moved in on the Sunday. On the Monday I locked the front door as I left for work, giving it a push to make sure. Instead of moving off I stood for a moment, the hairs on the back of my neck prickling. When I looked at the next door chalet I almost fainted. Jeff was looking right back at me through the window. He smiled at me, his little boy smile. I looked away. I hurried up the road, dry mouth, heart pounding, legs wobbly.

The chalet belonged to a man who lived down south. He stayed the odd night when on business in the area. He'd obviously fallen for Jeff's hard-luck tale if he let him stay there while he was away. I couldn't make my mind up what to do for the best stay, or go. Jeff wasn't a villain, he was usually law abiding. Eventually I made the decision to stay put, I was sick and tired of running away. I changed the lock as a precaution. It was a weird set up, quite unnerving, the chalet walls were paper thin and I could hear Jeff moving around, playing music, TV . . . the same went for him presumably. When I had a visitor—my mum, Sarah, Jenny, or Ilse—the sound was muted instantly. I visualised him with an ear pasted to the wall. This went on for about five or six weeks.

Jenny dropped in one evening and we shared a bottle of wine. Jenny used to be Jim before she had her sex-change operation. I was jealous of the pert boobs they gave her. She came from a middle-class background of doctors and teachers; her grandfather was a famous explorer. She had lots of backbone and character; before her sex change she'd been a Sandhurst-trained army officer. It was a long route to packing fruit for £2.50 per hour, but not my tale to tell. We were laughing about something when Jeff started hammering on the wall. We ignored him, but resorted to whispering. She stayed another half hour or so and we had a good look around before she left. All was quiet. No sooner had she gone than Jeff was at the front door banging on the glass and shouting. I trembled from head to toe but refused to open the door. He yelled that we'd been taking the piss out of him. Speaking through the locked door I informed him that contrary to his belief the universe did not revolve around him, his name had not cropped up. I told no lie, it hadn't until he started banging on the wall. He went back to his own chalet and turned his television up full blast. Silly bugger probably got jealous over the Jim bit; even though we all knew Jenny had never been with a woman.

The guy who owned the chalet came down a few days later while I was at work and my mum told him about Jeff's harassment so he asked him to find somewhere else. Jeff moved into a Department of Health and Social Services-run B&B a mile down the road. I breathed a sigh of relief; the strain of being stalked was grinding me down. He was still drinking in all the local pubs, telling whoever would listen that he still loved me and hoped we'd get back together. Knowing he believed that, I prayed he wouldn't go blabbing my business at the same time. March, April, May and June passed uneventfully. Fear of the consequences of what Jeff might do still made me reluctant to go out with the gang on Saturdays; the town was too small to hide. I knew full well that I was still allowing a man to rule my life, even if it was by proxy; I just couldn't cope with the mayhem that would surely follow if he discovered me on a night out. I was content, I had a roof over my head, a job, money to pay my way, no state handouts, so I could hold my head up.

For no other reason than they liked each other's company the gang decided to have a rare mid-week night out at one of the surrounding villages. Knowing there was no danger of bumping into Jeff it was a rare opportunity to act like the free woman I actually was, so I said I'd join them. There were twelve of us. Derek drove us in the van. Martin volunteered to stay sober and drive us home. It was a lovely little country pub and they had a few acts on, country and western mainly. We sang, we laughed, joked and joshed each other without let-up until closing time. I was with friends—I could have passed out and woken up safe at home, fully clothed, person and handbag untouched. I relaxed totally and had the nicest night ever. It brought home to me how much I'd been missing, shutting myself away as I did.

The work force expanded owing to new contracts at the factory. Derek and Sarah started going in their car and Martin became official van driver. He was notorious for his lack of sense of direction and sure enough, the first day we hit Boston he went round and round the roundabout looking for the turn-off. This was to become a regular occurrence. We'd all be sitting in the back with big watermelon grins as we approached the roundabout waiting for him to get it wrong. In six months he only disappointed us twice, to a chorus of boos. On Saturdays someone else drove; it wasn't the same when they got it right first time!

A couple of months later we all met for another night out and another great time, though Martin was missed—he couldn't get time off from the night-club. Somehow it ended up with a few of the gang coming back to mine for coffee and sandwiches, which turned out to drag on a bit so I sent them home. Old George was last to leave.

'I can go home happy now,' he said.

'Why?'

'Martin asked me to look after you.'

'Huh?'

'He said I was to make sure no harm came to you.' Ah, bless him.

I wasn't sure how to take this. Had it been any other man I'd have known what the score was. Martin was such a nice person, known for his kind heart and consideration; he might have meant George was to look out for the old granny. Just as I was mascot for the men, Martin was mascot for the women at the factory, Fina included. They all adored him, he was chivalrous in the extreme, would do anything for them, young or old.

I've never heard a single soul say a bad word against him yet to look at him you'd think he'd cut your throat for a dollar. The shaved head made him look like a Russian prisoner from the gulag. He wasn't that tall, but had huge shoulders and was as strong as an ox. The two Andys put his name forward for the arm-wrestling contest when the town held their annual fête; the prize was a barrel of beer. It was a beautiful July day and people came from the surrounding towns and villages. Martin tried to get out of it, shy to be the centre of attention, but Andy and Andy wanted the barrel of beer and kept him in a headlock until his name was called. Everyone was laughing at their antics and the atmosphere was lovely. The contest went on for ages, the men seemed to get bigger as the afternoon progressed. Martin really got in to the swing of it, grinning as he demolished one after the other. Those of us who knew him could tell he was tiring. His shaved head was getting sunburnt so big Andy plonked a Kleenex on it, shoved a bottle of water at him and said:

'C'mon, you can't stop now man. Quit pussyfooting around. We're thirsty.'

The crowd laughed. Martin didn't let them down; he beat all-comers from the county, the gang cheering him on. The two Andys were pissed for weeks.

In the canteen one day one of the Skegness women said she thought Martin and I were well suited, we both had similar personalities.

'Well suited for what?'

'Well you're an item aren't you?'

'Don't be daft! I'm old enough to be his mother. You know how friendly he is, we're just good friends as they say.'

She seemed surprised she'd got it wrong. Thinking of it later, I supposed we did get on well.

Martin brought me a pallet of grapes and took his time unloading it. Fina shouted,

'Martin! How come every time I see you, you always standa next to Lynda?'

Poor Martin—stuck in the spotlight, all eyes on him. No one

was more shocked than I was when he replied, 'Because I think she's the most marvellous woman I ever met.'

His face lit up as he turned and smiled at me. Fucking hell! The whole factory cheered and wolf whistled, as if someone had just scored a goal. I was scarlet. Fina smiled, shook her head, walked out the door. A day of surprises. And so Martin declared himself.

'Well, are you gonna get it on then, you two?' Sarah asked as we ate our sandwiches.

I laughed. 'Don't be stupid Sarah. The age gap's too great. I'm sixteen years older than him. I was only four years older than Jeff, he thought I was Methuselah.'

'Martin's not Jeff. The two of you get on so well, no one notices the age gap. Look at Rick and his missus. Twenty-five years between them,' Sarah insisted.

'It's different for men. He's considered a bit of a stud, something to be admired. When it's us we're just cradle snatchers. Or desperate. Or sex mad.'

'Yes please!' Sarah joked. 'Martin's not a boy is he?'

I responded that the gang might accept it; people who didn't know us would laugh. Sarah shrugged:

'So what?' She took another bite, then a mouthful of tea. She splayed her hands wide:

'That's their problem. Anyway Lynda, how many *proper* relationships do you know?'

She had me there. Some relationships appear to be OK, so long as you don't look too closely. I couldn't think of one that would survive a microscope.

Apparently, Martin had let it be known, as far back as Christmas, that he fancied me. I was the last to know. Now that he'd shown his hand publicly, however, the factory constantly chivvied us to get it together. All except little Andy who was disgusted by the idea. He liked me well enough in his own miserable way, but not as a love interest for Martin. I suppose it was bit like discovering your mum and dad did it. Martin still hadn't said anything directly. He later told me he'd been scared to death of me.

I think I'd already fallen in love with him one night at a dance. A teenage Down's Syndrome girl at the next table complained to her mum that no one would dance with her. Martin was on his feet in a flash, extending a hand, nodding towards the dance floor. Sarah and I glanced at each other, damp eyed. We watched as they twirled around the dance floor, having a great time, beaming smiles on both their faces. After a couple of dances he escorted the girl back to her mum, kissed her hand, gave a little bow. The girl kept coming over and stroking his shaved head, which she found amusing. Little Andy teased Martin about the new girlfriend, Sarah told him to shut his face or she'd shut it for him, everyone laughed. Martin took the teasing in his stride.

'I like to boogie. I was just having a good time enjoying myself . . . you should try it sometime instead of sitting there with that miserable face of yours.'

He grabbed little Andy's nose and pretended to twist it off, then added,

'Any woman deserves the right to be treated like a princess, why should it be any different for her?'

Sarah and I said, 'A-a-h,' in unison, then burst out laughing at one another.

Derek made my mind up for me when he was dropping me home one night. Sarah had enlisted him to act as matchmaker.

'I can't Derek. There are things you don't know about me. I'm not quite the person Martin or you all think I am. Thing is, Jeff knows all about me, sooner or later it'll all come out.'

Derek put his hand on my arm and said, 'Jeff's already done his worst. He rang me months ago, going on and on. I put the phone down on him in the end. Me and Sarah don't think any the less of you. The past is nobody's business but your own.'

I burst into tears; it was the kindness that did it.

'Oh, God Derek, I'll never be free of it. Does Martin already know?'

'No. We thought it's for you decide whether you want to tell him or not.'

We looked at each other for a moment.

'You know Lynda . . . Martin is one of the good guys. You might just discover he's also broadminded. All that matters is he's crazy about you. I tried to tell you that the night of the Christmas party.'

Eventually, we did 'get it on', as Sarah would say. Forget all that love at first sight rubbish. Love is so much easier, sweeter, when you've known each other a while, have mutual respect, but above all like each other. I recommend it.

There were two flies in the ointment of our love. The first was Caroline, the woman Martin had lived with for nine months. Martin wasn't one for bad-mouthing anyone so what little I knew of her and their circumstances I learnt indirectly. At one point the Andys had ragged him unmercifully when he began taking Mondays off to see his kids; they accused him of letting the team down. In reality, they missed the horseplay. I heard him tell them Caroline did not want the kids at her house so he stayed in a caravan on Sunday nights so he could have them to sleep over.

The intimate bits, the things most women really want to know I got from Sarah. Being a small town everyone seemed to know everyone's business. Caroline worked part time in a café in town, was a bit of a hard nut, and drank a lot. Because of her drinking her husband had walked out on her and her two kids. She was dead jealous of Martin's wife who was supposed to be drop dead gorgeous; that was the reason Caroline didn't want her bringing the kids to see him. I could relate to that.

Martin's wife had been carrying on while he was working nights as a security guard in the town. I think the kids may have dropped her in it, but when it all came out the wife booted him out and her lover moved in. The owners of the arcades clubbed together and bought a caravan for Martin to live in, which he shared with the site guard dog, a particularly vicious Rottweiler by the name of Rocky.

Martin was heartbroken over losing his children. Caroline was still coming to terms with her husband's desertion. Two lonely people took solace in companionship. Martin, being as shy as he was, meant that Caroline had to make all the moves. She sent her kids to ask him to dinner. He was too polite to refuse and it went on from there. Working nights proved inconvenient owing to Caroline's young children; it also meant Martin couldn't sleep during the day so he went to work at the packing factory. He sat in weekday nights babysitting for her while she hit the pubs. They were not in love, but they shared a bed and a home and the months rolled by regardless. He gave Caroline all his wages from the factory and worked weekends on the doors for money for himself. However, she had made a fatal error in showing her hostility to Martin's kids. He told her he would look for a place of his own. She probably thought he was too nice to do it and he also had no chance of getting the money for a deposit.

There is truth in the belief that you cannot help whom you fall in love with, I discovered. It's not to my credit that I hardly gave Caroline a thought; I had her fixed in my mind as a nasty, scheming person, undeserving of any attack of conscience. They'd only been together a short time, were not married and there were no children from the union. When I did think of her at all it was only that she took karate lessons, was as hard as nails and had a vicious temper, according to Sarah. I hoped I never had to cross swords with her.

Talk about a fast mover, we'd only seen each other socially twice when Martin asked if he could move in with me. I sighed. His face dropped. Straight away he said,

'It's OK, I'll move into a B&B.'

It was not his way to apply pressure. We were walking in the factory doors the morning he asked me. However, because I loved him and he'd not insisted, by the time the shift ended I relented.

People who know me well seem to hold the view that I should not tell about my past, but should let people like me for who I am. How could I not? It stands to reason the world and his mother don't need to know, but a relationship based on lies and deceit is doomed before it starts. How would I explain my fear of the dark, the nightmares, the sudden panic attacks, the fear of strangers, January, sparklers, bonfire night, crowds, social situations, women with curly hair, tall thin Irish men . . . anyone with an Irish accent, diverse sounds, sights and smells? If there's one thing almost as bad as having a past, it's living in perpetual fear of it being discovered. I believe any man has the right to know what exactly he's getting into anyway, especially in my case, when his life could be in danger.

Normal, well-adjusted people take happiness for granted. I had been putting off spilling the beans for purely selfish reasons. I'd been basking in the glow of Martin's adoration, the love in his eyes. He made me feel like a *good* person. I was so happy I wanted the novel experience to last a while longer. I was dreading the disillusionment I knew would surely follow, was frightened of what I would see in his eyes when he looked at me then. Now is never a good time but it was time to quit playing the fairy princess. I said we needed to talk before he moved in. He looked wary; talking wasn't his bag.

Nothing but ruthless honesty would do, I decided. Martin was deserving of nothing less. Even to my own ears the subject matter sounded disgusting, seedy and shocking, utterly divorced from the lives of ordinary decent folk. As I spoke, I was thinking did this—or that—really happen. Was I really involved in something so dreadful? Did I really waste the precious gift of life in that way? Heaven knows what Martin must have been thinking. I held nothing back in the telling, didn't want any secrets to come back to haunt me. My palms were sweating, my chest felt tight and I had a nervous tick on my right eyelid as I awaited his reaction. He was a hard man to read. He listened without interruption. When I'd finished, he said,

'Is that it?'

God, how much more could there be.

'Right. Its all out of the way now, I'll never mention it again', he said.

He hugged me to him, whispered in my hair, 'Let's have a brew, eh?'

Thank the Lord for tea.

*

The day he left Caroline he arrived earlier than planned, while I was having a cuppa with Ilse. One look at his face and even she could tell he was upset so she said she'd leave us to it.

'I hope I never have to do that to a woman again,' he said, as he put his suitcase down. He sat looking at it, all the colour drained from his face.

He'd had quite a showdown with Caroline. She'd ranted and raved, cried and begged him not to go. She hadn't let him go without a fight, though. She wouldn't allow him to take his car; she put the keys down her bra and told him he'd have to fight her for them. She couldn't drive so he'd been giving her lessons. He felt so guilty he told her to keep it. He was deeply upset she'd taken his leaving so hard. It sure took the shine off his moving in. We sat facing each other across the room, trying to think of something to say that wouldn't sound banal. I suppose we were both wondering if the other was worth it.

On the Friday he handed me his un-opened pay packet.

'What's this?' I asked stupidly.

'I always gave Caroline my wages.'

'I'm not Caroline. You earned it, you keep it.' I handed it back to him.

'I've always kept my woman.' He handed it back to me. 'I've got my bouncing job for pocket money.'

'Not this woman you won't. It's your money; you worked hard for it. Keep it.'

He seemed quite put out, as if I'd tried to belittle him in some way. The experience was foreign to me. I'd never as much as seen a man's pay packet before, let alone had one presented as a gift. It made me feel respectable, a woman worthy of a man's hard labour. My throat constricted, I looked at his open face and said,

'We'll split the bills fifty-fifty. And give up the bloody doors; you don't need the job anymore. I don't want you getting a bottle over the head.'

He gave notice at the nightclub and worked his last weekend; I sat home worrying for his safety. He was sweetly old fashioned and felt uncomfortable with my continuing at the factory. It wasn't that he felt emasculated by my working, but he believed that 'women should be looked after and cherished'. Ah bless.

Martin swore he would love me until the day he died. I, being older and by now a little wiser didn't believe it for a minute, though I didn't doubt his sincerity. But what the hell, I'd grown to love him—whatever love means, as Prince Charles once said—and somehow the fact that I was sixteen years his senior did not seem to matter. Martin was happy in his own skin, didn't feel threatened if I shared a joke with the men on the line. I loved going to work then; I would have worked for nothing. When I said this to Sarah she said,

'Jesus . . . you must have been starved of normal friendship.'

Martin courted me, bought me flowers, made me laugh on a daily basis. I never realised how seductive it is to have someone utterly besotted with you and he adored me. A woman at work said,

'I'm seriously concerned about Martin.'

I asked why. 'Every time I turn round I see him standing looking at you with a silly grin on his face. He's like a love struck teenager.'

We both turned to where he worked and sure enough, he was.

He grinned and placed two hands over his heart in a Chaplinesque manner. If I heard a pallet being moved I'd follow the sound and he would blow me a kiss and mouth 'I love you'.

He held some odd ideas about women. He was passionate about the animal kingdom and the survival of the planet. Any compliments he paid invariably related to animals. Lying beside me in bed he told me I had eyes like a giraffe.

'A giraffe!' I giggled.

'It's meant as a compliment,' he replied defensively, 'you've got the same eyelashes.'

I was eating an apple and he remarked my hands were 'tiny, like a squirrel's.' When I complained my hair was a mess he responded, 'No, I like it. It's like a lion's mane.' I told him if he ever mentioned elephants or rhinos we were history.

We were playing 'getting to know you'; he started it. Given the kind of men I used to know it wouldn't have been over-dramatising had my first question to a prospective lover been: 'Have you ever killed anyone?' Second, 'Have you ever raped a woman?' Third, 'Have you ever beaten a woman up?' Their questions would invariably be 'How many men have you slept with? Question one, two and three. To which I'd reply, 'Well . . . leaving out my job, not as many as most women.' Trouble was they couldn't see past my job.

Martin began by asking me what my favourite film was. *Casablanca*. He didn't comment, probably too young to have seen it.

'What's your favourite song?

'REM, Everybody hurts.' He pulled a face.

'Favourite book?' he asked, looking at the bookcase.

'*To Kill a Mockingbird*'. No response.

'Right, now you,' I said, 'what's your favourite film?'

'*The Sound of Music*.'

I burst out laughing.

'Favourite song?'

'Devil woman, by Marty Robbins.' I was unacquainted with both.

'Favourite book?

He frowned. '*The Guinness Book of Records: Hit Singles*.'

That just about says it all. There were no sides to Martin, what you saw was what you got. I was probably the only person in the western world not to have seen *The Sound of Music* at the time; now I could almost reel it off, verbatim. The same goes for 'Devil Woman'. I wrote it out for him when he was doing a karaoke with his sister. It spoke volumes about the type of woman Martin was attracted to; I hoped I wasn't included!

*

It was my rotten luck to bump into Caroline when I was shopping on my own in the Co-op. I spotted her over near the frozen foods. She was leaning into the freezer, talking to her young son. I made a U-turn, hoping she wouldn't know who I was. No such luck. I stood wavering in the next aisle, debating whether to leave or keep to the other end of the store. Leaving would have been the greater danger; the exit was too near the frozen foods. I decided to stay. A bad move. Next thing I knew she was in front of me. I desperately needed tomatoes, I suddenly remembered, looking at the bottom shelf. Caroline wasn't fooled. She threw her basket on the floor.

'Oi you!'

I couldn't pretend I was deaf, you'd have heard her in the next county.

'Yes you, you fuckin slapper!' Oh God.

'Can't you get a man your own age, you old c . . .?'

I wished I were dead. If there's one word I absolutely loathe it's the C one; it should be made illegal, punishable by having the offender's mouth sewn up. I was scared, no doubt about it, but the worst part was the sheer humiliation.

'I'll go to prison for you,' she shouted.

Her little boy was shaking. So was I.

'I'll do time for you, you c. . . . I swear it.'

Shoppers stood frozen to the spot as if playing statues.

'I'm sorry.' I mumbled, almost hypnotised by her yellow feline eyes, nice in a cat, repellent and intimidating in a person. She was a dead ringer for *Coronation Street*'s Janice Battersby, apart from the eyes. Terrified and embarrassed though I was, I still had space in my head to wonder how on earth someone as gentle and polite as Martin could be mixed up with someone so rough.

Caroline wasn't having any of it. We had an audience by now. The store manager, who had always smiled and said, 'Good morning/evening, Madam', came and knelt right beside me on the floor, pretending to straighten the cans on the lower shelves.

'Sorry?' she shouted, letting fly a fresh string of expletives, ending with, 'I'll willingly do time for you, you old c . . .'

I cringed. I felt like slapping her to shut her up, for my sake and for her little boy who appeared to be in shock, but any residue of guilt I'd felt because of her evaporated as I stood listening to her vile mouth.

'That's for sure,' I finally retaliated.

'You will if you come anywhere near me.' I put my basket of groceries on the floor and left the store on shaking legs. At least I didn't run.

Lying awake regurgitating the day's events, it dawned on me that Caroline never once said she loved or missed Martin. All she'd harped on about was money, money, money, what would she do without Martin's wages.

'I don't know. I haven't got his money,' I'd retorted.

'Course you have, you fuckin c. . . . Why else would you be with him?' she bellowed, yellow eyes raking me over from head to toe.

Of course I couldn't go near the Co-op again for the shame of it all, which was a nuisance, it was the only grocery store in the town.

Martin's wife, Lisa, brought the kids to see him the following day. She wanted the low-down on the Co-op fiasco; the town was buzzing with the scandal. I could understand Caroline feeling threatened by her. She was indeed drop-dead gorgeous, a figure to die for, long black hair down to her backside. As I was old enough to be Lisa's mother I felt a bit threatened myself, but I looked upon her as an ally; we both had reason to dislike Caroline.

'Why did you let her get away with showing you up like that?' she asked.

'What else could I do? I wasn't expecting to bump in to her. I was stuck in the aisle; I'd have had to pass her.'

'I'd have hit her with a tin of beans if she called me what she called you. I owe her one for the way she treated my kids.'

'I was a convent girl!' I replied, in mock horror. 'We don't go brawling in supermarkets!'

I liked Martin's kids, eight-year-old Jodi and ten-year-old Lee, on sight. They were well mannered, sweet, well behaved, though I'd expected nothing else. They were very easy to love, which was a relief. I'd be seeing a lot of them. Martin was a great dad, he adored his kids, they in turn worshipped him.

*

The other fly in the ointment showed up a few days later. I casually answered the door one evening and got the shock of my life. I screamed and tried to push the door shut but Jeff wedged it open with his foot. Martin pushed me aside and wrestled him off the doorstep. I slammed the door shut, rushed to the telephone and dialled 999. As I called it in, I watched through the window as Jeff grabbed a long-handled hoe from the outside bunker and jabbed it in Martin's face. Martin planted his feet apart in a boxer's stance and tried to get in under the hoe to throw a punch but couldn't dodge it. Martin and Jeff circled each other like gladiators for a few seconds then disappeared from view.

I shook and shook, praying for the police to hurry. Seconds passed, though it seemed like a lifetime. I was terrified out of my wits that Jeff would badly injure Martin or that the police would be too late to stop Jeff kicking the door open to get to me. Martin ran up the path covered in blood. I opened the door rapidly to let him in and slammed it shut even quicker. Jeff was one second behind him, still clutching the hoe. Jeff gave one almighty push on the door. Martin and I put our full weight on the other side to keep it shut. The one on the outside has the advantage when a door opens inwards and we were in danger of losing the battle when the police arrived and yanked Jeff away from the door. Martin had blood streaming down his lower face where Jeff had hit him with the hoe; it had sliced through his top lip.

It seemed to take forever for the three police officers to subdue Jeff; he was like Samson pulling the pillars down. Each time they had him under control he broke free again and lunged towards the front door, causing me to jump behind the sideboard. Ilse was first out for a ringside view; the rest of the residents soon joined her. The odd thing was, because I was watching it through the large chalet window it did not seem altogether real; it was as if it was projected on a huge movie screen, frame by frame. A replay of another old movie at that: the violence, the blood, the fear, the sound effects, the chaos. Not again, please let this end.

Martin stood motionless beside me without speaking. I stole a look at his face; it was devoid of expression. After the longest period of time the cops had Jeff upright, his hands behind his back and were attempting to handcuff him, without much joy. He wouldn't stand still. You could safely say it was one time the prisoner really did resist arrest.

'Are you happy now Lyn? See where you've brought me?' Jeff roared to the window.

Eventually they managed to cuff him and they led him away to the police car, still struggling. They earned their pay that day; it took a while to force him in the back of the car. I thought they'd gone so I went outside and started tidying up the garden tools, as usual, but I'd forgotten they had do a U-turn to get out. When they passed Jeff stared at me, I lowered my eyes. I'll always remember the look on his face. He looked like a lost, tortured soul.

The nearest hospital was fifteen miles away and we had no car so Martin stitched his own lip from the inside. I had my hand over my mouth as I watched, my stomach was heaving. He asked me to cut the thread just above the stitch, my hands shook so much I cut through the knot instead so he had to re-stitch it. Unbelievably I did exactly the same on the second stitch. He didn't even shout at me. The next four stitches I managed to cut right.

*

It's as plain as the nose on my face now that the pain suffered by all those involved—Caroline, Jeff, Martin, my fellow workers—was down to me. Relationships end, people split up, every second of the day someone somewhere in the universe suffers a broken heart. It's how they deal with it that matters. Joe or Jane Bloggs will weep, endure the pain, grieve, lick their wounds, then go on with the rest of their lives, a little sadder and wiser. The Joe Bloggs of the world always scared the hell out of me and it took forty years to work out why.

I wish there was a way of making men who sexually abuse children understand the enormity of the long-term damage they do, long after the physical scars have healed. The abused child grows up to be an adult who feels worthless, used, cheap, dirty, tainted, abnormal, not *nice*, unworthy of respect, unlovable, not good enough. It sticks, like a piece of chewing gum chewed for too long. When you try to dispose of it, it comes out in long gluey strands; the harder you try to escape it the more it clings. You can't wash it away. Should you get it on your clothes or in your hair the only way to get rid of it is to cut it out. Only death will put an end to the feelings of utter worthlessness.

Because I was damaged goods, I was only good enough for someone who was also a second-rate reject from society. I only felt validated when someone loved me, but who, except a needy man could possibly love someone already tarnished and soiled by childhood. The Joe Bloggs might want, but they don't need. It was my choice of man, in this case Jeff, which had brought the violent movie to the little seaside town. Like me, Jeff was a loser in life; I was the last woman on earth he should have gotten involved with. As for Martin, all he wanted was to love me; he ended up covered in blood, with a scar he will carry forever.

*

And so began my life with Martin. Jeff went to court. Martin and I weren't called to give evidence; we'd already decided against it. Nevertheless, Jeff was convicted and fined £175 (his first ever conviction), for resisting arrest, and was ordered to pay Martin £150 compensation. I bet that stuck in his craw.

Caroline and Jeff met up. He told her all about me and between them they spread it all round town. Well, all's fair in love and war so I couldn't complain, yet I could not live with the knowledge that people now knew the worst. Martin and I also knew we'd never have peace while we lived at the chalet so we decided to move from the area altogether.

We would both miss the gang a lot. Apart from the trouble with Jeff they had been very happy times, had eased me into a normal life. We promised to keep in touch with Derek, Sarah and the rest of the gang. Fina wished us well and said she hoped we'd be happy!

I called to say goodbye to Jenny, who'd become a very good friend. Jeff used to drop in on her at all odd hours hoping to bump into me. He kept mithering her to pass on messages to me but she'd steadfastly refused. Now that I was leaving she felt safe confiding in me that Jeff had broken down and admitted he'd treated me so badly to punish me for being abused by my father. I listened in shock as she told me Jeff had confessed that his twin sister and been abused by their father when she was very young. No wonder Jeff refused to discuss my experiences. Jeff's mother was a schizophrenic who had frequent breakdowns and when she was hospitalised her husband would go to the pub, then go home and molest his daughter.

Jenny was mystified over why Jeff had waited more than forty years before breaking his silence. I considered this as I dwelt on the fact that I'd harboured such a grave secret myself and concluded that perhaps the trauma of our break-up had unleashed it all for him.

The last I'd seen of Jeff, apart from the day with the hoe, was the day I'd left the hotel carrying the bunch of flowers, having refused a reconciliation. Jenny said that was the day he had boarded the train and gone to confront his father. Whether he did actually strike his dad is unclear, but a scuffle took place which brought his mum on the scene. They rounded on her and told her to leave the room. Jenny said his mum would not have known about the abuse, she'd been too ill at the time. Jenny was unsure how the confrontation had ended.

Jeff then went on to see his twin sister and told her he knew what she'd gone through. She broke down. She had carried the burden all those years without telling a soul. She told Jeff she felt no-one would believe her. She'd been unaware that he had lain awake in his cot watching, listening to her pain; she thought he'd slept through it all. They'd both lived in perpetual dread of their mother's next breakdown. The twins held each other and cried. Poor Jeff. Poor sister.

Though no longer of consequence between us, I was still shattered Jeff hadn't shared with me the hurt he must have felt. That he hadn't trusted me enough. I only hope that by confronting his father with what he'd done and confessing to his sister that he shared a small part of her burden, it proved cathartic for Jeff, and that the twins found a sort of peace within themselves. I now understand why his twin sister was always so contained, why she'd left her office job and gone back to college to study psychology, why she constantly scrubbed her hands, why she repeatedly cleaned the house when it was spotless already, why her wedding photograph shows her being led down the aisle on her father's arm unsmiling, virginal as a Bride of Christ in plain white satin, not a scrap of lace, make-up or adornment. And why she divorced her Italian husband because he liked the occasional drink.

In a weird way, discovering why Jeff had treated me the way he had, helped me believe I had not deserved it. I felt I could move forwards emotionally as well as bodily. I vowed I would never again allow myself to become anyone's scapegoat. I thanked my lucky stars that Martin came without baggage.

My mum cried the day we left the chalet. I did too. We'd seen each other almost every day and were learning to build bridges. Or rather, I was learning to forgive. With me moving so far, we knew we wouldn't be seeing much of one another. I hated being on the move once again, I was worried sick that I'd never be able to put down roots, but with Jeff around, I had no choice. So, only a year after I'd arrived at the seaside I was on my travels again, minus the man I'd arrived with and my beautiful dog. New beginnings.

12

Martin, can I ask you something?' he nodded, keeping his eyes on the road.

'When I told you we needed to talk before you moved in with me did you have any inkling what I was going to say?' It is always easier to broach a sticky subject when you don't have to look directly at someone; I'd chosen my moment carefully. We were travelling along the motorway on the first leg of our new life.

'Nope. Not a clue. Why do you ask?'

'Just wondered, that's all.' I said casually.

In actual fact, I'd been picking away at it like a scab. To my mind, his reaction on hearing something so heinous had been unnatural; he had not asked a single question. We drove in silence for a few miles. I nodded off.

'I suppose I was a bit relieved, if truth be known,' he said, apropos of nothing.

'Relived about what?' I sat up.

'You know. What you said earlier.'

'What I said about what?'

'When you said you had something seriously bad to tell me when I was moving in.'

Oh that. 'Why did you feel relieved?'

'I thought you were going to tell me you were dying of AIDS or something *really* bad like that.'

'Jesus!' I looked at him. 'What would you have said if I had been? Run for the hills I suppose!'

'No, I wouldn't actually', he said matter-of-fact. 'I'd have died with you.'

I stared at him curiously, waiting for the joke, but his face was impassive. I checked myself over for a sprinkling of fairy dust, lay back and watched the countryside slip by without commenting.

We were going to live with Martin's father, Tom. Tom had lived alone since Martin's mother had died, when Martin was ten years old. He had had a couple of relationships in the intervening years but 'couldn't take to any of them'. He was lonely, and looking forward to having some company. We didn't have sufficient funds for a deposit on our own place; work had been scarce at the factory for a few weeks before we left.

My mum had surprised me by giving me back all the board money I'd given her when I'd stayed with her while waiting for Jeff to vacate the chalet. I bought us an Audi 80 with it. It was an old banger but it looked tidy and drove like a dream. I liked it because I'm scared to death of speed and if Martin drove above sixty-five miles an hour, it made a right racket. I'd be nodding off real peaceful like, then old Betsy would start to shudder, I'd say, 'Martin!' with my eyes still closed and he'd ease off on the accelerator. He was dead chuffed to have wheels again, but had taken a great deal of persuading to accept it. We needed a car to move away, I argued. I couldn't drive so he'd have to be my driver. I'd left all my furniture at the chalet because my mum was renting it out to old George, one of our work colleagues. As usual, all I had with me were clothes and books.

*

Tom ran a very well-kept house, unusual for a man living alone. He kept an allotment so there was always plenty of fresh vegetables, chicken and duck eggs. He cooked some great meals. He did his best to make me feel welcome. He always made a point of asking what I fancied for dinner and treated me to chocolate éclairs; nothing was too much trouble for him.

Although Tom was kind and I had all the comfort I needed, I could not settle. Fifty is not an age for living on someone else's floor. I don't think Tom was keen on his son living with someone so much older. Martin told me that one day when they were waiting for me in the car Tom said as I walked towards them, 'Lynda looks well for her age doesn't she?' Martin agreed.

'What are you going to do in twenty years time when she's seventy?'

'What did you say?'

'I said I'll be twenty years older myself.' Bless his little cottons.

Tom made a point of showing Martin the daily page three girl as we ate breakfast and asked his opinion on her attributes. Martin would say he wasn't interested. Fibber. I was trying to get an angle on the dynamics between the two of them; there seemed to be quite a lot of tension. One morning he held the paper up for Martin to see the daily offering, Martin carried on eating.

Tom said, 'She's your type isn't she?'

Martin cast a cursory glance and muttered, 'Not really.'

Tom smirked. 'I thought you liked them with small tits and long black hair.'

I could have cheerfully wrung his neck. Martin flushed. Tom watched him like a hawk hunting prey for a moment before lowering his head over the paper.

'It's lonely hearts in the local paper tonight. Never know what you might find,' he said, his eyes scanning Miss Whoever. There was a sudden charge of electricity in the air. I felt myself grow warm. I could have wept for Martin.

'I'm fixed up,' Martin said softly, the tone of his voice at odds with the colour suffusing his face and neck. 'What about you Dad? Perhaps you could find someone to keep you company.'

The room was deathly still; the only sound the central heating boiler. I realised I was holding my breath. Tom folded the newspaper slowly.

'How dare you disrespect me,' he said quietly.

He leaned back in his chair slowly, folded his arms and pinioned Martin with a stare that could have melted the North Pole.

'How dare you disrespect me?' he said again, waiting for an answer. Martin stared fixedly at his plate. I counted the stripes round the rim of mine. Tom got up and left the room with the newspaper under his arm. Martin and I sat without speaking, eyes downcast.

I don't think I liked Tom very much after that incident. Not on my own account, but he'd shown a cruel streak in putting his son on the spot. I'm also sick and tired of hearing the word 'disrespect' issuing forth from the male mouth. You disrespect me . . . Christ! As if, they have a monopoly on respect. I've heard many arguments between women, but I've yet to hear the word 'disrespect' bandied about.

Martin was highly deferential to his father; he'd only stood up to him once before in his life. When he was a teenager Tom had ordered him to empty the ashtrays even though he knew Martin was pathologically anti-smoking. Martin, full of teenage hormones, had refused saying the smell made him sick. Tom blew smoke in his face; Martin decked him. Since that grotty episode, Martin had never again breached the invisible parental line.

I was dismayed and saddened by the display I'd just witnessed and aware it was my presence in the house that had caused it. After the little show, I knew my suspicions were right. As Tom is no longer alive, I feel at liberty to say I knew that he felt I was better suited to him.

On one occasion, we went to Martin's workplace to bring him the lunch he'd forgotten. Tom placed an arm on my shoulder as we walked on the building site; I stiffened, but was too embarrassed to object, him being Martin's dad. Tom's proprietorial arm had the desired effect, as he had intended, because Martin told me later that a workmate said,

'Your dad's got himself a young bit of stuff hasn't he?'

I hooted with laughter when I heard this: 'What did you say? No, I've got an old one!'

'No, I said, "That's my woman." '

Martin refused to crack jokes about the age difference. I did it all the time, which he found extremely irritating. He said he loved me—'that's that'—age wasn't an issue.

*

Martin got work straight away in a small company that made top-class reproduction wooden furniture, all hand finished. Being the man on whom the words 'work ethic' could have been based, Martin sanded the pieces so enthusiastically he almost sanded his fingerprints off. I shuddered when I saw the stumps of his bloody fingernails.

I felt awkward on my own in the house with Tom once I knew he saw me as a prospective stepmother for Martin. I took a job in a bottling factory packing jars of cook-in sauces and tins of salmon and labelling on the conveyor belt. The pace was much slower than the fruit factory; well, they'd no Fina to crack the whip. I missed the gang; there wasn't much of an atmosphere. The bottling was another revelation. It should have been called re-bottling by rights. We soaked jars of a well-known cook-in sauce well past their sell-by date in huge metal baths full of cold water. When the labels were soaked off, we stood the jars on draining mats to dry, wiped the gunge off the lids, and then relabelled them with an up to date label. Some batches were as much as a year out of date. I since think twice before buying any brand of cook-in sauce because surely they were not the only company to use such tactics. Working in the food industry causes you to eye just about everything you put in your mouth with suspicion. I was working through an agency and within a matter of weeks the work had dried up; they promised to ring in a few days when some new contracts came up. Two weeks later and still no word.

I called in to see Martin at work and was appalled at his working conditions. I don't know what I had expected but there were half a dozen stables open to the elements, men sanding pieces of furniture in each, sawdust everywhere. Wind whistled through the open doors, but because of the sawdust they couldn't be closed. All the men were frozen. It was like something out of a Dicken's novel, one step away from the workhouse. He worked from 7.00 a.m. until 4.30 p.m., Monday to Friday, and 7.00 until 1.00 on Saturdays. He came out with £104 a week. After my visit, I made him pack it in.

The year was 1994 and it was still possible to scout for jobs, just, so we got in the car and visited some factories and left our contact details. We took jobs in a tomato-harvesting plant. We started at 6.00 a.m. We picked tomatoes from the vines. The slightest hint of red or yellow, off they came. We walked down the aisles, one on either side of the vines pulling the tomatoes and placing them gently in our carts. Being a greenhouse it was lovely and warm. We were grinning at each other through the vines, mouthing 'I love you', and congratulating ourselves on landing such cushy jobs. The vines were a bit sticky, but after the freezing fruit factory, it seemed like bliss.

'If the gang could see us now,' Martin smiled through the vines.

'Mmm,' I smiled back.

I saw them in their thermals, standing on cardboard boxes, their noses dripping.

'I hope Fina's arse is frozen!'

Martin whistled and I hummed as we worked along the aisles. Each time we reached the end of an aisle, we gave each other a little kiss before starting the next one.

Then the sun rose. The temperature rose. Our body heat rose. Once again, I was wearing the wrong clothes. I had on a polyester blouse under a long acrylic jumper (to hide my bum and bought for warmth when I worked at the fruit packing), and within a short time we were sweating profusely, covered with green from the vines. My hair was long and curly and proved such a hindrance as I leaned through the vines in pursuit of tomatoes. With the increase in temperature the vines grew steadily stickier and stuck to my hair like Velcro. Martin stopped whistling, I ceased humming, and both of us longed for break time.

When we sat down in the canteen, I burst out laughing when I noticed for the first time the green rivers of perspiration trickling down Martin's shaved head in stripes. Everything we wore from the knees up was covered with green. The heat in the greenhouse sapped all our energy and we were exhausted by lunchtime.

It reminded me of the childhood story of the argument between the Wind and the Sun. If I remember correctly, the Wind claimed he was so powerful he could force this old geezer to remove his overcoat. 'Nonsense', replied the Sun, 'I'm stronger than you.' The Wind disagreed. 'Prove it to me,' says the Sun. The Wind blew, the old man buttoned his coat, the more the Wind blew, the deeper he huddled in his coat. Then the Sun did his bit, he shone and shone, radiating heat until the old sod was perspiring so much he was compelled to remove his overcoat. As a perpetually frosty arsed six-year-old I disagreed with the outcome; I knew the cold Wind was stronger than the Sun. I wished I were back in the cold factory.

The day passed all the same and we finished work at 2.00 p.m. Now I knew why it was such an early start. I soaked in the bath for ages and after washing my hair, I was still finding bits of green on everything. The bathwater looked like a stagnant pond; the towels wouldn't come clean in the wash.

I was dreading Tuesday; we both were. I borrowed Martin's green ex-army cotton shirt and a pair of his green combat pants and off we went. My outfit became quite trendy for women years later, but at the time I felt like a bloke. Even wearing the right clothes, with my hair tied back in a ponytail the second day was no easier than the first. It was fine for the first three hours, though like laboratory mice we'd learnt what to expect so we couldn't enjoy those hours knowing what was to follow.

Matters weren't helped by the appearance of the Sun Goddess. She was about twenty years old, breathtakingly beautiful, with hair of spun gold, like the princess in a fairy tale. I don't know how she did it, but while the rest of us sat down for our tea break covered in green slime like creatures that had walked out of a swamp, she wafted into the canteen like a Cecil B. De Mille starlet, ready for her close-up and not a hint of green on her palest blonde hair. I was green with envy. To this day I do not know how the delicately tanned vision managed to remain perfect. Perhaps she picked the tomatoes by osmosis.

We did not stay in the job because the wages were abysmal. We were paid by the amount of tomatoes we picked, not by the hour. Neither of us were afraid of hard work—we really grafted—but when we looked in the wagon at the end of the shift to assess how much we'd earned I was convinced there was a hole in the bottom with a chute leading straight back to the vines, where the tomatoes reaffixed themselves. I swore (jokingly) that the Sun Goddess managed to stay clean because she was nicking our tomatoes. The employers were aware the wages were low and the turnover of staff was astonishingly high.

What finally did it for me was having to wash my hair every day. I grew up in the fifties when 'Make Friday night Amami wave-set night' was the order of the day. Women only washed their hair once a week, as we had to go through the rigmarole of setting it in rollers and sitting under the hair-dryer hood for an hour or more if we had long hair. I followed slavishly, even though I inherited my mother's naturally curly hair. Now I just wash and wait. Though the days of rollers are a distant memory, when I got home from the greenhouse I was stuck indoors every afternoon waiting for my hair to dry, having never learnt to blow-dry it.

We wouldn't have left the job to go back on the dole, but the agency rang and asked if we were interested in a job involving quality control. That had been Fina's job and I quite liked the idea of working in a white overall in a nice clean environment. Quality control of what, I enquired. 'Carrots.' Fine; I envisioned myself pointing at ugly misshapen carrots that displeased me and having them removed from my offended sight. I was quite looking forward to the job.

It took us ages to find the place on the Monday. As we were driving down a dirt track road I thought there had been a mistake in the directions we'd been given and was getting worried we'd be embarrassingly late for our first day. We came to a large barn with a tractor and a few cars parked outside in the mud. My heart sank. I couldn't see an office anywhere. There was a raised platform in the barn with a rickety old conveyor belt running the length of it. Four men were hanging around waiting for the belt to start up. I looked around the yard and saw four trailers of very dirty carrots. A car pulled up, three men got out and began donning overalls over their jeans. The farmer came to welcome us; he said they'd never had a woman sent to work there before. By now my heart was in my hiking boots but I shrugged and said, 'Right Martin, let's get on with it.' As we walked up the slope to the conveyor belt I was silently cursing the guy from the agency; he'd have made a great estate agent. When the belt started up it sounded like an old horse-drawn cart being pulled along a rutted field. The farmer backed one of the trailers up to the start of the belt and a worker began throwing the carrots on. Martin turned to me and smiled, his face showing a mixture of encouragement and apology.

As the carrots made their slow ascent one of the men explained what we were to do. We were to remove any large carrot tops by swiftly slicing them off on blades which were imbedded in sawn off fence posts nailed to the platform on either side of us. He demonstrated . . . one carrot in left hand, slice top off on left-hand blade; one carrot in right hand, slice top off on right-hand blade—left-hand slice, right-hand slice, left-hand slice, right-hand slice. He made it look easy. Right, here goes. A large carrot trundled towards me like a victim to the guillotine. I picked it up with my right hand and drew it across the blade. I missed it entirely. I repeated the procedure; a green feathery bit fell off. I did it again; another bit of greenery bit the dust. I held the offending carrot with both hands and managed to lop off a quarter of an inch of hardtop. I had another couple of goes with the same carrot and the same result, then thought sod it, and threw it on the belt. Martin was working steadily beside me—left, right, left, right—skiing skilfully with both hands. I picked up a slightly smaller carrot for my next attempt and drew it over the blade; I'd have had more luck with a cheese grater for all the top I managed to cut off. I really tried my damndest but I just hadn't the strength to pull the large carrots over the blades, and when I did I wasn't fast enough and the pieces clogged up the blades and I then had to use a knife to push them out. I kept my head down to the task, too embarrassed to look up, but I could feel the men taking sly peeks to see how I was coping. Martin didn't open his mouth, he knew me well enough.

I sneaked a quick look to see how the men worked, they all made it look easy, even the little runt at the end. I psyched myself up and renewed my efforts, but conceded that I would either have to use two hands for the big carrots or settle for medium-size ones, so I sort of bluffed it but did the best I possibly could. Slivers of carrot flew in all directions and before long we were covered in carrot peelings: hair, pockets, socks and boots. After attempting to decapitate a particularly obnoxious, woody one and suffering a sympathetic smile from the guy who'd showed us the ropes I decided, bugger the big ones and went for the small ones, some as tiny as my little finger, that didn't need doing., I tackled the occasional large one just for show. The men pretended not to notice. They chatted while they worked; I found I needed every ounce of concentration for the carrots.

It started to snow. At least the fruit factory had a wall and a door, I complained to myself. The toilet was an Elsan in a shack, with no running water; the stench was overpowering. At lunchtime, Martin apologised for the conditions and asked if I wanted to go home. I've never known if my stubborn streak was due to being Irish or having to prove a point because I'm a woman, but I refused. I'd have severed a limb rather than walk off the job in full view of the men. I told him I'd stick it for the rest of the day.

Unfortunately, at the end of the day one of the men said, 'Don't suppose you'll be here tomorrow. Not women's work is it?'

I wish he hadn't said that. He might as well have slapped my face with a gauntlet and challenged me to a duel. All day long I'd chivvied myself along with the comforting thought that I only had to get through the day. Now, of course, I felt obliged to turn up the next day, and the one after that. In that vein, we worked right up to Christmas Eve. I did not intend to go back after the holiday though. I dumped my Barbour jacket, which had taken on an orange hue and looked rather odd.

We had Martin's kids to stay over the Christmas and it was quite a houseful, what with the rest of their family dropping in. It was wonderful to see Martin interacting with his children. They were an extremely tactile family and very affectionate. They told each other a million times a day they loved one another, by the time the kids left I'd been added to the list. They were always playing games or horsing around, no couch potatoes there; they automatically included me in what they were doing, I was exhausted by the end of the holiday. My usual idea of a good time is to be left in peace with a book—no chance in that family—but I enjoyed it. We told Tom we were going to see my mum as a blind and Martin drove me to yet another prison to visit Chris. Though Martin was non-judgemental, I don't think Tom would have been.

Surprisingly, Chris was in good form, unlike his mother who was depressed as hell seeing him in his prison garb for yet another season of good cheer. He had us in stitches with his caustic witty thumbnail sketches on each of the prison officers who watched our every move.

Memory is a strange thing. Unexpectedly, an image of me carrying the unborn Chris floated in my mind as I walked towards the visiting table carrying a tray with three cups of tea and a small mountain of chocolate goodies for the prisoner. I saw myself pulling a long black hair from my head and weaving it, one plain, one purl in the rib of his matinee coat as I knitted, something I'd always done when I knitted anything for the kids, so they'd have part of me next to their skin. Chris turned to smile at me as I put the tray down. I chewed on the inside of my mouth to keep from blubbing. He hated when I started to cry.

'Don't Mum, please!' he'd say the moment he spotted the tell-tale watery eyes. 'I really don't need this every time. Let's just be happy eh?'

Only a complete imbecile would question why the life I'd wished for him turned out the way it had, and I was bowing under the weight of maternal guilt. I was glad Martin was with me; Chris was so busy entertaining he was oblivious to the fact that I was on the verge of breaking down in tears. He always argued he could have fallen foul of the law whatever his background. We'll never know but I'm convinced he's wrong.

Joey, as usual, had migrated as part of the nomadic life he had chosen to live. No-one knew where he had moved to and I reconciled myself to another Christmas without contact.

*

I didn't know it then but the carrots were to be the last job I had for quite a while. With the job ending at Christmas, before I knew it, January was upon me and instead of sneaking up on me as it usually did, it came at me from behind like an assassin with a sledgehammer . . . whack! One hit and I dropped.

One minute I was in the kitchen crossing days off the calendar waiting for the agency to ring with a job offer. I drew a line through the ninth of January my eyes dropped to the following Monday, the sixteenth. The sixteenth! My heart rate increased. It can't be! I closed my eyes for a moment. When I opened them the calendar was the same. It can't have come round so soon! Just seven days to the anniversary of the murders. My hands shook. I looked at the biro in my hand as if I'd never seen it before, my thoughts whirling. I looked at the date again hoping I was mistaken. I drew a line through the month of January as if it would disappear off the calendar. When I could still see the dates, I started to cry.

Tom, who'd been watching me in bewilderment, asked what was wrong. I said I didn't feel well, felt a bit dizzy and needed to lie down. I stumbled up the stairs to bed where I lay shivering. It was as if a dense fog entered the room; it descended on me, trapping me to the bed. I stayed holed up in the bedroom for two weeks, only leaving the room to use the bathroom. Poor Tom didn't know what to make of it all. I knew it was the height of bad manners to take to my bed when I was a guest in his house, but I literally couldn't move. Martin told him I was suffering from depression; he of course knew the truth.

When I did rejoin the household I went to the supermarket with

Tom, cleaned the house and other mundane things, but I didn't feel right. I should have known the past could never be forgotten. I was right back where I started; scared to leave the safety of the house. Pretending to be normal, making polite conversation, constantly acting, living under Tom's roof proved to be too much of a strain. I told Martin we had to find a place of our own and he agreed. We heard of a caravan going for rent that took DHSS tenants. We weren't keen on the idea of living in a caravan but it was somewhere to start; we said we'd pretend it was a holiday. It was a long way from Tom's house, which suited me fine. We rang them and they said we didn't need an appointment to view, just come with our gear and two months' advance rent. Great. Off we went. New beginnings.

Not this time though. It was a dreadful place, as soon as we set eyes on it we knew. There were ramps every ten feet or so, always a bad sign. People were sitting outside their caravans burning wood to keep warm, like hillbillies.

'Is that really necessary?' I enquired, pointing to the gas cylinders chained up outside the vans.

'Yes, the gas bottles will be nicked. Oh . . . and don't leave your windows open or you'll be broken into.'

Lovely. Every unsmiling eye in the place was on us as we slowly drove up and over each ramp. Betsy's suspension went as the back end sagged under the weight of our belongings; Martin muttered under his breath about my books. If I had been the crying type, I think I'd have burst into tears at that point.

People will probably think 'who the hell does she think she is?'—what with her being on the game an' all, as Steve once said—but we didn't belong there. Martin was a well-brought-up farm boy. Having grown up in children's homes and convents—architecturally beautiful buildings—I developed a hunger for beauty. At fourteen, when I went to live with my mum she was well on the property ladder in a lovely five-bedroomed Victorian house. When I set up home I always rented in the private sector, until I left Craig Nelson. Though I then ended up squatting in a flat in Ballymun for a year, I hardly ever saw it. I was insulated because I worked at night, slept in the day, taxied everywhere and ate in restaurants, so it was just a place to lay my head. I never mixed or shopped locally. Ballymun did have some redeeming factors—the flats were quite spacious, they had balconies where you could sunbathe in the nude if you were so inclined and the under-floor central heating was wonderful. That kind of property in the private sector would have been quite sought after by yuppies, though the flats were most unsuitable for children.

Our caravan was sited at the top of the hill, which pleased me as you could see for miles. My pleasure was short-lived when I discovered that we had no water most of the time because the pressure wasn't enough to get up the hill. I got talking to a lovely Welsh girl who lived in the next van to ours. She was like a fish out of water. She was in hiding from her husband who used to rough her up. She told me the owners of the site charged her extra rent because she had a little boy. I stared at her in incomprehension. Why?

'Wear and tear of the van,' she replied.

'But they're penalising you for being a mother!' I exclaimed angrily, my sense of injustice outraged.

She too was always short of water so I used to collect her water container when we were going to the garage to fill ours. Her van had been broken into before we arrived. I asked what had been taken. Some bread and milk and a tin of custard.

'What?'

'They're only kids,' she explained.

Most of the kids were hungry because the parents had to pay the excess money out of their giros for the wear and tear of the vans. What a bloody con. Looking at the state our van was in I thought the previous tenants must have been the Waltons . . . with dirty fingernails. I was deeply unhappy about the sheer unfairness of such a tax on parenthood and couldn't wait to get away from the place. The van stank because there was never enough water to flush the toilet properly. I never felt clean and the pong put us off our food. The worst was the hostility from our fellow campers; I don't know whether it was because of old Betsy (who looked as if she'd cost real money), but I never once saw a smile on a single face as we drove through in the six weeks we stuck it out.

Once again, fate smiled. It arrived in the shape of Tom who had discovered a better caravan site near to his house. I wasn't proud this time; I was in his car in a flash to go check it out. The site was beautifully landscaped and had well-equipped separate shower blocks for men and women and two blocks of separate toilets. The couple who owned the site were gypsies and had built a lovely house on the site. She was about the same age as me, a lovely friendly woman who didn't want to face any more winters travelling in a caravan 'with me old bones playing me up'.

There were a few travellers' touring caravans hooked up to the mains electricity. They were top-of-the-range aluminium, chrome, stainless steel or whatever they're made of, which probably cost as much as a small house. At the other end of the site were ten old, but serviceable, static caravans let out to people who were on benefits of one kind or another and we rented one of these. Unlike the gypsy hook-ups, these had running water and flush toilets, a small miracle after the previous dump. For twenty quid I bought an old washing machine with a wringer from the Salvation Army charity shop and I couldn't have wished for anything else from life. I dug the little plot surrounding our van—to the amusement of all on the site—and planted it out with tulips and daffodils for the coming season, nicotiana for fragrance, alyssum, perennial geraniums and a few dahlias.

There wasn't a lot of mixing between the travellers with their beautiful expensive vans and us, the trailer trash. The former all worked hard for a living while we sat around waiting for our giros to drop on the mat. Still, we got along well enough with them, they were very cordial in the main. Now and again the gypsies would employ one of the men from our end for the odd day, fitting carpets or whatever. We were only there two weeks when Martin landed a job with Wimpy, the builders. I signed on the dole and stayed home waiting for him, my only link with the outside world. Though as usual I kept busy, busy, busy and he was most impressed when I re-lined his ancient leather jacket with a remnant of luxurious burgundy silk. But I couldn't get my act together to go out in public.

Mind you, I wasn't unhappy, I was more than content with my life. I had a roof over my head, food, good health and a man I loved who idolised me. I must also have had amazing powers of self-delusion for I had no idea that what I was content with, the life I had carved out for myself, was lacking in anything. I did not know that I should want more. Fulfilment. Odd word really, when you think of it. Full . . . fill . . . I was unfulfilled and unaware of the fact. Perhaps if Martin had not loved me so much I would have known something was missing from my life. As it was his love settled round me like a quilt of finest down, nestled into every nook and cranny, made me feel safe and warm, no cold bits infiltrating.

Martin was bent over a jigsaw puzzle of a Goya nude; he commented that Goya had painted her with a loving eye. I asked what he meant. He pointed out that she should have a little fold of fat here, a few wrinkles there, had she posed like that in real life. I saw what he meant.

'That's what you've done with me. You've painted me with a loving eye. You think I can do no wrong,' I smiled lovingly at him.

'Nonsense. You're a good woman. I just love you,' he said simply.

Love is a strange phenomenon, when one such as I can be described as a 'good woman'. If he read the eulogy at my funeral people would think they were burying a saint and on my headstone: 'Here rests a good woman.'

The year at the caravan was one of the most contented either of us had ever known. Martin had suffered a lot of sorrow in his life, with his mother dying when he was so young and then losing his children, wife and home. The winter was awful. There was ice on the inside of the windows when we woke in the mornings and all our clothes went mouldy in the wardrobes, but it didn't really matter because we were so much in love. We'd had our name on the council housing list since we'd lived there and were expecting to wait years, but because of the damp were made an offer after eleven months. We didn't want to go really, in case the spell was broken. It had been a very happy year, but winter would come again and I would have breathing problems because of the damp. What I didn't know was that I actually had asthma; I had yet to be diagnosed. It must be hereditary because my mum got it in her fifties.

The woman who owned the site didn't want us to go either. She complained that every time she got a decent tenant they left; we took it as a compliment. We accepted the offer of a very nice two-bedroomed flat in an up-market village twenty miles away. New beginnings. The woman from the site gave us two narrow foam mattresses out of a caravan they were scrapping and apart from that all we had moving in were two deckchairs, a small table and the washing machine, but we couldn't have been happier. We were like a couple of newlyweds in our first home. I did the decorating while

Martin was at work. I was pretty ace at it by that stage because I'd decorated a three-storey house, room by room, for a woman I used to clean for, while being pulled there and back every day by Monty on his lead.

Nights would find us sitting with our deck chairs touching, holding hands like a couple of teenagers as we watched the telly. We slept on the floor on the foam mattresses, the best sleep I had had since Mountjoy Jail, where they had similar mattresses. It was six months before we could afford a settee and a year before we got a proper bed; it was second-hand at that, Sally Army again. We had trouble getting it up the stairs to the flat and, when I went to make it, I discovered it was a king-size and our sheets were too small. Not that it mattered; neither of us was into things very much.

Tom died a few weeks after we moved in. Martin was distraught. I administered tons of TLC to help him cope with his grief.

My mum rang to tell me Joey had been in touch, looking for my new address so I got Martin to drive me up to Liverpool to see him and Linda. He and Martin hit it off. Everything seemed to be fine between Linda and Joey. I was content just knowing where he was. We used to talk on the phone a lot and I visited him for Christmas and his birthday. They came to us a couple of Christmases, but Linda was a Liverpool lass who hated to be away from her family. Then he got six months in the nick for stealing and by the time, he was released; Linda had found a new man. Joey was devastated; he went to the dogs and ended up living in a hostel. Mothers are always the last to know. Linda later told me Joey had started doing cocaine and became very aggressive and argumentative, so she was not entirely to blame. I always liked Linda, it's sad when your kids' relationships end.

I went to Liverpool every few months and kitted Joey out and gave him a few bob. It was not much because the money wasn't there but I felt like I was doing something. He still worried about Linda's welfare and kept tabs on her to make sure she was not being ill-treated. I pleaded with him to come home with me but he wanted to stay near Linda, hoping for reconciliation. He could not accept it was over. The rest of the time, I did what mothers do; I worried.

I was in a charity shop buying work jeans for Martin and got talking to one of the volunteers and she said they were desperate for help. I told her my mum worked for Oxfam and I don't know how it went from discussing my mum's work to being roped in myself, but somehow I found myself volunteering to help out one morning a week. First, I had to be interviewed by Ann, the area manager. Ann said they were looking for a shop manager and asked if I was interested. I was tickled by the idea of me managing anything and I told her she had to be joking. She assured me she wasn't. The job carried a salary. Would I at least think about it? I told her I couldn't manage myself let alone a shop.

I could have kicked myself. What had possessed me to volunteer? It would mean interacting with people on a personal level and I only ever really talked to Martin. I had a panic attack when I got home. I argued back and forth with myself. Should I? More importantly, could I? What harm could it do? I'd given my word I'd be there, they were nice people, they needed help. They wouldn't want me in the shop if they knew who I was. They weren't there to judge me, they just wanted someone to help in the shop for goodness sake, not someone to adopt their grandchildren. I argued the toss. Martin said it would do me good to have women to talk to. I saw the sense of this. I decided I'd go.

I was as nervous as hell, but apart from the butterflies, I did not have a panic attack as I would under normal circumstances. I needn't have worried. The woman I worked with on Mondays, Marjorie, was very friendly and helpful. The customers were nice too; most of them were regulars. Even the huge antique till wasn't a problem. None of the buttons did what they were supposed to. No matter which one you pressed the cash drawer shot out like a bullet, so you had to move out of harm's way at the same time; a bit like old Arkwright's in *Open All Hours*. We had some fun with it. The morning flew by and I enjoyed it. It was great to be busy; I looked forward to the next Monday.

Before I knew it, I was working all day Monday and Thursday mornings; volunteers are thin on the ground. Glenda worked Monday afternoons. She never stopped yapping. She said herself she suffered from verbal diarrhoea and she never listened to a word anyone said. I come from a yappy family—my mum and my sister never draw breath—but Glenda was something else. She was the most egocentric person I ever met. She was totally unshockable, though that could have been a result of not listening; you could have confessed to poisoning your whole family and she would have forgotten it by the time she got home.

On Thursdays I worked with Moya, the sweetest eighty-year-old that ever lived. Though she was old, her mischievous brown eyes were those of a ten-year-old. She had never married, though judging by her looks and personality she must have had plenty of admirers in her youth. She lived with her sister who was also a spinster.

Moya looked like a negative of a badger, a fluffy halo of snow-white hair with a dark brown stripe clean down the centre. Stupid me didn't realise the brown stripe was, in fact, nicotine. Moya smoked like a chimney. She wore acrylic or nylon sweaters and black or brown polyester slacks, heavily embroidered with cigarette holes. She would shuffle outside and sit on the window-sill to have a smoke half-way through the morning. I would tell her she was lowering the tone of the shop as I plonked her mug of coffee beside her; she had a wicked sense of humour. She was so cute I felt like wrapping her up in cotton wool and taking her home in my pocket.

She was crossing the road to the shop one morning and fell over a ramp. A window cleaner came to her aid and called an ambulance. As she was carted off to hospital she asked the window cleaner to let us know in the shop. The hospital rang to tell us she would not be able to make it to work, she had sustained a broken nose and her face was badly smashed up. That was typical of Moya, thinking of others. She used to arrive at the shop by taxi, paid from her own purse. After the fall Ann insisted the charity paid the fare but Moya took some persuading. The time came when she fell whenever she set foot out of the house. She'd sit at the till looking like a victim of domestic abuse. In the end it was no longer practical for her to come to work. We all missed her severely.

I went to visit her when she was convalescing in an old folk's home after yet another fall, and as I walked in there I was hit by a strong smell of cigarette smoke. I stopped a care worker and asked for Moya, he pointed down a corridor. I should not have bothered asking, should have followed the tobacco trail. Moya sat in an armchair puffing her head off. I gave her a box of her favourite liquorice allsorts. She handed them to a man next to her, and by the time I left, she had given them all away. Sadly, pushing ninety, she died recently, proof that smoking does kill . . . eventually. I hope heaven has plenty of ash trays.

Whenever Ann came to oversee the shop, she badgered me, in the nicest possible way, to take the manager's job. I always laughed it off. It was one thing to be there as a volunteer; I was too inept for the responsibility of running the place. I did not have the confidence anyway. I was mystified that she couldn't grasp the fact that I was hopelessly unsuited for the job. Luckily, I was let off the hook within a short space of time when Ann found herself a new manager.

Gill was a petite blonde with a very caring nature who nurtured the elderly volunteers and was a tireless worker. I looked forward to the days she worked and came to consider her a friend. Sadly, Gill's daughter contracted Crohns disease; as the illness worsened, Gill was compelled to take a lot of time off work to care for her so I filled in for her at the shop. Some weeks I worked five days. I loved the place; it was very laid back with it being a charity shop. All the volunteers were elderly—apart from Wendy, who was a student—and, it was a social outing for them where they met others like themselves; and the tea and biscuits we consumed at the till reflected this. Older people are in the main a far gentler generation. They were interesting company, with a wealth of experience between them, and I felt enriched by the time I spent with them.

One morning I woke up full of joy knowing I was going to the shop. As I showered, I did an autopsy on the sensation, a habit I'd grown into since I met Martin. I felt that if I could isolate the happiness particle I could put it in the bank as insurance against the bad times. I concluded my state of bliss owed itself to the knowledge that I'd become a part of something. I belonged in the shop . . . I was a member of the team . . . part of the charity. I had finally found my place in society.

13

Just when I'd reached a stage in life when I wasn't expecting fate to throw any more shocks my way, I arrived home from the shop one evening to find Joey waiting in a car outside the flat with a girl whom he introduced as his wife. They had been married just three weeks and he had decided it was time for her to meet the mother-in-law.

In a state of shock, I welcomed them in to the flat, told them to make themselves at home, and went to make coffee. I stood the mugs on the draining board, and set about peeling extra potatoes and vegetables to add to what I had prepared that morning, while I waited for the kettle to boil.

We got married three weeks ago. A wedding in the family. Joey is married. Joey . . . married.

I tried to get my head round it. I would have put money on Joey remaining a bachelor until the day they carted him off in a coffin. He certainly had no reason to view marriage as a worthy institution. Joey was the first of my three kids to tie the knot. I wondered what Martin would make of it when he got home from work.

I totally forgot I was supposed to be making coffee until Joey shouted through, asking if I had gone to Brazil for the coffee beans. My children never cease to amaze me. There's me tossing and turning unable to sleep nights grieving for Joey over the loss of Linda, his substitute mother. He arrives, married, to a girl eleven years his junior I didn't know existed.

Dawn was only eighteen, but while her face was bare of make-up (something Joey hates), she looked older, a picture of innocence lost. I thought her cheeky, hard and brittle, but kept my counsel. She already had a five-year-old daughter whom her mother looked after.

Dawn appeared bored to tears the whole time, as if she couldn't wait to escape, distinctly under-whelmed by the mother-in-law. Her eyes, when she looked at me at all, were as cold and flat as pebbles. I saw her smile once, then wished she hadn't, her teeth were black. I could not understand how an eighteen-year-old could have such rotten teeth. Ha! Shows how little I knew.

The newly-weds were lethargic and uncommunicative. I wondered why they'd bothered to tie the knot. They never seemed to be hungry, maybe it was because they were so much in love. After the life I'd led I can't believe I was so clueless and naive.

The next day I was sprinkling fish food in the tank in the kitchen and Dawn leaned across me, opened the cupboard above my head, helped herself to a packet of chocolate biscuits, closed the cupboard door, and walked out of the room without as much as a by-your-leave. Joey grinned and rolled his eyes at me. I shook my head, but held my tongue. I wouldn't dream of helping myself to a breadcrumb in my own mother's house without asking permission, let alone anyone else's.

They stayed a few days, the first and last time I ever set eyes on my daughter-in-law. It hardly needs saying the marriage never stood a chance. I don't want to humiliate Joey so I won't go into the doings of Dawn. Let's just say she caused him a tremendous amount of pain. Though they were only together a wet day, he carried a torch for Dawn for years. He couldn't move on if he wanted to because she kept coming back to him. Dawn would bugger off and do her thing, hear through the grapevine Joey had a few shillings, turn up out of the blue, stay with him until the money was spent, then take off again. On 4 July, she was ringing his doorbell at 6.45 waiting for his birthday card to arrive in the post; she knew I always sent money. He hadn't seen hide nor hair of her for months. I smiled when I heard this; I could see the funny side. Joey loved her so much he didn't care that she came for the money; he was just glad she was there.

The only time I felt truly sorry for Dawn was when Joey told me that she'd broken down in tears a few hours after the wedding, which was by special licence, saying, 'What have I done! I don't want to be married!' I asked him why they decided to marry in the first place. He said that he felt sorry for her because she'd had such a shit life. He wanted to make her happy. Joey does have a sense of humour but I held back on the smart retort; he takes affairs of the heart seriously.

'You want to see her face when I asked her, Mum. It lit up like a little kid's.'

'You're such a softie,' I sighed. My heart swelled with love, my eyes ached.

'I don't get it from the stones on the road.'

'Don't blame me for your lousy choice!' I teased. 'Was it worth it?' He laughed ruefully, and then admitted he would do the same again.

Considering Dawn got married on a whim (wearing Joey's tracky bottoms and t-shirt because they couldn't afford a special outfit), in front of two strangers hijacked as witnesses, who could blame her for feeling let down. I felt like weeping when I thought about it, poor kids.

Were I to fight Dawn's corner I'd have to admit Joey is no saint to live with himself. He suffers from depression; anyone unfortunate enough to share life with a depressive will know what hell that can be. He's quiet, introspective and serious, also rather argumentative, has been since he was a child. Hardly a young girl's dream.

Long after Dawn left him, he thumbed a lift a hundred miles to visit her in prison only to have her get up and walk off when she discovered he hadn't brought her any drugs. He always said he'd take her back no matter what she'd done. I know the social workers could come up with all sorts of reasons and excuses for Dawn's behaviour and I am usually sympathetic to the cause, but sod all that, it's too close to home to be objective.

Three months after their wedding, Joey was in the nick again. Dawn did a runner as soon as he got locked up, which meant he had nowhere to go on his release. I lay staring at the ceiling at night, worrying what Joey would do when he got out. I envisaged him walking out the prison gates to nothing and no-one. Abandonment is a terrible feeling. Without being asked, Martin, bless his soul, offered to drive me to meet Joey the morning he got out of Walton Prison.

Joey looked fit and healthy when he walked out the gate at 8 a.m. carrying a black bin-liner containing all his worldly possessions. Because of the early hour, we drove around aimlessly for a while. Our first port of call was McDonalds for breakfast; Joey had been looking forward to it. Then we set off on a quest to find Dawn. I was unhappy about it, no good could come of it, but I kept it to myself.

We drove the length and breadth of Liverpool throughout the day looking for Dawn. At the same time, Joey was trying to sort out a place to doss down until he got a place of his own. Martin and I asked him to come home with us but, again, he wanted to stay near his woman. Joey called on anyone he could think of who would possibly know Dawn's whereabouts while Martin and I sat outside in the car waiting.

As the day progressed Joey was spending longer at each port of call, Martin and I twiddling our thumbs in the car. I was fed up, but kept it myself. I didn't want to spoil his release day by kicking off. Martin, Mister Nice Guy, did not complain once, he was always happy just to have my company, but I bet he was seething secretly. By 7 p.m., after sitting outside a high-rise block for over an hour waiting for Joey to emerge I'd finally had enough. Martin had to get up at 6 a.m. for work and we had a 160-mile drive ahead of us. Joey asked us to drop him down the road from Dawn's sister's house.

I got out of the car to say good-bye. I hugged him then held him at arms' length to look at him as I trotted out my final maternal admonishments.

'Oh my God!' I recoiled in horror. The pupils of his eyes were like pinpricks.

'What's wrong with your eyes? What have you done?' He looked like something from a graveyard in a cheap horror film.

He shook his head. 'Nothing, mum. I'm just tired.'

I stared at his eyes, full of fear for him. He was like a stranger standing before me. He gazed off in the distance, unable to face my concern. It was probably my imagination, but he seemed to be standing in a shadow. Maybe it was the soul-catcher closing in. In spite of the warm summer evening, I shivered.

It hit me that whatever Joey had taken, he had done so under our noses while we taxied him around. Apparently, Martin and I had taken a day off work to drive him to drug dealers. I felt a surge of annoyance. I was too exhausted after the long drive to the prison and the day hanging around in the car to let rip at him. If I'm honest, I felt betrayed. I kissed him, got in the car, and we drove off. I craned my neck to watch him until he was a dot on the path, so upset I did not wave.

Joey's pinned eyes were the first inkling I had that something sinister was afoot. What an idiot I had been in believing his biggest problem was women. Judging by his graveyard eyes, I knew that his life, so my life by default, was never going to be the same again. I chewed it over with Martin on the way home; neither of us knew enough about hard drugs to figure out what Joey had taken. Joey's love life was now the least of my worries. It paled into insignificance against the knowledge that he was doing drugs.

*

Time marches on regardless of whether your world is coming apart at the seams. The shop and the volunteers were my salvation in the dark days that followed. Especially Glenda. Because Glenda did not have conversations, rather one-woman monologues, she didn't notice my smile was forced, or that I moved around in a fog. She held court at the till, yakking non-stop from the time she stepped over the threshold at 9.30 in the morning until she waved goodbye to me as I cashed up at the end of the day.

Work occupied my time, kept me busy, and giving me less time to think about Joey's drug involvement. No-one at work knew what I wrestled with; they would have been shocked. All their children led decent, ordinary lives. Their kids had been blessed with stable backgrounds and united families. They had gone to school, university, had good jobs.

By very virtue of the fact that they worked for a charity, the volunteers were a caring crew. As I grew to know them, it became clear that in spite of their sheltered lives they were not small-minded or mean-spirited. Had they known about Joey's drug problem they would have been concerned and supportive, but I could not confide in them without explaining the underlying reasons for it. It was yet another dark secret to keep.

I kept my past well under wraps; the volunteers never pried but took me at face value. Who, anyway, would believe I had so much to hide? I was hardly your run-of-the-mill volunteer.

The answer to the riddle came a few months later via one of Craig Nelson's vile letters. It started something along the lines of 'just thought you'd like to know your son is a heroin addict begging on the streets of Liverpool, thanks to you', and followed on with a litany of recriminations. The shock waves sent tremors through me. It didn't help that the letter of reproach held more than a grain of truth.

Craig's letter was intended to hurt and it was bang on target. What pierced my heart was knowing he'd seen our son in the gutter and walked by. How could he do that? In fact, Craig must have stopped to talk to Joey long enough to prise my new address out of him. How he could go home then and play the good daddy with his new family is beyond me; this is the same man who keeps a written record of what he calls his Indictments of Society. Maybe he should read it sometime.

Joey's tale is a long road of hostels, prison and the descent into heroin addiction. It makes me dizzy trying to piece it all together, to work out the sequence. I had not heard a word from him since Martin and I met him on his release from Walton. When heroin takes over, keeping in touch with family is bottom of an addict's list of priorities. I'd need a satellite navigation system to keep track of him, but when I eventually caught up with Joey he said he'd been selling the *Big Issue*, not begging. I believed him. He would not have been able to affect that wheedling tone and the downtrodden, submissive body language they use; he was too angry by far. The heroin was a different story.

You hear parents say they had no idea their kids were doing drugs, and other people saying 'Who are they trying to kid?' but it's true, you don't know. Hard drugs weren't an issue when I lived on the wild side. People drank, smoked dope, took a few pills occasionally, just as they had in the sixties. A few did a bit of recreational cocaine, that was about it. Heroin was just rearing its very ugly head around the time I hung up my working boots.

I did know one heroin addict back then, Sonny, a prostitute. Sonny was an extremely attractive country girl, bubbly, buxom, and vivacious until she got into heroin. I saw her two years or so after she started taking it: she'd aged fifteen years, her lovely white teeth had turned brown, she was haggard, ugly and looked like an X-ray.

Worst of all she had no personality; it was as if her psyche, her ego or whatever makes us unique, had died along with her veins. We were all so ignorant of heroin then; I thought her decline was due to the dreadful man she'd picked up with who had introduced her to the drug. It was so obvious that no-one in his or her right mind would use the stuff if that was what it did to you. Sonny was not the first woman I'd seen deteriorate rapidly after falling into the clutches of an evil bastard. Now I'm so much wiser, I realise Sonny was exhibiting the classic signs of prolonged heroin usage.

Eight years later, I realised that Dawn was already a heroin addict when she married Joey. Joey had tried it a couple of times and decided it wasn't for him, but once he married Dawn there was no looking back; the honeymooners had been doing drugs in the bedroom of my home. Their anti-social behaviour at that time now made sense. As did Dawn's rotten teeth. Joey had been an apprentice then, smoking heroin as opposed to injecting. I had asked them not to smoke around me because I'd given up, so they were confined to smoking in the bedroom. I'm glad I did not know because it gave me a few years of ignorant bliss.

*

Gill came to work very subdued one morning and announced she'd decided to hand in her notice. The strain of looking after her daughter while holding down a job was proving too much. We were shocked by the news; Gill was a good manager and we hated the idea of having to get used to her replacement. Gill startled me by saying she wanted to recommend me for the job, it would mean she wouldn't need to feel guilty about handing the volunteers over to a stranger. She saw how panic-stricken I was and dropped the subject.

Ann, our area manager got on my case again, insisting I'd be good for the job, I was adamant I couldn't do it. Ann however was like a terrier with a bone and kept the pressure on until I weakened and agreed to an interview; by law the job had to be advertised.

Martin pointed out I'd been doing the job in Gill's absence; he believed I could do it as well as the next person. Feeling loved is the foundation stone of confidence, I've come to realise. Growing up in a loveless home meant I had no confidence at all. Then along came Martin who showered me with love and compliments at every turn.

Some of it must have stuck to me without my realising because I began to see a glimmer of possibility that maybe, just maybe, I might be able for the job.

That didn't stop me from feeling nervous on the day. I sat opposite Ann and another interviewer with my stomach churning, a dry mouth and felt like an utter fraud. I'd given two references, the supervisor from the bottling plant and Gill, at her request. When the interview ended, I could have slept for a week. I told Ann how scared I'd been. Because she knew nothing, at that stage, of the kind of life I'd led, she wasn't to know what a major turning point it was for me, far more than a job interview. She said she didn't know what I was fearful of; I'd been doing the job for the best part of a year anyway. She had more applicants to interview, but she'd be in touch. I honestly did not believe I stood a chance; the other applicants seemed far better qualified.

Ann rang me later in the day to tell me the job was mine. I was dumbfounded. Someone thought I was respectable enough to front the flagship shop. Nice society had judged and not found me wanting. I had made it. I made a pact with myself that I would give good value for money.

Gill warned me it was a part-time job with full-time responsibility. I quickly discovered she wasn't exaggerating. Sorting donated goods, some for rag, some for wash, some for pricing, culling old stock, pricing new, dealing with customers, keeping the shop tidy any fool could do. But juggling volunteer rotas and making sure they were well looked after, coping with a stream of drunks, druggies and shoplifters required a little more skill, though I managed quite well because the volunteers were such a decent lot. They had hearts of gold and any one of them would help out at the drop of a hat. The drunks I was used to, thanks to living with Jeff for four years; the shop-lifters I could spot a mile off.

I loved every moment of the working day and would arrive early and finish late, reluctant to turn the sign to 'Closed'. Had the shop gone bankrupt I'd willingly have worked for free. It was such a novelty to be paid for something I enjoyed doing. I still lived in fear of being unmasked when I contemplated where I had arrived from, but always managed to push it to the back of my mind. Sometimes I felt I was soaring over the rooftops, so complete was my happiness.

It wouldn't have been the same if I worked for M&S or Woollies, where you just stood, smiled, and served customers. The fact that it was a charity shop is what made the difference; it was like a little community.

We had some great regulars in the shop. Scottish Jeannie, with her little dog Rosie whom we pretended not to notice because dogs weren't allowed. Jeannie, a hard-up pensioner in her eighties called in every pension day and bought small gifts for half the neighbourhood: a book, a stuffed toy for a child down the street, a shirt off the bargain rail for an out-of-work man in the next block. Her motto in life is give, give, give. We all knocked the price down on what she bought. Not that it helped her because she'd shuffle back later with a sandwich, or a couple of cakes she'd bought from the café, and put it under the counter for me and I couldn't stop her doing it.

Madge, whose husband had recently died, called in every single day for a chat. She couldn't reach her shoes to tie her laces so she'd shuffle in, sit on the stool, and hold her feet up for me to tie them. She'd sit for a while until she got her breath back and then trot off to buy the daily newspaper. We were the only people she saw, one month to the next.

Another regular was a young man in a wheelchair who'd pull up outside and mime through the window for me to bring some trousers out to show him. He went through them at a rate; he was incontinent so they had to be a dark colour. I'd take three or four pairs out to him, he'd ask which were the trendiest, and I'd throw in an extra pair as a goodwill gesture.

Mavis, a proud woman who'd been in the Women's Royal Air Force in the war, dropped in most days. She was in the early stages of senile dementia and would stand and cry because she'd forgotten something, or done something silly. She locked herself out of the house twice and we arranged for someone to change the lock for her. I used to joke that I must have had juvenile dementia as I'd been that way all my life, to try to jolly her along. Mostly it worked and she'd leave smiling.

A young woman with two children under four dropped in most days. She had to stay out of the house for as long as possible as her husband worked the night shift and would be trying to sleep. She looked so weary. One of us would take her boy to look at children's books to give her time to try clothes on.

Then there's Chanel. What a character, seven-years-old going on nineteen, with very definite ideas. She was a regular book buyer. Her mum would recommend one for her, Chanel would enunciate loudly and clearly that she wouldn't read it, she wanted that one instead. You couldn't help but be filled with admiration for such an opinionated little person. Once, I selected a book. 'How about this one Chantal?' She looked at the book I offered, but made no move to take it. She frowned, placed her right hand on her forehead, and said exasperatedly: 'Chanel. My name's Chanel, not Chantal.' C-H-A-N-E-L' she spelt out slowly, because she was dealing with a fool.

Keeping my face straight, I apologised for my mistake and explained we had many customers through the door and it was difficult getting all their names right. She forgave me.

'OK Lyn. It must be difficult to remember all of them.' She took the book from me, smiled, and conceded graciously, 'Anyway, Chanel and Chantal are a little alike.'

Thereafter we became the best of friends. She would call in to show me her paintings on her way home from school, or her new clothes. Her mum said she refused to enter the shop on my day off.

We had a few lousy regulars too. I've been threatened, abused and spat at, all grist to the mill with my background. One girl, a junkie, threatened to get me after work when I barred her for stealing: 'I'll send all my friends in to see you,' she promised. I stood my ground, but didn't retaliate; I didn't want a situation in front of the customers. Olwyn, our accountant, happened to be in the shop at the time and surprised me by giving the girl a mouthful and threatening her with the police. The girl looked right through Olwyn then turned to me and said, 'You fuckin stuck-up cow. You know fuck-all about real life and real people. Why don'tcha do us all a favour and fuck off home to your knitting!' She spat at me as she left the shop. Olwyn put her arm round me protectively, mistaking the hand over my mouth and my heaving shoulders for nerves.

Every day was different, there was always some anecdote or funny incident going the rounds from the shop to the offices or the other way round. I cannot resist making people smile, though I come unstuck occasionally. I came back from banking the takings one day and one of our regulars, an Austrian man whom I couldn't stand, was waiting for me; he wanted me to reduce the price of a vase he'd taken out of the window. This man quibbled over every penny, which got up my nose; our prices were already rock bottom. I refused. He stood erect and said very correctly:

'I sought you ver a lady I could do business viz. You disappoint me.' He reminded me of an SS officer the way he was standing.

'Oh goody. I love disappointing men.' I retorted walking past him to straighten the hangers on the shirt rail.

A woman at the knitwear spluttered, I noticed a man looking at the trouser rail guffawing, his shoulders moving, a couple of students tittered.

Playing to the gallery, I continued. 'Men have been such a disappointment to me all my life.'

I noticed Glenda desperately trying to catch my eye. And then I saw the Austrian's wife straightening up from the floor where she'd been looking at the shoes. She looked daggers at me.

We had many students through the door but thought nothing of it until one of our regulars, a student, said he'd recommended everyone on campus to come to the shop for the entertainment; he likened us to the Fawlty Towers of the charity shops. He said Glenda and I made a great comedy double act. I think he meant it as a compliment. I've been in many charity shops where you get the feeling you are unwelcome; you'd be shocked if they cracked their faces with a smile.

On one memorable occasion, Sandra, our newest and youngest volunteer and I were pricing donated stock at the till and she asked me what I thought of a shabby blue velvet jacket someone had left on the counter. I pulled a face. 'Not much.' Sandra stood holding it out for me to have a good look.

'It's tatty isn't it?' she grimaced; nodding at the torn lining She went through the pockets, used tissues, scraps of paper with phone numbers, two biros, some loose change. The money she put in the till, the rest in the wastepaper basket. 'Shall I bin it?'

'Yeah. No, on second thoughts, price it up. Ann might have sent it.'

'No one is going to buy it. It went out with the ark.' Sandra sniffed. 'Would you walk out with a man wearing that?'

'Students might buy it as retro.'

'There's retro and there's retro. I wouldn't use it for a duster,' she said stubbornly. We didn't nickname her 'Little Hitler' for nothing.

'No one's asking you to wear the sodding thing. Just put a bloody ticket on it.'

'How much?' She wrinkled her nose in disgust.

'Four-fifty.'

Sandra put a label on it and hung it up disdainfully. A young man came out of the changing room and stood looking through the suits on the rail. 'I've got one just like this,' Sandra and I turned to look at the man. He was holding the blue velvet jacket.

'This is just like mine. It is mine!'

'Oh! I seem to have acquired a ticket on it.'

Sandra and I put our hands over our mouths simultaneously in paroxysms of laughter. The insults we'd heaped on the jacket! I wanted to apologise, but we were laughing so much the words wouldn't come out. Sandra, in hysterics, began rifling through the rubbish bin looking for the stuff she'd emptied from the pockets as the man looked on. I daren't look at her. The man was a very good sport, faced with two helpless gigglers he was soon laughing as much as we were. He was an art teacher; he'd bought the jacket recently from Oxfam, he said, it had cost £10.

'You were done,' said Little Hitler.

'Sandra!'

I was useless at delegating; they all knew me too well. Once, I'd worked on my own all day and had a party of day-trippers late so didn't have time to finish pricing up the order Ann had sent, so I left Glenda a note.

'Dear Glenda, had a coach trip in p.m. I'd be very grateful if you'd price-up a few of the items in the box if you get time. Lyn. PS. This is a crawling letter.'

When I arrived at the shop two days later the stock was untouched and there was a note taped to the till.

'You must be joking! Glenda.'

I shook my head and laughed. Glenda had been there since grandpa was a lad and did things her way. She was there to talk, not work.

Occasionally, memories from the past filtered through my head sometimes, as if to say don't get too carried away with yourself, we're still here. Proof that the past was merely in hibernation came when I arrived at work one Saturday to discover we'd had an attempted break-in the night before. The gate at the rear of the property, which was always locked from the inside with two large bolts and a key-lock, was swinging open. There had been no obvious attempt to force the back door; the security combination lock and the alarm system probably acted as a deterrent.

On Monday Sally, our boss, decided that though nothing was taken we had to notify the police, if only for insurance purposes. She told me later that the police were on their way to lift fingerprints from the crime scene. She wasn't to know the impact her words had on me. I felt sick to my stomach picturing my ten dainty digits and two palm prints, immortalised in ink in my teens, flashing up on the police computer when they tried for a match.

I rinsed the empty milk bottles out in the sink, then sauntered out to the back gate and put them in the crate. As I straightened, I hurriedly wiped the latch, handle and lock of the gate clean with a tea towel, all the while keeping an eye on the upstairs windows over my shoulder in case I was spotted. I strode to the back door, working quickly I wiped the combination lock and the door handles, inside and out, with the tea towel, then the surrounding glass. My legs were like jelly. I went to the cloakroom and sat on the toilet seat, splashed cold water on my face, neck, and wrists and waited for my heartbeat to slow and the shaking to pass. The police never did take fingerprints.

I know there is a Statute of Limitations whereby fingerprints and criminal records are supposed to be destroyed after ten years or something. So they say, but I did not trust it. If that is the case, how is it that newspapers are able to unearth and print criminal convictions since the year dot when some big-time criminal is convicted of a major crime. Even though the police had not followed up on the attempted break-in I felt very unsettled. I'd have been out on my ear if the powers that be discovered I'd had convictions for prostitution as a teenager.

A couple of times the police came to see me concerning shoplifters, once over a young volunteer I'd caught stealing from the till. I died a thousand deaths while they were there. I sat at an angle, hoping the cop would not notice the faint blue-black dot on my cheekbone, which was actually a heavily camouflaged tattoo. Any cop would spot a Borstal Spot at a hundred paces, pan stick or not. The crime prevention officer probably thought I had a crick in my neck and had difficulty turning to face him.

*

Considering how many people we cross paths with in a lifetime its odd how infrequently we meet someone with whom we feel an instant rapport. As soon as I set eyes on Ann, the area manager, I felt I'd known her for years. Ann is blessed with a keen sense of humour, which probably had a lot to do with it; I can't be doing with anyone who has none. She's down-to-earth, says what she thinks, hates hypocrisy, people who give themselves airs and graces, and has a heart as big as the moon. She'd go out on a limb for you if you were in the right, but you wouldn't want to fall foul of her. Her soft accent is like a lullaby, should someone on the receiving end of her tongue fail to notice the flint in her eye it takes a while before they realise they are in the dog house. She started her career as a midwife before becoming a ward sister in a hospital maternity unit. I cannot think of anyone who could instil more trust in a pregnant woman, and I bet she ran a tight ship on the ward.

Ann visited all the shops on Mondays; she worked it so that she could take her dinner-break with me. We had our lunch in my office, a room smaller than a broom closet, the door open because she hates enclosed spaces. We'd be in stitches the whole time, shushing each other in case people heard us through the sliding doors.

Martin called me a teacher's pet when Ann asked me to go on management training courses with her; the organisation could only afford to pay for two. I must admit I was a bit flattered. I was excited too, me, going on a management course! The first one we attended, Ann picked me up at the crack of dawn, and we talked all the way. North Shields was still shuttered, not a soul in sight when we arrived. We drove around looking for a cup of coffee while we waited for the conference hall to open. We were always first to arrive wherever we went.

There's something about a long car journey along a motorway that induces a lowering of barriers, especially after dark. Ann is a good listener and I hardly noticed I was imparting morsels of information from my past; nothing too shocking just snippets of this and that. We went on a few different training courses and we really got to know each other well. I'm not sure we learnt a great deal on the courses—I think you learn more in the workplace—but it was a day out and the food was good.

All the shop managers were compelled do a first-aid course. The courses were staggered; you couldn't have all the shops without a manager at the same time. As usual Ann and I took ours together, not that she needed it. I worried about exposing my chunky knees when it came to putting one another in the recovery position, I couldn't stop laughing as Ann swaddled my lower half like a baby. As for the bandaging, by the time I'd finished with Ann's 'broken' arm she looked like a deformed mummy. The nursing profession had a lucky escape when I decided against following my best friend into nursing when we left school.

Each shop had to have a designated first aid person. I was blessed because our assistant manager was the designated one for our building. The offices were closed on Saturdays though, so it was down to me then. My volunteers were under strict instructions not to dare fall ill on Saturdays.

The worst thing that happened was when a three-year-old trapped her tiny fingers in the shop door. My first aid training flew straight out the top of my head. I took the girl to the cloakroom and ran her fingers under the cold tap; I sang 'Rockabye baby' as we watched the water run, the only thing I could think of. Next, I dislodged Glenda off her observation post and sat the girl on the high stool near the till while I rummaged around for the biscuit tin; some first aid. The child's poor little fingers had indentations from the doorjamb and were turning blue. I handed her a chocolate marshmallow. She still had tears in her eyes but she'd stopped crying. I said I thought a plaster was called for, I knew it wasn't really, but kids love them. She nodded enthusiastically. She was thrilled to bits when she saw the blue plasters. I wrapped a couple over the small fingers, she asked me to put one on her other hand. I asked her mum for her details because I had to write the incident up in the accident book, the little girl was most impressed as I wrote her name.

Ann and I always 'got' each other. Just a look was enough. Someone would say something, or something would happen and

Ann would look straight at me deadpan: I'd lose it. I'd plead with my eyes, stop! She'd look back real innocent. It was all right for her; she could control her giggles.

Personally, I'd have had Alexander Graham Bell shot at dawn, but when I first got the job I had sent letters to Ann concerning the shop via our van driver. She had rung me, 'Hey up Lyn. I got your letter.' There was a pause, and I realised I had done something odd. Thereafter I surrendered to the telephone. I'm convinced Ann was born with a telephone joined to her ear, perhaps she's a descendant of old Bell. If Ann had cause to ring me we'd spend ages talking (my end would need decoding if I was in the shop with customers listening).

Sometimes, when Ann felt overwhelmed by the sheer volume of donations, she sent the van to collect me and bring me to the depot to help her sort it. I liked those days, away from them upstairs at head office. We got on well with them actually, but it was nice to kick our shoes off while we worked, chatter, and share a joke without worrying about customers earwigging.

Ann decided I was to be her deputy, filling in for her when she took her holidays.

'You're deputising me! Where's me sheriff's badge?'

'I'm serious Lyn.' She replied in a tone that brooked no argument.

I was in a state of panic. I knew what Ann's job entailed. It carried a lot of responsibility, too much for yours truly anyway. I tried to get out of it, pointing out that other managers had longer service, and were far better suited to the job—Wilma for instance, a retired schoolteacher, well able to keep the unruly mob in check. Ann would not be swayed.

'You can do it. You always underestimate your capabilities.' Martin agreed.

'I thought you were supposed to be on my side.' He laughed, said a couple of weeks a year wouldn't kill me. OK, I could bluff it a week at a time. Which is exactly what I did. Ann made it easy by cancelling job interviews and juggling a lot of other stuff that could wait for her return, and leaving written instructions. Just as well, I soon found out my organisational skills left much to be desired.

Working on my own at the depot was a very different ball game.

No wonder Ann felt isolated and needed company, it was a very lonely working environment. In addition, I still hadn't a clue what I was doing most of the time. I was fine sorting the donations and putting up the orders for the shops, but the phone rang incessantly. I'd stare at it full of hate, wishing it'd disappear, hoping whoever was calling would change their mind if I ignored it long enough.

It was lovely being back on my own turf the following week; I'd missed the volunteers and the regular customers. The spectre of Ann's next holiday was pushed to the back of my mind, the last one quickly forgotten. Except that Ann was inconsiderate enough to go and get breast cancer and was compelled to take almost three months off work.

The area manager's job, in this case deputy dog's, was to oversee the shops, deal with staff and volunteers and any problems arising. You also had to organise the van drivers, deal with the ragman, the bag drop man, New Deal trainees and members of the public. On top of all that, plough through mountains of donated goods and select a decent order twice a week for all the shops. I didn't mind the sorting; it's what we all did in the shops, though not on such a grand scale.

The managerial side of things was easily sorted; I worked upstairs sorting stuff and left the others to their own devices. I was not cut out to be a boss. I solved the problem of personality clashes between the drivers by letting them get on with it. I felt like slapping one driver, a poor hard-done-by, over-worked moaning Minnie, so I stayed out of his way.

What I hated most was being compelled to work with my worst enemy, that dreadful instrument of torture, the telephone. The other shop managers were kind enough not to bother me too much. I'd ring round the shops Monday mornings to ask for the figures for the week's takings, to be kept in another book, and ask what they wanted me to send in the order. People rang in with donations, mostly furniture, books and bric-a-brac, and these were to be written in the driver's collection book. I had scraps of paper with addresses on them, scattered all over the place. In another book we had a rota for deliveries of furniture sold in the shops. Yet another book was kept for wheelchair hire.

If all went to plan things were fine, but customers would ring complaining our van was late, they had waited in especially; some had taken the day off work. I was good at the old mollifying and conciliation though, having had plenty of practice with one loser of a man after the other down the years. I mailed a couple of get well cards to Ann, underlining the 'soon'.

I had to interview a prospective volunteer who wanted to work in one of our shops. I was petrified merely thinking about it. As luck would have it Hilda, a volunteer who came to help sort, arrived just ahead of the interview and offered to sit in on it. I looked at Hilda's black woolly hat, an inch of white hair peeping under the rim; it looked like a dead cat sleeping on a doily.

As soon as he appeared at the top of the stairs, it was obvious the interviewee was nervous. The weather was touching freezing point yet he had a film of perspiration on his forehead and his eyes darted nervously round the room. I had been forewarned he was getting over a mental breakdown; volunteering was a precursor to getting back to normal employment.

His wife accompanied him. Apparently, she went everywhere with him because he was unable to cope on his own since his breakdown. I asked them both if they would like a cup of tea or coffee, first no-no of interviewing I should think, but it was all I could think of. They declined. They stared at Hilda's woolly hat. I looked at Hilda helplessly. Hilda started chatting to them as if she had met them on a day out at the park. What bus did you arrive on, how far have you travelled, where do you live, how many children have you got etc.?

Graham, the interviewee, sat stiffly, blinking constantly behind large owl-like spectacles, feet close together, hands loosely folded in his lap, as if it were a proper interview, looking from me to Hilda. His wife stared at Hilda. Hilda sat with her coat and woolly hat on, wiping her nose against the cold of the room, her boots off because 'I'll feel the cold when I go out.' She wore two pairs of socks under the stirrups of her trousers, her feet stretched toward the bottle-gas heater.

The interviewer proper, who had yet to open her mouth, sat with both hands warming on the heater, clad in an overcoat, scarf and a fleece jacket thrown over her shoulders. The four of us huddled up near the heater like Russian prisoners granted a pit-stop en route to the salt mines.

It quickly became evident that missus was the boss. She did the talking, asked the questions. Graham came across as very shy. His wife sat ramrod straight, as if she were the one being 'interviewed'. Getting two for the price of one was unexpected and a bit disconcerting; I fished around for something sensible to say and came up empty.

Ann always did interviews in a proper office, but as I couldn't be in two places at once, we were surrounded by boxes of books, clothing, numerous boxes of bric-a-brac, old electrical goods, records, music tapes, videos, bedding, knitting wool, a hill of drinking glasses, pictures, piles of jigsaw puzzles, boxes of shoes, boots, slippers and enough handbags to open a store. The scenario was so surreal it took every ounce of self-control I had to keep a straight face.

Hilda's interviewing repertoire was grinding to a halt so I pulled myself together and asked Graham a couple of pointless questions, then asked which shop he wanted to work in. He looked to his wife, she shrugged. Graham fidgeted and blinked rapidly.

'Where do you work?' he asked nervously. I thought, I bet he wants to make sure he's far away from mine, but I told him a little about each of the shops.

'I'd like to work in yours,' he responded when I'd finished.

He looked at his wife for reassurance; she nodded. The three of us sat looking at Hilda's woolly hat, wondering what to say next.

I asked Graham and his wife was there anything they wanted to ask, there wasn't. I told them we'd be in touch as soon as we had received his references. As they left, they both took a last look at Hilda's woolly hat as if reluctant to lose sight of it.

By working a six-day-week moving between my own shop and Ann's distribution depot I managed not to screw up, but I was relieved when Ann returned. She sent me a massive bunch of flowers. The card read: 'Thanks for looking after my interests in my absence.' It's a good job she was not there to witness Graham's interview.

We, or rather Hilda and her woolly hat, must have had something because Graham did come to work in my shop where he proved invaluable. He told Glenda it was the oddest interview he'd ever had.

14

Three years passed quicker than a click of the fingers, or so it seemed. Previously, I'd greeted each new day grudgingly like a death row prisoner, relieved to be alive, while facing yet another excruciatingly empty day. I discovered I was actually quite good at what I was employed to do. Ours was a happy shop, we all got on really well, unlike some of our others where there was bickering among the volunteers, or between the managers and the volunteers.

Then once more the past came knocking at the door. A man who worked for a sister charity had stolen a sizable amount of money from an elderly man he visited and the newspapers were full of it, calling for stricter regulations of charities regarding visiting of the elderly and the vulnerable. Rightly so. Guidelines and precautions were already in existence relating to care workers in residential care homes, why not for charities. In response to the bad publicity our Head Office decided to run all of its paid employees through a criminal records check. I knew my number was up.

Shop manager was the most respectable position I had ever held; the thought of leaving was breaking my heart. Martin knew what the volunteers and the shop meant to me. He kept giving me cuddles, reassuring me how much he loved me, trying to make up for the loss of my place in the world.

Weeks went by without the subject of a criminal record mentioned again and I hoped it had died a death. No such luck. I called in to see Ann on my day off when I was out with my dog, Toby. She always had some biscuits waiting for him. We had a cuppa downstairs in the furniture shop. I was on the point of waking Toby who'd fallen asleep on my foot when Ann said casually,

'See we're all going to have a criminal record search done by the CRB next week.'

'Mmm,' I murmured, equally casually. She knows! I got the butterflies, my hands started to shake in panic. We both stared out of the window for a while at nothing in particular.

'I'm going to have to leave if they do,' I said softly. I was surprised to hear my voice; I hadn't intended further comment.

'Why?'

'Oh, Ann.' The words sounded strangled.

Ann stared out of the window, waiting, sensing something of importance was about to happen. I took a deep breath.

'I had convictions for prostitution when I was a teenager,' I said baldly, the words ricocheting round the room.

I turned my head aside to avoid the snapshot of myself shivering on a street corner that rose in my mind, as if Ann could see it too. Shame of my past washed over me as I watched my newfound respectability disappear as easily as a sandcastle when the tide comes in. If Ann was shocked, her face did not betray her.

'Well so what? It doesn't affect the shop, does it?'

She was being kind of course. Strangely, once the words were out I felt as though I'd been holding my breath underwater. In all the talks we'd had, I'd always held back, changed the subject frequently when something like the miners' strike, the summer of such and such a year, all those 'remember when' conversations arose. I must have appeared thick, but I could not say I was out of the country at the time without explaining where I was, what I was doing.

Over the next few days, Ann and I did a lot of talking. Not once did she say or do anything to make me feel any different; we had a secret was all. She pleaded with me not to be hasty, not to leave. She would back me to the hilt. I don't know what Ann said to Sally, our boss, but I still had a job. They didn't want me to leave; I was a 'valued member of staff'. How about that! Sally promised that my past would remain a secret from the rest of the staff, and that my CRB papers would be kept in the safe.

A couple of months later Sally came downstairs smiling and handed me some papers.

'Your CRB check came back,' she said, the corners of her mouth twitching.

I scanned the documents quickly. I flipped the page over again and read the sentence twice to make sure I wasn't seeing things. Under 'Previous criminal convictions', it read 'Nothing found'.

I looked at Sally, her lips were still twitching. We grinned at one and other. I closed my lips tight, pulled my thumb and index finger over my mouth in a zipping motion. Sally nodded in agreement, lips turned up at the corners.

Initially I felt embarrassed when Sally passed through the shop. She still occasionally came down from her office to talk to me when I'd shut up shop for the day as she'd always done; the awkwardness was from my side purely. However, Sally, a Londoner, had a cosmopolitan outlook on life and people's foibles; while she may have been surprised by my shady past, she did not think less of me as a person. Because of that, the awkwardness soon faded and what people knew somehow no longer seemed important. After a while, I hardly thought about it. Ann and I carried on as if nothing had happened.

*

Aside from the shadows of the past, a constant I must live with until I die, the cloud on my horizon was the fate of my kids. I even had a plan of action for dealing with the suicidal impulses that accompanied most of January. It was all very well giving in to the darkness and taking to my bed to ride out the storm, but after another such terrible January I saw that everyone else had to suffer alongside me. In particular Martin, who crept about the house like a mouse, and came home to find me in bed with the curtains drawn. I did manage to make him his pack-up and cook him a dinner, but that was as far as it went. I could barely manage half a dozen words of conversation in a day. Martin was of the present, the future, he bore no culpability for the past, and it was unfair of me to make him suffer too.

The next January I decided not to be so self-indulgent. My strategy was to work my way through the anniversary of the murders, pushing the memories, the horror and the guilt behind me one day at a time, like an alcoholic. I was doing a good job of it too. I was going to work earlier, tidying the rails, dusting, cleaning and washing the bric-a-brac before we opened up. At closing time, I hung around, taking my time cashing up, anything to delay thinking time.

On the fifteenth of January I washed all the paintwork in the flat before going to bed. On the sixteenth I took Toby for an unaccustomed late night walk. We walked miles. When I got home I washed all the windows. A waste of time as it turned out, I could not see the muck in the darkness. When I looked at them in the morning light, I saw they were smeared. On 17 January, I washed them again before retiring.

Stupidly, I thought I was alone in knowing I'd survived another anniversary, having learnt I coped better if others did not know it was that time. They'd only be on tenterhooks, tiptoeing around me, waiting for me to fall, better not to mention it. Until Martin put his arms round me and asked, 'OK now, my love?' peering at me with concern.

I nodded. 'I didn't know you knew.'

'Course I remembered. I love you. My job to know . . . silly.'

On the eighteenth of January I was reading the evening paper before going to bed, the ITN news was on, the sound muted, when the words '. . . in a fire in . . .' grabbed my attention. I jerked my head up to look at the television. The shell of a burnt-out house filled the screen briefly. For one horrible moment I thought I was hallucinating. The garden of the house looked just like the one at my old house, the one Steve and I had lived in. I scrabbled around for the remote control but by the time I found it the item was finished. I looked at the clock, it said 10.04. Must have been the main news item, then. It was the national news, not local, so someone must have died. Reason told me it could not be my house. It did not prevent my heart hammering against my ribs.

'You're going January crazy again. Get a grip,' I chided myself. The shock of seeing a house that looked the same as mine, destroyed by fire, in the city I'd lived in, on the eighteenth of January, when John Cullen had set fire to the Lynchs' house on the sixteenth of January, was such a freakish coincidence. It did look like my old house. Having said that, the garden was buried under a pile of burnt timbers and blackened furniture the fire brigade had dumped there, it could have been any garden.

I did not take my eyes off the TV screen for the next twenty minutes, even during the advertisements in case I missed the recap at the end.

Dolores' presence in the room was strong—she'd come to wait with me, she hated to miss anything. I almost said hello. When the newscaster came back on, I perched stiffly on the edge of the settee, the remote control in my hand.

'A mother and four children died in a fire in a house in . . .' The newscaster's voice was disembodied as I stared in horror at the burnt-out house on the screen. The camera panned to a long shot of the property. I saw the gate that Steve had made to keep the kids out of the back garden. '. . . arson is suspected.' My heart was thumping so hard I thought my ribs would fracture. It cannot be true. You've conjured this up. It's trickery. Just a trick of the imagination.

I knew I would not be able to get through the night without finding out for sure. I rang my sister.

'Hi Sam, sorry it's late.'

'I was up anyway. I'm sorting.'

I interrupted. 'The fire on the telly, where the kids died. They only gave the area. Was it Bedford Avenue?'

'Yes. Isn't it terrible? Those poor children.'

My stomach lurched. 'Sam, please tell me it wasn't number forty-nine.' I kept my eyes tightly closed, holding my breath.

'Oh', she sounded surprised. 'I don't know. I've only heard it on the news. They never said. I haven't seen the paper.'

'Oh my God Sam. It is . . . I know it is. I knew it . . . I knew it . . .'

'Lynda what's wrong?'

'It's arson isn't it?'

'So they say. What makes you think it's your house?'

'I bloody saw it on the telly. I saw the trellis . . . the clematis I planted . . . the gate to the back garden Steve made. Oh God. I don't know what to do.'

'What can you do? Why are you . . . ?' Her soft gentle voice, trying to work through her thoughts.

I felt like screaming at her.

'It must be dreadful knowing somewhere you've lived ha . . .'

I cut through her. 'You don't get it, do you? It's January.'

'Get what? What does the month have to do with it?'

'John Cullen killed the Lynches in January.'

'What's he got to do with it? He's locked up.'

'Is he? How do we know that? He could be roaming around with a firelighter in his pocket for all we know.'

Sam digested this in silence.

'Just because he's locked up doesn't mean anything. He could have paid someone else to set fire to it. Those poor kids are dead because of me. Too much of a coincidence, Sam.'

'I think you're over-reacting Lynda.' As ever, the calm voice of reason. 'That was years ago. Anyway, you moved out four years ago.'

'Sam, I am not over-reacting. It could be fifty years, years are nothing to him. He waited years to get Dolores. You don't know him . . .'

I closed my eyes to blot out the image of John Cullen's face, his eyes smiling . . . that smile, as he lifted the machete over my head.

'Vengeance is mine sayeth John Cullen . . . it's not The Lord's. It's the eighteenth of January. I know the fire was meant for me.'

'Lynda! Stop it!'

'He's going to go crazy now he didn't get me. I'm telling you.' I was so scared my voice was a squeak. 'He'll haunt me and stalk me till I'm dead.'

Sam did her best to soothe me; her words floated in the air, all I heard was, 'Yes, it was Bedford Avenue.' She promised to buy a local paper the next day and post it to me.

I let the phone fall from my fingers and collapsed on the settee. Please God. Please God. Please God. Not again God. Please God, not again. I didn't know what to do. I was alone because Martin worked nights. Even if I rang the gym where he worked, he wouldn't answer the phone. I wished I had a pack of cigarettes. There was no point in going to bed. I spent the night pacing and thinking, waiting for Martin to come home. Dolores never left my side.

Martin was shocked with my news. He didn't seem to believe I was over-reacting. I told him I was going to ring the police, he offered to wait up with me, but I sent him to bed. I took comfort from his presence in the next room. At 7 a.m., I rang the police and asked to be put through to the murder squad but was told they were not available until later. I left my phone number and asked them to call me back urgently. A sergeant from the murder squad called me back later that morning. I asked him if the fire was at number 49. He confirmed my fears.

'I used to live in that house. Was the fire intended for them do you know?'

'What exactly do you mean?' he asked guardedly.

'Look, it said on the telly it's arson. What I'm asking is was the house the target . . . or the woman and her kids?'

'Why should the house be the target?'

'I lived there before that family. I moved into that house when I came from Dublin. It's the eighteenth of January. It was the sixteenth in Dublin. I had to leave . . . I was a witness in a murder trial. I gave evidence against a man, and the murder was in January—and it's January now, it's me he wanted to kill . . . the children are dead because of me . . . the fire was for me . . . the kids . . .'

'Whoa! Slow down.' The sergeant interrupted. 'Just calm down . . . calm down.'

I took a couple of deep breaths. There was silence on the other end. I could hear my ragged breathing.

'Now . . . slowly. Just who is he? Who did he murder?'

'His name's John Cullen. He killed three women in Dublin. On 16 January. He murdered them by setting fire to . . .'

My voice cracked, I saw John Cullen's bent shape leaning in the downstairs window of the house in the darkness of the night. I saw myself running for my life, Dolores's screams in my ears. The sergeant waited in silence.

'Now do you see why I'm scared?'

He made no response. He said he would contact the police in the Republic of Ireland and check it out. His tone was neutral, no intonation interfering with the serene process of the law. When I rang, I had presumed that one of the murder squad would travel to see me and was surprised when the detective did not suggest it. He did not hurry himself ringing me back. Two interminably long days went by and all that time I thought the mother and her children had been mistaken for me. The weight of their deaths crushing me; I was on my second inhaler by the time the sergeant made contact again.

The sergeant rang and told me he had talked to someone at police headquarters who had assured him John Cullen was still in prison.

'Okay.' I exhaled. 'What about one of his cohorts?

'No. I don't think so. Highly unlikely.' He answered decisively, giving me to understand that their enquiries were leading in a different direction.

'So the fire . . . the dead children and their mum are nothing to do with me?' I needed to hear him say the words.

'No.' He said briefly. It may have been a one-word answer but I bet he was thinking 'selfish cow'. I couldn't have explained to him how it felt to believe you are solely responsible for the deaths of five people, that they had been mistaken for you . . . that they had died in your place. The silence stretched between us as I decided whether I believed him.

'Thank you so much . . . thank you . . . thank you.' I said gratefully, and replaced the receiver.

I found out later, when I read the newspaper, that the police were following a definite line of enquiry even as I rang them. The boyfriend of the murdered woman was charged with the murders of her and her four children.

I avoided reading about the trial. I felt a cloying, fearful certainty, or fanciful notion depending on your point of view, that the new tenant, the murderer/arsonist had picked up on my nightmares. Had he? Had I left something of myself behind in the house? Had I left my nightmares? Had he been dreaming my dreams? Shaking like a leaf, I ran it past Martin.

'It is not your fault, Lyn. You are not responsible for this,' he said firmly. 'You've got to stop torturing yourself.'

He went on. I never knew Martin had so many facts at his fingertips, he must have compiled them from all the news and TV documentaries he'd been forced to sit through since he met me. He gave me the whole caboodle: combat troops watching comrades commit atrocities, concentration camp Jews 'helping' the Germans, men giving up their wallets and cars at knifepoint, women, and men 'allowing' themselves to be raped, men having to watch their women being raped, people turning a blind eye on public transport when a knife was produced.

'It's all down to fear, Lyn. We all feel fear. Animals feel fear. Look how Toby used to shiver when we got near the vet's. Big dog like him . . . and I had to drag him along the ground on his lead; because he knew what was about to happen . . . associated it with pain. What would Cullen have done if you had started screaming.'

I shuddered. 'He'd have killed me. He had murder on his mind, in his heart. No-one could have stopped him. He'd waited too long, his whole life was geared up for that moment.

'It's why he took a knife, in case he met with resistance.'

'There you go then. You knew that.' Martin said, stroking, soothing.

'It doesn't alter how I feel.'

'No, don't suppose it does. Think of it this way. If someone pulled a knife on me do you think I'd give up my wallet?'

'You don't carry a wallet.'

'You know what I mean. Alright, do you think I'd hand over my money.'

I considered. I did not want to hurt his feelings, tough nightclub bouncer.

'Yes,' I whispered.

'Too right. Of course I'd like to think I wouldn't.' Martin pulled me towards him and hugged me.

He said, 'I don't care what anyone says, when you're up against it you don't argue with the one with the knife. Anyone tells you different they're lying. The world is not full of heroes, Lyn. The odd time you hear of someone fighting back they're usually drunk, too pissed to know the danger they're in. The only reason we hear about them is because they get themselves killed.'

We sat silently, Martin's arms comforting, for a moment.

'Even if he hadn't had a knife that night I'd still have been too scared to run,' I confessed.

'Like I said . . . fear. Look what he did to whatsername, and that chap.'

'Teresa. Oh, God, poor Teresa,' I closed my eyes, but I could still see her young face, bludgeoned to pulp with the leg of a chair. 'And Tommy Carlisle. God, he almost killed him.'

'No, I forgot about her. The other one, the one he slashed in the face with a broken bottle.'

'Little Dolores. Poor little thing, she had such a pretty face too. It took five seconds for him to disfigure her for life.'

I thought about that. And I thought of how it had taken John

Cullen less than sixty seconds to scale the fence at the garden adjoining the Lynchs' house, slide the window and strike a match. Sixty seconds. Sixty seconds, my body rattling from hair to toenails, fingers gripping the chicken wire for gravity, praying for lights, people, God.

The darkest minute of your life only lasts for sixty seconds. I was now even more depressed.

Martin was just trying to be kind. I was moved that he'd obviously squirreled away so much data for just such a time as this. Regardless of that, we could have argued the toss all night and it wouldn't make a blind bit of difference to the way I felt.

The nightmares were back in full force. The break of day brought no peace. In the shop my mouth moved, words formed, miraculously sounds came out, yet all I saw in my head was my burnt-out house and the faces of the dead mother and children. My head was overcrowded, people from the spirit world, the little Asian girl who had died of breathing difficulties before I moved in, the mother and her four small children who perished in the fire after I moved out, the Lynches occupying the plot they'd laid claim to since January 1983.

I made a point of not knowing the victims' individual names. The past had taught me how traumatic it is to hear the Christian name of a murdered person. Their faces on the front page of the newspaper were more than enough. Every curve and plane, each hair and eyelash, was as familiar to me as the face I saw when I looked in the mirror, each tiny chocolate-sticky finger, each child's mucky mouth in the obviously un-posed photographs became as well known to me as any in my family album.

For months afterwards I started the day with a nauseous feeling in the pit of my stomach. I tried not to be morbid, but I couldn't stop it. The fact that it was January had made it worse.

Today, I can still see the bedrooms where they lay trapped, the small box room where I had sat on the floor to admire my wallpapering and listened to a dead child breathing. Only now I wonder had I in reality been experiencing a premonition, a sense of foreboding of what lay in the future.

Newspaper reports said the fire was so fierce the plaster on the walls burnt off to the bare bricks. I blamed myself, for asking Steve to put the wooden beams up in the living room and the fitted wardrobes, fearing they had made the fire take hold quicker.

Those poor people. They had lain in the same spot as I had. Rested their head against the same wall. Bathed in the same bath, peed in the same toilet, washed their dishes in the same sink, greeted the dawn through the same windows, put their books on my shelves, trod the same wooden hill to bed, sat beside the garden pond that Steve had started and I'd finished, walked the path that I had laid. In an odd way, I felt they were my family. Mandy always said it was an unlucky house.

15

Chris finished his eight-year stretch. I hoped he would put crime behind him and have some joy in his life while he was still young. Before the year was out, he was robbing banks again. He robbed a bank in London of around £4,000. He bought Gill a washing machine and a new cooker; with the rest he took all the *Big Issue* sellers out on the razzle and within days he had blown it all.

He walked past the same bank a few months later and a bank clerk recognised him and rang the police. The police were on the scene in minutes. They are always quick off the mark where money is involved. Granted, as a new member of the paid-up human race with taxes, TV licence and a mortgage, I realise property must be protected, I just wish they were as prompt when a battered woman is screaming down the phone for them to hurry while she is still conscious.

Chris was sentenced to ten years imprisonment. I appreciate the fact that he had to pay for his crimes but I couldn't help drawing a parallel between him and the white-collar worker who gets twelve months, if that, for embezzling £4,000. Had the same man upped the stakes and fleeced millions from his employees' pension fund, he'd have strung it out in the courts for years with the help of high-ranking lawyers, by which time he would have been too ill to stand trial. Then, he'd have a miraculous recovery once the trial was over and he'd walked off scot-free. I was full of pity for Chris's wasted life, and the ten dark years stretching in front of him.

At the same time, I was annoyed with him. I had not heard from him once he got out. I made no mention of it when I went to visit him at the start of the ten.

'Whatever happened to working for a living?'

Judging by the amused look in Chris's eyes the question was a joke, coming from me. What I did not know until my daughter Fiona enlightened me was that Chris had to finance a habit, so working wages would have been useless. That sure took the wind out of my sails. While he had only been out a wet day he got so hooked on heroin that he'd come close to having a leg amputated after becoming infected with a dirty needle. One addict in the family could happen to the best of families, but two?

I stare so long at schoolchildren it's a wonder someone hasn't yelled stranger danger. I see their happy faces, clear eyes, shiny hair, healthy complexions and I think, 'Mine looked like that once. How did they get from that to this?'

It's always the same answer. Joey insists heroin was his choice; I should not blame myself. He claims he would have found it anyway. Which is complete bollocks. Joey turned to heroin because it is an opiate. Opiates kill pain. Had he had good parenting he would not have suffered so much in the first place. He was twenty-nine before he turned to drugs. The pain just grew.

I do not know what Chris thinks. He hasn't said. Though he laughs his way through life, I don't think he's as tolerant or forgiving of my failings as Joey is. Whenever I come perilously close to lifting the lid on the past Chris's body grows still and he gets a wary look in his eye that makes me drop the subject rapidly.

Chris had just one month left of his ten-year stretch when the screws caught him with a mobile phone in his hand in the prison exercise yard just as a delivery of cannabis and heroin was thrown over the wall. He went back to court and got another eighteen months on top of the ten years. He has spent almost all his adult life in prison. The thought of it crucifies me; likewise, Joey's future. It dilutes the happiness I've known since meeting Martin. I reckon that is what the bible meant about women being born to suffer. I think it alluded to mothers.

Although Chris embarked on the same heroin boat as Joey, his plight did not impinge on my life with Martin in the same way. The fact is I saw more of Chris in prison than I ever did when he was free.

Chris didn't need a mother when he was out; he had a life, of sorts. He always managed to snare a 'good' woman; he wouldn't give the time of day to a girl who did drugs, or even an 'ordinary decent criminal' type. Chris's women are of a type: respectable, law-abiding, normally sensible, soft-centred, gentle and always attractive. He uses his good looks and charming personality like a weapon. I don't think he has ever known the pain of rejection at the hands of a woman, yet.

It isn't that Chris is cruel, or an intentional user of women. He enters each relationship optimistically and well intentioned. He loves women, he's affectionate and generous to a fault (albeit on the proceeds of crime), but he's too far down the path of self-destruction to pull back before he ruins their lives in his pursuit of a good time. My heart sinks when his latest conquest/casualty rings me for a chat when he's been arrested yet again.

Joey, on the other hand, was always on his lonesome; past hurts and the fear of betrayal were so strong that he'd opted for a life without women. When he falls in love, he falls hard; he wants it to last forever. Perhaps he drove women away with his over-protectiveness, something he applies to his pets too. Once, while visiting them, at 1.00 a.m., after Linda had gone to bed, he said, 'I'm off out. Fancy a walk?'

'Where are you going this time of night?'

'I'm going to look for the cat.'

'Why? He'll be back. You've got a cat flap.'

'I haven't seen him for hours.'

'He could be anywhere.'

'I know. I'm just worrying about him being out so long.'

'He's a tom cat. That's what cats do . . . they stay out all night.'

'I don't care. I can't go to bed 'till I know he's safe.'

'I don't fancy going out in the rain.'

'Didn't think you would. Just thought I'd ask to be polite. See you in the morning.'

He walked around all night searching, calling the cat's name. When he got back to the house, the cat was curled up in his basket fast asleep. Cats have more sense than to stay out in the rain.

*

'C'mon Toby, drug run.'

Toby knew what that meant. He was out of his basket in a flash, stumbling over his long legs in his excitement. I put a tenner wrap of heroin in an envelope and stuffed it down my bra. Toby jerked his lead off the hook and dropped it at my feet. My arthritic knees creaked as I bent down to pick it up. Toby waited impatiently while I secured the lead to his collar, then dragged me out to the back gate. I pulled him back and locked the kitchen door after us.

'Hope you know if we ever get caught we're buggered,' I told him as we hurried up the street. 'I'll be in the nick . . . and you'll be thrown in the dog's home . . . accomplice to a crime.'

Toby ignored me. He wasn't bothered; he'd never been in the nick, and a walk is a walk.

Toby led me all the way, we made the same trip seven days a week whatever the weather. I took the risk of holding Joey's stash for him and doling it out on a daily basis to regulate how much he took, mainly for financial reasons.

The trip took us fifteen minutes each way. We'd set off at 6.30 a.m., post the heroin through Joey's letterbox, back home by 7 a.m. to get ready for work. I cannot believe I have reached that stage, but I have.

It all started on Christmas Eve, just fifteen minutes off Christmas Day. Martin and I had opened a bottle of wine and were toasting absent friends. There was a knock on the window. I pulled back the curtain wondering who would be knocking on Christmas Eve. I thought I was hallucinating; Joey had his face pressed up against the window. What perfect timing! Thank you, God.

I rushed to open the door. I threw my arms round the prodigal and hugged him. Normally he would have squirmed—we are not a very demonstrative crew, though I am learning—but he just stood there and took it.

'Come in. Come in. I can't believe this!'

'Now then chap. This is a nice surprise,' Martin said pumping Joey by the hand. 'You know you've made your mum's Christmas.'

Joey was standing under the chandelier, which highlighted his shrunken cheeks, and made his already large eyes look huge. Wounded eyes. He was unshaven, his face and hands ingrained with grime. The clothes he wore were filthy and threadbare, his trainers worn and split. You could have mistaken him for a refugee from a war-torn Eastern bloc country. Except for his teeth. When he smiled they looked like puffed wheat in his mouth; unmistakeably the heroin addict's smile. As I rustled up some food, I could hear him and Martin laughing and I was brimming with happiness.

I asked Joey how he had managed to get to our house from Liverpool with no money. The state he was in I knew no-one would have stopped to give him a lift if had tried thumbing. He told me he had jumped on the train and hidden in the toilet, but the inspector had caught him. Joey pleaded with the inspector; he was homeless, destitute, wanted to spend Christmas with his mum, in a house. In the best spirit of Christmas, that kind-hearted man said that he could stay on the train all the way. He even brought a cup of coffee to Joey and wished him and his family a happy Christmas. It made me feel good about the human race.

Joey was so exhausted after weeks of sleeping rough that he slept most of Christmas day and Boxing day. He had not slept in a bed for months. He had been living in a hostel at one point, but had been ejected for beating up another inmate whom he had caught stealing from his room. It was like one of those cheesy feel-good Christmas movies that the TV companies push down our throats every festive season, only miles better.

When Joey eventually got up out of bed, he bathed and shaved and resembled himself, though he still looked very ill and undernourished. Martin gave him some jeans, sweatshirts, underwear, and socks. I asked Joey where he would have slept over the holiday if he had stayed in Liverpool. Some cities have centres for the homeless to stay for the festive season.

McDonalds doorways were the best, nice and warm, he informed me. However, the police moved them on all the time, so they went from doorway to doorway. He picked at his dinner; a toddler would have eaten more. That is something else I have gotten used to, the junkie appetite. Since he had not visited since Dawn left him, I asked why he had decided to come now, Christmas notwithstanding.

Joey confessed he was lonely—his buddies were dying or going in the nick one by one—but what topped it was when he went to collect his sleeping bag from its hiding place and discovered it had been stolen. He was at his all-time lowest ebb at that point. It was the best sleeping bag in the world, ex-army, filled with duck down, hood and all, which I had bought in the Army and Navy store. This was the time of the 'Sleeping Bag Wars' as the newspaper dubbed it with homeless people stabbing each other to death over stolen bags. When you think about it, it is tantamount to coming home to your house and finding it gone. Joey said he would head back to Liverpool as soon as the holiday was over. I pleaded with him not to go. I could not bear the thought of him sleeping in a doorway.

Martin went out of his way to make Joey feel welcome and asked him to move in with us. He saw how happy and content I was having him around. I went on at Joey relentlessly too. I could feel him weakening due to the lure of a soft bed, clean sheets, baths, hot water, heat and food that I dangled in front of him like a carrot.

'Just until New Year's day then,' he conceded, reluctantly. 'Then I'll have to go.'

A small victory. I know he had to go 'home' in order to collect his methadone prescription. As a registered addict, the methadone was supposed to last the week, but like a lot of addicts, he sold it on to buy heroin. Over the holiday he did manage to get by on methadone alone. He said it merely took the edge off the withdrawal symptoms and right enough he did have flu-like symptoms. It proved to me that it was sufficient to his needs. I have learnt that addicts do not have much concept of self-control. There again, who am I to talk, especiallly when it comes to smoking.

For my part, I was content just knowing where he was and not having to watch the weather reports too closely, worrying when snow, frost, or rain was forecast. Since I discovered he was homeless, I have had this dread that he would be found frozen to death in an alley, as had happened to one of his peers. Three of them had bedded down for the night after drinking copious amounts of cider, the homeless person's best friend. Joey, woken by the cold, got up and went for a walk to get his circulation moving. But one of the men died of hypothermia in his sleep. He was only twenty-five. I wept when I heard. And I smiled when I heard another friend had said philosophically, 'Ah well. He won't be needing this then,' as he pocketed the cider belonging to the corpse.

Like the ten green bottles they were falling one by one. If they were lucky, they got away with only having a leg amputated. If unlucky, they died from using dirty needles, injecting heroin that was too pure, or mixed with Vim, rat poison or even brick dust. Their health was bad already and because they neglect themselves so much they have no resistance to any foreign bodies coursing through their veins. Joey knew a girl who was operated on to remove a lump of concrete from a vein in her leg after an unscrupulous dealer cut the heroin with dry cement dust.

Joey set off on New Year's Day even though Martin told him the chemist would not be open. He was aware of that, but intended sleeping out so that he would be there for opening time the following day. He was gone for days. I failed to understand how anyone could leave a comfortable home and willingly sleep rough on the streets. But now I was even more worried than usual; up to then I had been ignorant of many of the side issues being a homeless junkie with a drink problem entailed. I did not appreciate fully the minutiae of his daily life.

I had slept rough myself as a teenager so I knew the despair—what it was to walk past a house aglow with a light, curtains open of a dark winter's night, to look with longing at other people's lives. I remember people sitting watching telly, someone setting the table for the family dinner, reading the evening paper, stroking a dog, tidying things away and wishing I lived there, that I was a part of it.

Memories fade round the edges with time and I'd forgotten how terribly long the days were. Walking, wandering, sitting for a while, walking, wandering, trying to find a way of making time go faster, filling the day somehow until it came time to find a place to lay your head once more, to dream. To dream of other people's lives. Now I sat with a book unopened on my lap, gazing straight ahead unseeingly.

Martin asked, 'Joey?' I nodded.

On my way to work, I passed a man sleeping rough in Sainsbury's car park. He had been there for weeks; the sight of him lying on the ground, open to the elements always upset me. I had wanted to do something, make some kind of gesture, however small, but I didn't like to approach him. He always slept with his back to the path, I guess it was the only bit of privacy he had. Now that Joey was sleeping under the same crisp morning sky I felt I had to act, the man was somebody's son.

The man lay on a slope which made walking treacherous because of the frost, so I picked my way carefully. I tapped him on the shoulder and said, 'I'm sorry to intrude, but I'd like you to have this.' I pressed a £10 note on him. He jumped in fright. He was wearing a flying cap with the ear muffs pulled down against the cold so he had not heard me approach. He was so shocked that for a moment he did not react, but when he came to his senses the note disappeared.

He did not look up at me, I was grateful for that; I felt dreadful encroaching on his private territory while he slept there. At a glance, I took in the fact that he was quite young, around twenty-five, and he had an almost empty bottle of spirits beside him.

He muttered something, I presume gratitude. I touched his shoulder in solidarity as I left. 'My own son is homeless in Liverpool.'

*

Joey arrived back with only half a bottle of methadone, which was meant to last the week. He had sold the rest. I was so relieved he had returned that I said I would give him some money for heroin rather than, as he planned, have him go back to Merseyside the next day. He jumped at the offer of course. Where will you buy it? Easy, he replied, just ask the *Big Issue* seller outside the local department store. If he does not know someone, no one will. Which proved to be the case. It took him forty minutes to score in a strange town. By a strange quirk of fate, I later found out that the man Joey scored off was the same one I'd foisted the £10 note when I came across him sleeping outside Sainsbury's.

Once again, however, I had painted myself into a corner. I could either let Joey go to Liverpool and do his own thing, thereby getting rid of the problem from my own doorstep, or help him out whenever he was skint, which was most of the time. That way, at least I could try to help him sort himself out. As a mother, I felt I didn't have any other choice. I had no idea what I was taking on.

I soon found out that being around Joey in the year AD (after drugs) was no picnic. Having a compulsion for cleanliness, the hardest for me to deal with was Joey's appearance and the smell in the house. As if being an addict was not enough Joey also had a drink problem. He quaffed White Lightening cider from sun up. It smelt disgusting. His motivation for keeping himself clean and tidy had vanished with the onset of addiction. He would stagger down in the mornings shivering in withdrawal with runny nose and reeking of cider and tobacco. His beard was as black as a pirate's and I had to turn aside because I could not bear to look at him.

And to think this was same son who BD (before drugs) hogged the bathroom while the rest of the house waited cross-legged for the loo. When you eventually got in there you would be in danger of passing out from the aerosol fumes from his various deodorants, after-shave and body sprays. He must have been more than partly responsible for the hole in the ozone layer. Now they were lined up along the sides of the bath like little soldiers, mostly unopened.

How Martin coped, I do not know, because Joey walked around the house like the Prince of Darkness, grunting when spoken to or answering in monosyllables. The only time he appeared happy was when he'd just scored, but the more he had the more he wanted and I knew that if I continued to finance his habit, Martin and I would be bankrupt. I was constantly drawing money from the ATM that was earmarked for bills. I told Joey I had to stop it. He shrugged, said fine; he'd get by somehow.

I went to see a drug counsellor who explained heroin addiction to me and, in addition, what I could expect from Joey. Nothing but heartache. The counsellor explained that heroin is so powerful that nothing matters, but the drug. I had already discovered that.

I came across an old copy of William Burroughs' *The Naked Lunch*, which is considered something of a classic. It made for painful reading. Burroughs had been an addict prior to writing it and in the book he told how during the throes of his addiction he had gone a whole year without washing. No-one visited (indeed who would want to), but if perchance someone had called and happened to die, his only reaction would have been to go through their pockets for money for heroin. Had I known nothing about addicts I would have thought he had written that tongue-in-cheek. Burroughs had the benefit of high intelligence and a good education so would have *known* there was a better way to live. He had the wherewithal to help lift himself out of the gutter; Joey was on a hiding to nothing in comparison.

In a John Grisham novel, a jailer tells someone that a heroin addict could do a ten-year jail term, get clean, and on his release would contact his drug dealer before he'd call his wife or mother. I had found it to be true, so no, it is not always the fault of the parents. But in Joey's case, what chance did he have with me as his mother?

All my kids have had great suffering in their lives. I have to hold myself responsible for that. But it was Joey who was exposed to the most dreadful things. It was Joey, as a helpless thirteen-year-old, who had dangled on a plastic clothesline over a third floor balcony witnessing his mother being slashed with a pair of scissors. Joey who, left to fend for himself, had visited me in hospital daily for six weeks when I lay with my broken foot in traction. Joey was living with me when I was caught up with John Cullen, when Dolores was murdered. It affected Joey tremendously. Dolores wasn't a stranger; she used to baby-sit for me when Joey was about nine years old. The kids loved her, she was such a softie, and they played her up a bit. Joey saw his mother arrested by the murder squad; he brought me clean clothes when I was being questioned in Kevin Street Garda station. Joey was deported by his mother for his own safety at the tender age of fifteen, when I was living under police protection awaiting the subsequent trial. Joey suffered greatly through having the misfortune to be born my son.

Two years ago, on Joey's birthday, I took him to the pictures to see *Veronica Guerin*. We were both subdued on the way home. The film was very good; Cate Blanchett's accent perfect, the acting superb. There was Dublin on the big screen—so vital, alive, atmospheric—and for Joey and me so frighteningly close. We knew some of the bad guys portrayed in the film. Going to see the film had been a bad move.

Joey had nightmares for weeks afterwards. Nightmares are nothing new to him but after the film they were relentless. I had a few sleepless nights myself. I could not get that song out of my head, the one they played over the closing credits of the film. I kept humming it, over and over.

*

When Joey became homeless, he was regularly beaten up by men who took exception to a homeless junkie having the audacity to show some spirit. He met their contemptuous gaze full on. His stubbornness was his only way of fighting back—a survival technique.

One night he was cornered by a gang of hoodies who demanded to know what was in the carrier bag he was carrying.

'None of your business,' he responded defiantly.

It was some old videos I had given him which he was intending to sell for a pound a go.

'Fuckin junkie . . . smackhead,' the mouthpiece shouted, and then they all jumped him. They gave him a kicking. Even as the blows and kicks rained down he never let go of the bag. Stubborn to the end. Guess it wasn't his lucky night. The cops arrived to break it up and the hoodies vanished through the maze of back streets. The cops confiscated the videos as stolen goods.

Beatings are a regular thing for addicts. People hate smackheads. But aren't they useful? Someone even lower down the ladder to take your anger out on. Interestingly, some of the kindest acts meted out to him when he was living on the streets of Liverpool came from Irishmen over on a few days' break. Some gave him money or fags. They didn't want to crush him underfoot just because he was an addict. Apart from two messianic Ulstermen who beat and kicked the guts out of him.

Joey was propped against a wall polishing off a can of cola when these two men came out of the train station. One backhanded the drink out of his hand, and the other knocked him sprawling on the pavement as they passed.

'Fuckin Scouse smackhead,' in a Belfast accent.

'Fuck you. Bastards!' Joey shouted after them, picking himself off the ground. They came back and leathered him; the first kick broke his nose.

It's difficult to feel sympathy for junkies. I feel affronted myself by the sight of dirty, smelly, cider drinkers occupying the bench near where I go to bank the shop takings. They are there at the expense of the pensioners who used to meet at the bench for some brief social contact. Now it has been stolen from the old people. What I cannot come to terms with though is the hatred junkies seem to inspire in certain people.

Liverpool was about to be designated European Capital of Culture so there was a 'clean-up the city centre' campaign in operation by the police force. Being a regular visitor there I would say they had their work cut out. Forget the fact that the service in shops, hotels and restaurants was atrocious.

June flew over from Dublin and we spent a weekend there once.

There was steam coming out of my bedclothes from the damp mattress in the hotel, not a cheap place either. I slept on the bathroom floor. June and I watched in disbelief as a completely toothless, tattooed woman slapped food on our plates in a top department store, while keeping up a conversation with her work colleague, without so much as a blink of an eye in our direction.

We passed street after street of boarded-up shops. At first I thought they were empty, then realised it was business as usual. The boards were replaced at close of business. The only thing I saw there that made me smile were the purple wheelie-bins. They were at least a splash of colour on the desolate landscape.

The thing that really hits though is the vagrants and beggars and dropouts everywhere you look. And junkies. So, Merseyside police had instructions to clamp down on the dregs, the homeless, the flotsam and jetsam, society's outcasts.

It must be a pain to come up with a legitimate criminal charge to arrest a person who is offensive to the public eye; the dirty, the unkempt, those 'wandering abroad without means' as the quaint charge was termed in the sixties. I am not sure if it still exists.

Someone high up in the police decided the simplest way to deal with them was to nick them all for begging. Rather clever really when you weigh it up: cost effective, easy to prove, difficult to disprove, almost no evidence needed, minimal paperwork, no witnesses to be called. Just 'You, you're nicked' if you don't like the look of them. It was a small charge, just a misdemeanour with a tenner fine. You are not even being particularly nasty to the criminal either. Not as if you are fitting them up, or nicking them for drugs or something. No big deal, they will never pay the fines unless you nick them again for non-payment and it's stopped at source from their benefits. OK, it is dishonest for an arm of the law to tell lies, but hey, it's a minor charge, it gets results. Nick them on sight the second they dare to pollute the streets of the city just by *being*. Stands to reason eventually even they will get pissed off and move to a different part of the city. Sod the residential districts, their problem; at least the city centre can wear its badge of culture. The city is being cleansed, reclaimed for decent people.

When they arrested Joey for this minor charge, I changed my views.

I had a call in the middle of the night from Joey to tell me he had just been released from police custody. He'd been arrested for begging. He had got off the train, exited the station and turned left when he walked, bang, into two cops who knew him.

'You're nicked.'

'What the fuck for?'

'Panhandling.'

'I've just got off the fuckin' train!'

'Bollocks. We've just watched you soliciting ten passersby for money.'

'There's not ten people on the street.'

'If I say there's ten people on the fuckin' street there's ten people on the street.'

They cuffed him. Joey was in a cold sweat by that time as he saw his dream of meeting his dealer evaporate. He had rung him as his train was pulling into the station. He tried appealing to the two cops. He told them he really had just got off the train, he was going to see his sister, he no longer lived in the city, and he was not homeless, lived with his mum.

'Fuckin' load of bull. You're fuckin' nicked.'

He became belligerent when they were too rough, shoving him in the back of the police car, so they drove to an alley out of sight of the CCTV cameras and battered him. He didn't mind the beating, it's a way of life to him. But they took his £44 drug money. They insisted it was the proceeds of begging. Liverpudlians must be the most generous people on earth then, he had a £20 note and two tenners. The police refused him a solicitor.

He got home late to the caravan so I did not see him until the Monday because I was at work. I felt sick when I saw his arm. One of the cops had stood on his hand and it was one enormous bruise. His breathing was shallow, his ribs purple. I took him to the hospital. The doctor was unconvinced the police had caused the injuries. He had a 'pull the other one' attitude. Why? Did he truly believe that Liverpool, or any large city, was *Heartbeat* country with kindly country Bobbies, a slap on the wrist for the wrongdoer? They are ordinary people just doing their job. But you can't spend too much time around the scum of society without it rubbing off. The police have to deal with it daily and must despise the people they come in contact with.

The doctor diagnosed cellulites. He was not happy with the arm, but prescribed antibiotics and told Joey to come back if the swelling got any worse. He didn't bother ordering an x-ray when Joey told him his ribs were painful.

The next day the arm looked as if it belonged to a sumo wrestler, oozing puss. No problem to Joey, he rode his bike one-handed scouring the town for heroin. An addict's daily lot. I, on the other hand, was devastated by it all. I had to cut his food into baby pieces, help him dress and worry, worry, worry he'd have to have the arm amputated. It would be ironic if it wouldn't be lost through intravenous drug use. I insisted he go back to the hospital, which he did in the end and was kept in.

He was still in pain with his ribs. After X-rays, it was discovered that two ribs were broken. There was also a query about his spleen. There was talk of removing the spleen, then the consultant decided against it. I'm not too sure of the reasons.

The arm had become infected in the first place because you can't get high on antibiotics so Joey hadn't bothered taking them, and hadn't cared to wash it because junkies are like rabid dogs with a phobia about water. He said he couldn't wash it as it was too painful and swollen, which indeed it was. He rang and asked me to bring him some pyjamas.

When I got to casualty, I asked a friendly nurse where I would find Joey. On hearing Joey's name, a young doctor writing at a table swung round on a swivel chair to look at me. His eyes slid slowly from the top of my head to my feet.

I stared back at the doctor without blinking.

He swivelled back in his chair and continued writing.

The action was so blatant it astounded me.

'Mother of a junkie', I knew he was thinking. The same doctor almost knocked me over as he passed me on my way out. I looked back at his white coat flying behind him as he walked.

'Tsk. Tsk. Manners,' I said to his back.

'Family gone, have they?' the doctor sneered, with a nod over his shoulder while I was still within earshot, as he pulled back the curtain of the cubicle Joey sat in.

I stood fuming for a few seconds. I'm frightened of confrontation by nature but when it concerns the kids I see red. The doctor's attitude riled me. I felt like going back and giving him an earful, only he'd probably have taken it out on Joey. I don't know what the doctor's problem was. Maybe he was sick to the back teeth of junkies, or working in casualty.

The media insist on giving people titles when reporting—schoolteacher, builder, shop assistant, caseworker, banker etc. Even old people are not exempt—retired butcher, baker and candlestick-maker and so on. The doctors' attitude made me feel as though I had been relabelled. I'd walked into the hospital as a shop manager; five minutes later I'd left the building with a new title, 'Junkie's Mother'.

They put an IV drip in Joey's arm and gave him transfusions of antibiotics every thirty minutes. In practice he took his meals at the hospital, occupied a bed, slept there. In between, he got dressed each day and went out to score. The nurses were fine about it. I would ring, apologising for my son's actions; they said it was what they had learned to accept from heroin addicts.

I looked up from serving a customer to see Joey grinning through the shop window at me on the sixth day. He said he'd been discharged. With his hand the way it was, he wouldn't have been able to cook for himself, so I took him home with me. There was a message on the answer phone from the ward sister asking me to ring her. Joey had gone AWOL—so much for being discharged. I did a bit of motherly moaning and he went back to hospital and signed himself out. It was arranged that a community nurse would visit him at home to change the dressings on his arm.

The waiting and worrying while he was in the hospital was almost more than I could stand. The powerlessness was the worst, having to accept that there was not a single thing I could do to make a difference. Little did I know this was the just the beginning. The local hospital is like a maze but I'd soon get to know all its nooks and crannies.

I've watched Joey deteriorate mentally over the years. There is anguish etched in his eyes in memories of the past; he is so haunted that nothing but heroin hits the spot. I still see the little boy who used to come and sit close to me, holding my skirt, if something scary came on the television. Now when I load the washing machine with clothes smeared with his lifeblood I want to howl like a wolf. You never get used to it. I look to the future with dread. Others, better parents than me, also look to the future with dread for their children. They too blame themselves and ask where they went wrong. Most of their recriminations are probably misplaced. Drugs are a scourge, an abomination in our midst. 'Abomination' is a word which always brought a smile to my lips, a bit too biblical for everyday use I always felt, but that is what drugs represent to me. Heroin is so powerful no amount of good parenting will win a person away from it.

*

I grew so weak and ill with all the torment that I was now convinced I had Hepatitis C, even if my blood test had proven negative. Martin was scared of catching the virus himself and became paranoid about towels, mugs, cutlery, plates and insisted Joey's be kept separate. He hid his toothbrush in the bedroom. I don't know why he bothered. With his puffed wheat sensitive teeth, brushing was the last item of hygiene on Joey's agenda. Martin bent the ends of a set of cutlery for himself so he could be sure at a glance they were his.

Joey did try to stay off heroin for days at a time; it was a huge effort for him and I was so proud of him. However, the methadone was never powerful enough and he always succumbed. He was still commuting between our house and Merseyside to buy heroin because it was a lot cheaper there. He never paid for his rail fare, just hid in the toilets until the inspector had passed. Often his illicit journey was interrupted when a member of the public cottoned on to him and complained to the ticket inspector, who would unceremoniously boot him off the train at the next stop. Sometimes literally.

A couple of times they threw him off without his belongings. I spent a lot of time on the phone to the rail company attempting to track down his mobile phone, his coat, his sleeping bag. He spent many a night kipping in the railway station of a one-horse town. They always got their money in the end when he went to court. When he finally reached his destination, he would sleep in an alleyway, up at dawn, scouting for a fix. While at home I lay awake worrying.

Apart from people imprisoned under brutal regimes where torture is a regular event, or refugees fleeing disaster or slavery, addicts must have the worst quality of life known to humanity. Every night I got in my warm bed, I asked God to watch over Joey, keep him safe, let him not feel the cold too much as he lay on the ground to sleep.

Martin was working six nights a week in a fitness gym at that time. He started at 10.00 p.m. and worked through to 6 a.m. so for two years he rarely got to see a soul, apart from me. I felt sorry for him because I had so much contact in the shop, so on Saturday nights I'd go with him. It being a Saturday night there weren't many people in, so he was able to finish early and spend the rest of the night at home with me. I stuck at it for a year. Having already worked my own six-day week on my feet, I would be swaying with exhaustion by the time we left the gym at 1.00 a.m. Vacuuming for four hours solid with an industrial cleaner is hard graft. We had a mortgage to pay on a house we were buying, or a two-bedroomed shoe box to be more precise.

Martin came up with the idea of offering Joey a tenner to go with him in my place. He felt Joey would gain a little self-respect if he earned his own money. I thought it an incredibly kind gesture. Joey surprised me by accepting. Martin reported that Joey was conscientious in his labour; I was rather proud of him.

Once, Martin left Joey's tenner earnings on the kitchen table with a note that read 'Joey, here's your money. Please, don't do it. We care about you.' Martin knew well the money would go on heroin. I felt a lump in my throat when I read it.

16

So it came to pass that Martin and I learned to live cheek by jowl with heroin addiction. Our dessert spoons disappeared; Joey used them to cook his gear. There were flecks of blood on the bathroom walls when he washed after hitting up. We had to keep a close eye on our towels in case we used his by mistake. I solved it by buying a set of dark blue ones for him. I told him to keep his razors separate from mine. Then one day I used one of his to shave my legs when he forgot and left it lying on the side of the bath.

I was half-way through my second leg before I realised the razor was a different colour to mine. I lay there staring at my unfinished leg with a sick feeling in my gut. I got out of the bath without finishing the task, stood with the towel round my shoulders, looking at the blue razor in horror. I thought of what I had read about hepatitis. I remembered what Ann had told me when I'd pretended to be blasé about it in the past, when I thought I might have it.

'Get it sorted, Lyn. Take yourself to the doctor for a blood test to make sure. Have you ever seen anyone die of liver disease? It's a dreadful death,' she'd said.

What would I say to Martin? I'd have to tell him. I was sick to my toes as I realised I would have to tell him I might have hepatitis. Oh Christ. Poor Martin. His worst fears realised.

He was deadly calm when I went downstairs and told him. He looked at me for a few seconds without saying a word, then took Toby's lead from the back of the door. 'C'mon Toby.' Toby was up in a flash, tail wagging. Martin put the lead on, opened the door, and followed Toby out without bothering to close the door.

I spent an anxious ten days waiting for the results of the blood test. Once more my guardian angel was watching over me. Never again did I offer the slightest protest when Martin moaned about living under the same roof as a junkie.

One night Martin and I were sitting in the living-room when there was a loud thump on the ceiling. Joey let out an unearthly moan. I froze in the chair, my hand over my mouth. Martin sprang into action, taking the stairs two at a time. He shouted down for me to fetch some towels—Joey had hit an artery. Martin stayed with him long enough to make sure he was OK, but he was seething when he came back down. I was still trembling in shock. It was not the only time it happened.

The only place Joey has not injected is his eyeballs; his veins are shot. Now I'm an oldie, the veins in my hands stand out and he jokes he'd kill for veins like mine. It was not unusual for him to appear in the doorway, boxers hitched sideways, holding his hands over a needle stuck in his groin, asking for a pen to mark a ring around the successful entry site. Twice I found him sitting in an armchair semi-conscious, a needle sticking out of his groin, and I thought he was dead. The sight still haunts me.

*

Joey arrived back from Liverpool one Sunday night just after I had gone to bed. Martin was still up. Joey knocked on the bedroom door and poked his head round to say hello. He looked shattered, eyes sunk in their sockets, dark shadows underneath. He obviously had a rough few days. The smell of cider wafted over me, making me feel sick. He was too weary and I was too upset to listen to a rundown so I told him to go ask Martin if he would rustle him up something to eat and that we'd talk tomorrow. I buried my head in the pillow to avoid the smell of alcohol. I heard raised voices coming from the kitchen and sat up in bed to listen. I heard someone running up the stairs. Joey burst in the room. He came and sat on the edge of the bed with his head in his hands.

'I'm leaving,' he spoke through his fingers.

'Why? What's going on?'

A chill crept up my back. I had goosebumps on my arms. I reached for my inhaler on the bedside table and took two puffs while he told me. Martin had stopped whatever he was doing when Joey walked in the kitchen. Joey was poised to open his mouth in greeting, before he got the chance Martin said, 'I want you out'. Then all hell broke loose.

I got out of bed, threw my dressing gown on, and went to investigate. I was completely taken aback. Martin had never said a single thing remotely negative concerning Joey. How blind I had been. Martin now let rip. Listing all Joey's grievances: his drug use, his drinking, smoking, his lack of hygiene, not having a job, his 'miserable fucking face'. I was almost as shocked by Martin's use of the 'F' word as by his outburst. I had never heard him swear.

Joey was shouting back. He would not be treated like an idiot, he was not going to listen to a lecture. It was awful. I watched my world crashing around me as the two people I loved slagged each other to bits.

'Stop this!' I tried to make myself heard above the racket. 'Nothing's changed in three days. What is this really all about?' I could see the hatred in Martin's face.

'He stole my pound.'

'What bloody pound?'

'The one with the hole in it.'

'What one with the hole in?' I asked in bewilderment.

'The one I kept in the kitchen drawer.'

'I didn't know it was a special one,' Joey shouted at him. 'I was trying to get a tenner together . . . I thought it was dumped in the drawer.'

'It's my property. You've no right to take it.'

'Jesus! I'll give you a bloody pound in compensation,' I yelled. 'I'll get the drill out and bore a sodding hole in it. World War Three starting over a friggin dud quid.'

'My dad gave it to me, if you must know,' Martin said.

'I thought it was dumped in the drawer because you couldn't spend it.' Joey said.

Martin was having none of it. He wanted Joey out of the house. I was fuming. I told Martin I would go myself before I would see Joey homeless again.

'Anyway. How come I never heard of this bloody pound with a hole in it? The one your dad's supposed to have given you,' I shot at him, my voice quavering with fury.

'I don't have to tell you everything.' Getting a bit brave aren't we, I thought. I was all for leaving. I've had lots of practice and dramatic exits are what I excel at, packing my bags and flouncing off in the middle of the night . . . with no particular place to go.

I looked at Joey, exhausted from sleeping rough for days, his dirt streaked face and filthy hands, and from him to Martin, white-faced with temper, his jaw clenched. 'I love them both,' I thought. 'How can I just walk out of the door? I don't want to lose either of them.'

'We have to sort this,' I said, bone weary.

Martin stated he absolutely refused to share the same roof as Joey.

'And I absolutely refuse to let my son sleep under the stars while I have breath in my body. If he decides for himself to do it . . . fine. I'd slit my throat sooner than make him.'

The hum of the refrigerator the only sound, the three of us stood glaring at each other in the small kitchen. It was Martin who gave in. He said he'd allow Joey to stay, but only on condition that he moved into the caravan at the bottom of our garden. He wouldn't allow him in the house while he was there under any circumstances. If Joey needed the toilet he would have to wait until Martin left for work. I despised him for that comment, but I was sensible enough to recognise that I'd earned a small victory, so I kept my gob shut. It was a solution of sorts, though far from ideal. There was no water in the caravan—a minor detail for Joey—but at least he had a roof over his head.

In a way, it was a relief. I wouldn't have to be forever opening windows to the winter air to get rid of Joey's cigarette smoke. Even though Martin had banned him from smoking in the house, he insisted in having a sly one in the bedroom. He only took a couple of drags and tried to blow it out the window.

Smoking was such an issue for Martin that I'd finally given up smoking after trying for twenty years. The crunch had come one night when sleep eluded me. I'd gotten out of bed, had a quick ciggie, and got back in bed and cuddled up to Martin's back for warmth. His body went rigid and he'd said, 'Don't mind me saying Lyn but you reek of smoke.' I'd thrown the covers back, stormed off in a huff, and went to sleep in the spare bedroom. I'd given up smoking for good a week later and now, ten years later I was still off them. A miracle surely. Now that I had asthma, I was glad Joey's smoking had been confined to the back garden.

It was cold and damp in the caravan with it being winter so Martin set up an extension lead from the house. I bought a small fan heater and a television for Joey to watch. The reception wasn't up to much with the indoor ariel so I got an outdoor one and Martin nailed it to our sycamore tree. Joey grew to like the set up. He could smoke to his heart's content and lie in bed watching telly. Bliss after being homeless, wandering around all day to kill time.

While I was grateful to know where Joey was I rapidly became ill with the stress of it all. I had to wait up until Martin went to work at 10.00 p.m. I'd let Joey in for a quick bath and to empty his portaloo. The rest of the time, I beat a path up and down to the caravan with Joey's dinner on a tray, a cup of coffee, tea, the newspaper, a container of water, a few sandwiches, all under the resentful, watchful eye of Martin.

It got really silly at one point and I was not even allowed to say the name 'Joey'. Literally. Martin kept the kitchen curtain closed and only used the front door. We had a back entry leading to the garden and Joey used this to get to the caravan. I tried my best to ensure their paths never crossed. I also had to somehow care for each of them without upsetting the other. If I spent too long in the caravan talking to Joey, I felt guilty when I got back to the house. If I was too long in the house, I felt I was neglecting my son. I did Joey's washing and ironing after 10.00 at night when Martin had left for work. I tried to dry his washing on the line before Martin got out of bed so he didn't see his arch enemy's shirts and trousers billowing in the wind like a taunt.

Martin would arrive home at 5.30 a.m. I'd get up and spend an hour with him before he went to bed and I took Toby for his walk. I couldn't resist tugging at the corner of the blind to see if there was any sign of activity coming from the caravan. Immediately there would be an atmosphere in the house.

I seemed to feel ill all the time. I got a bad bout of sciatica, which was very painful. I couldn't reach my feet. Martin had to wash them for me. He painted my toenails for me too, the tip of his tongue poking through his teeth in concentration. I drew the line at him having to pull my knickers up for me. I bought a device, which helped to pull my stockings on, and an aid for gripping things. I had two bad asthma attacks, ending up at the emergency department of the hospital.

On one occasion, I had an attack of asthma so severe I thought I was going to die. It was rush hour in the city and I was scared the ambulance wouldn't get through. Our car was parked outside so I rang Martin at work and asked if Joey could use it to drive me to the hospital. Martin said no, Joey wasn't insured. Joey didn't give a damn about that of course. I was so scared, neither did I. Martin said his own son, Lee, was working only ten minutes away, he would come for me. Lee got lost. Twenty minutes went by, I rang Martin. I could barely speak, like breathing through the eye of a needle. He agreed to let Joey use the car. Joey drove me to the hospital. After taking my stats, I was put on a ventilator. Joey stood beside the trolley, a bag of nerves, hopping from foot to foot. I felt sorry for him.

'Roosevelt died of an asthma attack you know.'

I raised my eyebrows in query.

'President Roosevelt.'

I gave him a look that said thanks a lot Joey.

'I'm just saying.'

I pulled my mask aside, gasped, 'Embolism actually.'

We smiled at each other, the danger over. When my condition stabilised I was allowed home.

The car was mine actually; my mum gave it to me when her Alzheimer's became so bad she no longer knew where the petrol tank was, or even that a car needed fuel. I didn't drive. I'd only bothered to ask Martin's permission because I knew he would hate the thought of Joey's hands on the steering wheel and so forth; I wanted to keep the peace. Martin would have stolen a car if he thought my life was in danger, so much for Joey breaking the law with no insurance. It brought home to me how badly our situation had deteriorated. I half-heartedly let fly at Martin when he came home because he expected me to; I didn't want to disappoint.

*

I was so tired, constantly. Utterly, completely exhausted. I went back to the doctor and asked for another blood test, still convinced I had hepatitis. The tests came back negative. After eight happy years at the shop, I seriously contemplated giving up work. I was yawning thirty minutes after getting out of bed in the mornings. Even the simple task of getting dressed exhausted me. So it continued. I was on the verge of walking out on Martin most days. The only time we were OK was when Joey was in Liverpool buying drugs. I could not help but see Martin in a different light after the incident with the car, when it seemed as if I had not really known him at all. It now seemed that his hatred for Joey was as intense as his love for me.

Retrospectively I know I expected too much of Martin. After all, how many men would welcome a heroin addict into their home? Some days I felt like leaving just to escape from the problem, if only for a breather; unfair, but there you have it. All that stopped me was our history. Somehow the months passed. Spring arrived, the time of year Martin and I loved the most, when everything in the garden was budding, work needed doing. I was so physically shattered I could barely put one foot in front of the other, let alone dig the garden. Martin resolutely refused to go in it while Joey was around.

'But Joey won't come out of his door while you're there,' I reasoned.

'I can smell him,' he replied, wrinkling his nose in disgust. 'I can smell him at five hundred paces.'

I kept my mouth shut. But I was fucking fed up.

Some people would say that the obvious way out of the whole mess was for me to ask Joey to leave. I could not do it. I wasn't about to fail him this time. The only alternative as far as I could see was for Joey to have a place of his own.

With addicts, you have to treat them like children. I personally escorted Joey to the city council housing department. What followed was surreal.

We got an application form, took it home and filled it in. I took time off work and handed it in personally, so they couldn't say it was lost. A month passed with no word. I sent Joey to ask what the hold-up was. He was told they had no record of him. He had not sent in a completed form. I took more time off work and took another completed form in. Joey was called in for an interview. He was told he'd been placed high on the list for housing because he had no running water and no toilet in the caravan. Weeks ticked by. Joey and I went back and told them the situation at home was in danger of becoming volatile. Martin had begun to make threats about what he would do if Joey weren't out of the caravan soon. A woman came down and took Joey to an interview room. He was out in a flash, shaking his head in disbelief.

'What?' I asked. He shook his head again. 'What? Tell me.'

I followed him out. He waited until we got round the corner. There he told me the woman had apologised, then told him he wasn't eligible for housing because he was homeless. I looked at him to see if he was pulling my leg. No.

This is how it went. If he were a tenant of the council they would house him. Because he lived in a caravan, he was classed as homeless so they did not have a duty to house him. I was so angry I left Joey standing in the street, turned around and went straight back to the council offices. I asked to talk to the same woman Joey had just left, but was told that as I wasn't the one applying to be housed I would not be seen.

'Then what is my son supposed to do?'

She told me that if he went into a hostel for the homeless the council would consider re-housing him.

'Why the hell would he move into a hostel with drug addicts and winos when he can stay in a caravan in his mother's garden?' Well, I wasn't going to admit my boy was no better.

She shrugged. When I got home, I rang up and complained. Someone with a little more heart suggested Joey approach the Salvation Army; they dealt with the homeless in the city.

'I see. Will they re-house him?'

'No. But if he goes to see them we may re-house him through them.'

Talk about Catch 22.

I've always had great time for the Sally Army since they put me up one night, along with nine-month-old Chris, when I ran out of the flat during one of Craig Nelson's drunken rages. When I rang they could not have been more helpful. They said to send Joey along and they would see what they could do. He went along a couple of times, at my request. The gist of it was that they helped homeless people to handle money, taught them how to cook, how to live indoors, how to cope with life and when they thought they were ready they would approach the council on their behalf, as they had more influence on them than the applicants would.

Admirable I'm sure, but with the domestic situation back home in danger of reaching boiling point I felt none of us had time to wait for cookery lessons.

I stewed for days. Dreams of blood being spilled filled my nights . . . Joey's . . . or Martin's. I went back to the city council and got a complaint form, one of those 'if you don't agree with our decision etc.' and filled it in. They only give you enough space to write what you had for breakfast. I wrote that I felt my son had been treated shabbily by the district council, what with losing the form, telling him he was top of the list, then telling him he wasn't eligible at all. I was in full flow by that stage so I had to continue on a separate piece of paper. I said I had thought of going to the press with the story. The only thing that stopped me was my reluctance to embarrass my employers. I named them, knowing they had kudos in the city. I ended the missive by saying that I felt my son would have been treated better had he come through the channel tunnel illegally. I've nothing against the refugees—I feel I am one myself—but our local rag is full of letters from irate residents objecting to 'foreigners' being housed and given benefits, and I wanted to sound like an ordinary, disgruntled member of the public.

Martin asked who I was writing to. I told him.

'You're wasting your time. We'll never be rid of him.'

A huge row erupted. I can't recall it all, but hurtful things were said on both sides.

The next day a woman rang me from the housing department to say she had received my complaint form.

'We've taken on board what you've said,' she said. She agreed with much of it: the lost application form and being told at one point that he was top of the list.

'So in view of all this we've decided to offer him a one-bedroomed flat.'

I immediately burst into tears. I thanked her sincerely, I meant every word.

I bought myself a bottle of Bailey's to celebrate. Martin made no comment. He felt it was too good to be true. The man of the moment barely reacted. All an addict is interested in is the next fix.

The flat needed a lot doing to it so I took a week off work in lieu of holiday to decorate it. I emulsioned the bedroom and the living room. It is to Martin's credit that he came over one day and emulsioned both ceilings and did all he could to help me make it look homely. Ann, my boss, helped by giving me a gas cooker and a kettle and let me buy enough furniture at a knock-down price. For the best part of three weeks Toby and I were backwards and forwards to the flat with curtains, cutlery, pots, pans, pictures, ornaments, odds and bods in the shopping trolley. Like all dogs Toby knew by the second day exactly where we were headed.

All this frenetic activity washed over Joey. He was in his junkie limbo, going about the daily grind of trying to scrape together the dosh for a deal, then going to score. Eventually it was all done. Martin and I moved all Joey's stuff to the flat in the car. I bought a load of groceries and stayed back with Joey to help him settle in.

I thought he'd be over the moon finally having his own place. In a way he was, but he admitted he missed the caravan and living in close proximity to me. It was the feeling of security he meant, but did not know how to voice it.

Eight months after he moved to his own place Martin's prophesy that it would look like a crack den proved false. The flat was clean and tidy, books and videos tidily stacked, clothes folded neatly, dinner dishes washed and put away. Granted, there were little flecks of blood everywhere, you'd have difficulty finding a spoon that wasn't blackened from cooking heroin, and you'd need to be careful opening the kitchen cupboards because one of them housed his 'works' (syringes, citric acid, surgical swabs), but the flat was a credit to him. Police who raided the flat were shocked; junkies don't usually show such domestic capabilities. It was just the old Joey showing through.

He'd made small strides. He gave up the cider and had taken to shaving most days (so the sprays were in use again). He'd gotten his teeth seen to—some had to be extracted and he needed dentures made—and still looked a good-looking man, especially when he smiled. It's been bloody hard work, and has not been an easy year, but I feel I have done something useful to help him, with his homelessness if not his drug addiction. He brings me his washing, as he has no washing machine. All his trousers have white patches around the groin area from the citric acid he uses to distil the heroin. When I'm ironing them, I get depressed, wondering what will become of him, who will care about him when I'm dead.

I knew it was only a matter of time before he was arrested and sent to prison because most days will find him shoplifting to get money for his drugs. If I'm honest with myself, stealing from shops may not be the worst he does to get money. I have seen how desperate junkies get. Notice how fast junkies walk . . . as if they were in the path of an erupting volcano. Last one out of town's a sissy. Smackheads are always on a mission, speeding about looking for something to steal, then rushing around looking for a buyer for what they have just stolen, next hurrying to meet their dealer, then scurrying to locate somewhere away from prying eyes to shoot up.

When Joey was on his last prison term, he went to the prison library and found my book *Lyn* on the shelves. He hid it on a bottom shelf.

'How awful for you,' I said, averting my eyes.

'It gets worse,' he responded.

He and his cellmate had been having a natter after lock-up. His mate said 'Right. I'm gonna check out now and read me book.' He took *Lyn* out of a carrier bag, climbed up on the top bunk and settled down to read. Unfortunately, the chap was a slow reader and my poor son lay in the bottom bunk for many a night dreading his cellmate joining up the dots, working out who he was, wishing he'd hurry the hell up and finish it.

I was too scared to ask Chris if it had happened to him. I had heard that it was a popular read in Long Kesh when it first came out. I can't think why. I expect the prisoners approached it hoping for a bit of titillation on the sex front; they must have been sadly disappointed.

I couldn't believe I'd just had my sixtieth birthday; I was officially a pensioner. I spent the next day in casualty having an asthma attack. Well it was January after all. We went to the pictures to see Mel Gibson in *The Passion of the Christ*.

As I was getting the tickets Martin piped up, 'Any reductions for pensioners?'

I shot him a look that would have melted an ice cap. The young man in the kiosk looked from Martin to me.

'Yeah. If one of you is over sixty.'

'I am.' I smiled self-consciously.

I took the tickets and turned to Martin.

'If you ever do that again I'll kill you.'

He smiled. 'Why are you ashamed of it? I'm not. Why pay top whack?'

I relaxed. 'Yeah. You're right. Sod it.'

I just didn't feel like a pensioner. There again, when I look in a mirror I marvel that men once paid me for my favours. Martin was now an old man of forty-five. Eleven years later and we were still an item, as Sarah would say.

Joey and I were walking to the shops and the talk got around to the passage of time.

'I know. I can't believe it's over a year since I came to yours. My life is nearly over and I've done fuck all with it,' he said bleakly, 'fuck all.'

The anguish in his voice pierced me. I bit down on my lower lip to prevent an emotional outpouring, not wanting to add to his pain. Mea maxima culpa.

'You're only thirty-seven Joey,' I said as we rounded the corner. 'Please don't say it's over.'

He shook his head in resignation. 'C'mon mum. I'm a junkie. I ain't gonna live much longer.'

Not trusting myself to speak, I reached across and stroked his face with my fingertips. He looked off.

'I can't believe I've lasted this long.'

He shook his head in wonder. We walked the rest of the way in silence.

17

Months passed in the blink of an eye. It goes without saying that Joey was still an addict. No shoplifting equals no money equals no gear. He solved the problem by allowing some drug dealers from Liverpool to use his flat as a base for their operation. The accommodation I had fought so hard for.

They had a safe house to sleep and somewhere to stash their supply and their takings, while they kept on the move using different addresses to sell from. These safe houses were, of course, owned by some sucker of a junkie only too willing for a whiff of the drug under their roof. Perhaps the close proximity of so much of the stuff was comforting; like the family dog loitering hopefully near the dinner table.

They used Joey's flat to work from: 'sitting off', as it's called in the business, watching TV, eating, drinking, smoking cannabis and waiting for their mobile phones to ring. When the order was rung in, they set off on their pushbikes, like pizza delivery boys, to meet the buyer. Dial-a-bag, Heroin Express. As flat owner, Joey was to get two bags a day for his trouble. I felt like hitting him when he told me.

Police were clamping down hard on the whole drug scene. Almost daily, local newspapers carried banner headlines detailing raids and drug busts alongside photographs of the perpetrators, all of whom looked as sick as parrots. And so young.

I have come to understand how attractive it must appear to a young person. You can make a whole lotta money selling something the buyer desperately needs: they are chasing you—begging for what it is you are peddling. Not exactly like trying to sell double glazing.

I was teeth-grindingly angry that Joey would not accept that he could be next on the list for a bust. Even if he happened to be out when they raided he would take the rap, it was his name on the rent book.

To add insult to injury the guy who ran the two scousers called to the flat to check on his employees. He was collecting well in excess of a grand a day from each of them, and he was moaning at the lads about their high expense accounts. He gave them a £100 a day each in wages, and let them take their living costs out of his profits. They lived on takeaways so I suppose it was a bit pricey. 'Sitting off' came under the expenses umbrella.

One of the dealers said 'Well, we have to give Joey something for sitting off and he's been saying he should get more than two bags a day for the risk. How much should we give him?'

'Oh we'll sort something out,' Mr Big replied breezily, thinking himself unobserved as he leant back in the kitchen doorway and raised the index finger of his right hand in the air. Bastard.

When Joey told me I was furious. With Mr Big, for his taking-the-piss attitude, and with Joey for putting himself in the situation of having to put up with it.

All that risk for a lousy tenner deal a day. I harangued him about it, pointlessly as usual. He shuffled around the flat moving things from one place to another, then putting them back to where they had been, refusing to make eye contact. He mumbled something.

'And why the hell don't you get some sodding fixative for those bloody teeth instead of just sucking them in all the time!' I snapped.

'It ain't that,' he said, baring his mouth wide in a grimace revealing little wraps of heroin between his teeth and gums.

I won't pretend I was shocked—I was way past that—but I was seething. I screamed at him in fury, mixed with desperation.

'Get rid of them!'

'Aah mum. I'm only selling a few bags for them now and again.'

'Just get bloody rid of them,' through gritted teeth.

'I can't, never know when the cops might gimme a pull.'

'I mean get RID of them! And the bloody dealers.'

Even as I ranted I was mentally giving up on him. He slumped on to the settee, raised his eyes to heaven and shook his head wearily. I stood with my hands on my hips, towering above him, wishing he was small enough for me to smack him on the legs as you would a child, and say, 'no, naughty, go to your room!' Not that I ever laid a finger on him when he was a kid, but you know what I mean. Instead I straightened up, took a deep breath, walked to the door and left him to it. I went home to cook dinner for Martin.

Drowning in despair, I could not get to sleep that night. I even prayed, feeling like a hypocrite as I did so; like a lot of lapsed Catholics I only use prayer when I'm desperate. I tried my best to get off the whole Joey, dealers, drug thing, tried to think of something else, but my thoughts were like a bloody Cruise missile, tracking me, bang on target, however hard I tried to escape.

So, the dealers were getting a bit lazy and were reluctant to venture out if the telly was good, or it was raining. Joey had always said he would never stoop to selling drugs; now he was justifying it on the grounds that it was different now he was an addict himself, only selling to other addicts he knew. Pretty it up as much as you like, I told him, it's still drug dealing. What next? I wondered, as I tossed and turned.

Before too long Joey became even more unhappy with his lot if such a thing were possible, because the Scousers had become lazy and were no longer bothering to go home to their safe house and had taken to staying at his most of the time, so he had no privacy, something he values highly.

He developed another blood clot in his leg which nevertheless did not prevent him from hobbling around, riding his bike, as he went selling drugs for them. But eventually the leg swelled to such an extent that he could barely walk. Martin and I drove him to the casualty department where he was admitted as an in-patient.

He was kept in for a few days and isolated from other patients, which is standard practice. Who would want to share a ward with an addict? Fortuitously for him he had the drugs with him, which he had been going to sell for the dealers, so he was hitting up every day he was in there. I could not condemn him for it; he was in a great deal of pain. If you are not a registered addict (and at the time he was not) it is not hospital policy to prescribe methadone, which he needed just to feel 'normal'. That's before you are talking pain relief. Normal painkilling drugs are useless to him of course. One hospital doctor told me that whatever they gave him would be ineffective because he had such a high immunity after years of heroin addiction. He likened it to an eyedropper in the ocean.

Martin was not happy when one of the dealers called to the house asking for Joey. He was looking for the drugs, not Joey. I told the guy that he was gravely ill in hospital and threw in a lecture about them using him. He asked me if they could have the keys to the flat. Under no circumstances, I told him and asked if I looked like the village idiot. They went to the hospital anyway and asked Joey for the keys and he told them they hadn't a prayer of getting them from me.

I knew Martin had every right to be annoyed over the dealer coming to the house; he was paying half the mortgage when all is said and done. I was even more furious because it was all my doing, yet I felt obligated to Joey.

I seized the opportunity to go to the flat and change the locks. The dealers were out doing what their job description demanded of them, now they no longer had Joey to do it for them.

The place was a tip. No one had bothered to tidy up after themselves. The kitchen was awash with empty beer cans, overflowing ashtrays, dirty dishes and newspapers. If nothing else, Joey always prided himself on a tidy home. I set to cleaning the place from top to bottom, scrubbing, scouring, washing, vacuuming, disinfecting and bleaching until it gleamed and it smelt lemony and fresh. I filled two bin liners with empty takeaway containers, beer cans and newspapers, emptied and washed all the ashtrays. I placed a pot plant I had brought with me on the coffee table as a welcome home pressie. Then I locked up and headed for home with a definite spring in my step. New beginnings.

Three days later, I was preparing dinner when I had a call from the hospital to tell me Joey could go home. Great news, I told the ward sister. It was very wearying going to the hospital, shopping for groceries, cooking and standing in the shop all day, rushing home to walk Toby, well, strictly speaking he walked me, he was so huge. A cop once stopped me and asked if I had a licence for him and when I said he ought to know dog licences were no longer necessary he replied, straight faced, that it was against the law to walk a horse on a public pavement.

There was a pause. 'We can't discharge him unless he has

somewhere to stay, and he says his flat is upstairs. Obviously he can't climb the stairs,' sister said. 'He shouldn't walk at all or there is a danger the blood clot may travel.' Oh dear.

'Thanks for calling sister. Will you tell him I'll come to collect him as soon as I finish dinner?'

I replaced the receiver slowly. I ran my fingers over the windowsill in pretence of dusting, stalling to give myself time to think, before turning to face Martin who had been listening to the conversation, jaw set, fists clenched.

'We have to talk . . .' I began.

He raised his hand, palm up, to stop me.

'He can move back in the caravan,' he said as he rose from the couch. He walked into the kitchen sighing. Thank you. Thank you. Thank you God.

Until the day I die, I will never underestimate how magnanimous a gesture Martin had made.

*

Back to square one. It tore me apart to watch Joey, pain etched on his face at the slightest movement. He could not put any weight on the leg at all, it had turned black and had swollen grotesquely—reminiscent of a dead hippopotamus floating on a riverbed in a wildlife film. He had to wear shorts because dressing was too agonising, not that he would have gotten into his jeans, the leg the size it was.

He was to give himself twice daily injections in his stomach to thin the blood, I think, or to stop the clot from moving and travelling to his lungs. I had to badger him to do it.

'It hurts.'

'You're a bloody junkie! Whaddya mean it hurts?'

'That's different,' he smiled wryly. 'There's no gain.'

'Course not—it's only keeping you alive,' I agreed. 'Whereas the other's gonna kill you—no contest really.' We smiled at one another.

Once more, I ran myself ragged up and down the garden path, to and from the caravan fetching and carrying. It was harder this time with Joey being so incapacitated. I had to carry the chemical loo to the house to dispose of the contents and this could only be done when Martin was at work. I did not want to give him too much to moan about, and the smell was pretty bad in spite of using the chemical which was supposed to degrade the waste and mask the pong. If I allowed it to get too full it spattered with a whoosh all over the new bathroom carpet as I tilted it towards the toilet, and when it plopped down in to the bowl it was like a tidal wave, spraying in all directions, up over the walls. More than once I was showered with the contents.

So, Toby was still taking me for long walks morning and night, I was on my feet in the shop all day, grocery shopping and lugging it home on the bus, hiking it from there to the house and then cooking dinner. The garden path to the caravan was in danger of erosion, yet my energy levels soared because I knew my son was safe, as was his safely locked-up flat.

Martin kept his cards close to his chest through all this disruption, refusing to talk about the situation. I suppose if I'm honest I have to admit I wasn't in the mood for a showdown, and had there been one I would have left him. Loyalty is important, but I owed a greater loyalty to my son. I gave him life, guilty-as-charged and the blood clot could have killed him. Once again no contest. I would have done likewise for one of Martin's kids in the same predicament, albeit reluctantly.

Now that I had Joey as a virtual prisoner in the caravan, I embarked on a mission to get him re-registered as an addict so he would be prescribed methadone. You can get it easily enough from registered addicts who sell it on because they preferred heroin but I wanted him to get it legally so he would not have to break the law to finance it. He had, of course, blown it all months previously by repeatedly missing appointments with his counsellor, and not calling to the chemist to get his meths. His excuse was that he hated being supervised by the pharmacist as he swallowed the green nectar while Joe public looked on. I saw his point; I would have hated it myself, but he must have put up with a lot more when he was hustling money to buy drugs. The other excuse he used was the highly addictive aspect of methadone. Bloody Nazis.

Some of the top-ranking Hitler elite were heroin addicts who, with war looming and supply routes in danger of being closed off, set the best German scientific brains to work to come up with a substitute and a new star in the galaxy was born—methadone. I suppose the war escalated too quickly, for the silly sods never got around to sorting the addiction molecule—too busy working on blueprints for other weapons of mass destruction.

In reality Joey had been using too much of the real stuff to need a substitute. There was a long waiting list to get back on the course so in the meantime he had to carry on using H. Unfortunately I was at work when his supply ran out and he dealt with the situation by using his mobile to ring the dealers and giving them back the keys to his flat so they could take up where they left off.

It hardly matters what my reaction was, I've run out of suitable words. Just like an old gramophone needle, on and on and on, stuck in the same old groove. I hit rock bottom. So much for new beginnings.

They were both giving him a bag a day. A mixed-race lad named Carl would bring it in person each night as he was on his way home from 'work'.

I took to leaving the garden gate open so Carl could straight to the caravan without me having to set eyes on him. I know he was somebody's son, but he was not mine, and it doesn't equate that because my son was an addict I had to like all junkies. I would hear the gate while I was cleaning up in the kitchen, then grit my teeth and watch through the curtains, throwing daggers in his back as he made his way down the path to the caravan. He didn't have a cocky walk or anything—though he strolled—I just hated what he represented. What irked me most was having to tolerate it. Sure I could have said no and let Joey score elsewhere—blood clot or no he would still have gone—but moving around could have killed him and I just was not callous enough to let that happen.

Two of the dealers went back to Liverpool, homesick I guess, they were only kids after all, which left Carl on his own. He began having trouble with supply, which meant Joey was in deep shit. Users never let an obstacle get in the way of a fix, so he somehow struggled onto his pushbike and set off to hunt some down.

I was so shocked to find an empty caravan. I stared at the space the bike had occupied under the kitchen window. On the verge of tears, I stood in the doorway of the caravan surveying his medicine from the hospital—the Fragmin, the bandages, the syringes, the useless painkillers he had thrown on the bed. Had he been a diabetic and left behind his insulin I could not have worried more. I pictured the blood clot on the move with every step he took. I fretted, paced up and down the garden path, in and out of the house, worry, worry, worry. Toby shadowed my every move; he adored Joey too; he used to head-butt the caravan door until Joey let him in. Another nail in Joey's coffin in Martin's mind.

Martin was unsympathetic; who could blame him. So I had to underplay my feelings. I was terribly angry also, but anger does not cancel out maternal feelings. The edges become blurred when I look at Joey: I see the child and want to protect that child; I see the junkie and want to smash my fist in his face. I suppose the time could come when I will look at him and see only junkie. For both our sakes, I hope that day never arrives.

Once he made a brief visit as I was working on this book. He could see what was on the screen.

'Whose life is this?' he laughed. 'Mine or yours?'

'Mine, but I can't have a life of my bloody own, it's all wrapped up in yours!' I'd replied, with more than a ring of truth.

I feel like the mother whose child has been abducted. I always cry with the parents when they attend that terrible press conference begging whoever has their child to let them go. My son has been abducted by Heroin. I can't function while my son is missing. Please, give me back my child.

It took him four hours to score. His leg had swollen alarmingly, the pain of exertion had brought him out in a cold sweat and he shivered uncontrollably. He eased himself onto the caravan couch, lay back in exhaustion, closed his eyes and lay there, breathing shallowly. He looked like a corpse. I felt as if I was at a private viewing. Something had a hold of my heart and was squeezing it so hard I had difficulty breathing.

I was so relieved that the blood clot had not killed him I only gave him the briefest nagging session before closing the door on him and leaving him in peace. Toby was on watch patrol beside his bed, fraternising with the enemy. This time I thanked God for his safe return. It made a change not to be asking for a favour.

The next day I went to the post office and cashed his giro while he slept. I called round to his flat and shouted Carl's name through the letterbox. He came downstairs and opened the door warily.

'What's wrong?' he asked, taking a step backwards.

'Nothing's wrong, I've come to buy something.'

I pushed past him and made my way up the stairs. When I reached the top I turned and waited while he locked and bolted the front door, then I walked into the living room. He followed apprehensively. Crossing to the window, he pulled the curtain aside, looked left and right, up and down the street then repeated the action.

'No need to worry Carl, I'm only here to buy gear for Joey.'

He looked nervous, eyes flicking round the room.

'I know you've got some, because he rang you and asked you to bring some over.'

He stroked his chin nervously, eyes still flitting, thinking.

'For God's sake Carl, I'm on the level. He's got a blood clot that could kill him if he moves, and he was out last night on his bike with his leg dangling to the ground trying to score . . . for four hours.'

He shot me a look, still chin stroking, then looked towards the window.

While he deliberated, I sized him up. Carl was a good-looking lad of around eighteen. Clean, impeccably groomed, well dressed, clear-eyed, healthy. Obviously no drug user he. A film was showing on the TV with two black guys arguing, and a distant part of me registered how Carl with his caramel-colored skin must have felt a long way from his multi-racial Liverpudlian home. I felt a surge of sympathy. He perched on the edge of the settee and pulled a wad of kitchen paper-towel from the pocket of his jeans with trembling fingers and unwrapped it, exposing the root-of-all-evil.

'How much have you got?' I asked, as I sat down beside him and took my purse out of my handbag.

He did not answer right off, kept his head bent, his fingers scrunching the paper.

'Enough,' gruffly. Tough guy suddenly.

'Would you have £100 worth?'

He nodded. I opened my purse and counted out £100 and placed it in the no man's land between us. He made no move to touch it. He started counting the wraps, which even to my untrained eye were of uneven sizes. One, two, three—he dropped one—his hands shook so much. I glanced at his face, eyes blinking rapidly, sweat forming on his forehead, real edgy, yet sort of vulnerable, to my maternal eye. I leaned across, touched his arm fleetingly and said softly:

'I'm not setting you up Carl, relax. I'm just a mum with a very ill son.'

'Nah. It ain't that, I'm just trying to find the biggest,' he said, with a shrug of his shoulders. Aiming for coolness he was fooling neither of us. Hypnotised by the shaking of his hands I watched him count the rest of the wraps, bringing it up to ten. I hadn't planned it and surprised myself by saying:

'What about some extra for bulk purchase?'

The tremors increased. He nodded.

'I was just gonna say that', he said. He dropped another two bags in my hand.

We looked into each other's eyes for a couple of beats then he dropped another wrap on me. I picked it up and handed it back to him.

'No. Thirteen's unlucky Carl.'

I did not want to take advantage of the fact that he was scared I might be setting him up.

He followed me downstairs to lock up after me. The flat was spotless and I thanked him for keeping it clean and tidy; he did not have to when all's said and done. As we said our goodbyes I think we were both relieved that the ordeal was over.

Neighbourhood Watch was out in force as I walked down the street. It was that kind of area. Heavily tattooed men with bellies hanging over jeans, yelling at packs of marauding pint-sized delinquents-in-the-making; equally tattooed girls-cum-women either impossibly skinny or vastly overweight, lounging in gardens, sitting on doorsteps smoking, hanging over fences. They all fell silent as I passed, then kept me under observation until I turned the corner. Joey was flabbergasted when I got back home and told him what I had done. I had him ring Carl to assure him he had nothing to worry about.

As for my drug-buying episode, I am not proud of it, but if I had to, I would do it all over again. I was as nervous as hell carrying the drugs in my bra on my way home to the caravan. I was scared in case the cops had the flat under surveillance and stopped me as I was leaving and charged me with possession of heroin. It was not the arrest, court and possible prison sentence I feared—been there, done that—but the loss of respect from my work colleagues, most of whom had probably never done anything naughtier than pee in the bath.

Joey was something of a 'Cause' with Ann the area manager and the volunteers. They were all mums themselves and they used to worry about Joey alongside me. They bought him sweets, biscuits, presents for Christmas and birthdays, out of the kindness of their hearts. However, me buying drugs was another story. Obviously my job would have been on the line, even though 'them upstairs' (the boss and the office staff) knew Joey was an addict, head office would not countenance a whiff of scandal and everything I had strived for—my respect, my standing in the community—would have been up the Swannee.

Eventually Carl went home to Liverpool because he missed his girlfriend and his little boy, which came as something of a surprise to me. He hardly looked old enough to be a dad. They say when cops start looking young you're getting old, same goes for drug dealers I've decided. Christ I'm old. I believe he was always laden down with presents for them on his trips home, spending all the profits he made from dealing. I was glad when he went because I had taken to worrying about him too. He dropped off the keys to the flat to me before he left, which earned him respect in my eyes; he could have walked out and pulled the door out after him, or worse. On reflection, Carl was far too nice to waste his life dealing drugs. I hope he and his little family find a way out of the sewer.

It turned out to be a long hard struggle, but after many phone calls and a lot of pleading, chivvying and forceful argument, I was successful in getting Joey back on the rehabilitation programme. The doctor in charge put him back on meths and I breathed a sigh of relief. I was almost as hooked on heroin as much as my son was; at least by association. It was so liberating to be free at last.

As Joey gradually recovered I bought him a walking stick and he began to hobble between the caravan and the house. I was so happy and relieved the danger was past. A son on the road to recovery. A son who was no longer injecting poison into his veins. No more Class A illegal substances in my life. What more could I ask?

Martin had been pretty patient for the ten weeks or so that Joey had been back in the caravan, until the day Joey dropped his walking stick to the ground to demonstrate the punches Rocky Marciano had thrown when he knocked out someone or other in a boxing match. That was it. If he's fit enough to box, he's well enough to go home to his own flat. I could not blame Martin; his nose had been put severely out of joint as I lavished care and attention on Joey and had kept his own counsel throughout. But still waters run deep.

Joey was not ready to go it alone. He had only been off heroin and back on the meths for eleven days; he was in the danger zone. Even if years had elapsed the outcome would probably have been the same.

Martin drove us to the flat. He's not a gloating kind of person and he did his best not to show it, but you could tell he was over the moon, which got up my nose. I was starting to lose my feelings for him. I know things had been hard for him but when you love someone you have to take the rough times too. I'm forced to admit though that I don't know how I would have reacted if his son had landed on my doorstep and put me in the same situation

The loneliness of the flat hit Joey as soon as we had left him. I was barely through my front door when he rang me on his mobile on some pretext, which did not bode well. He had been gone only two days when he called to see me and my heart sank as soon as I set eyes on him. His eyes were pinned and I could tell straight away that he'd had gear. (Heroin user's pupils become like pinpricks when they have had a hit—really ugly to look at.) I felt so betrayed. I don't think I even bothered to register a protest.

He took to using heavily again. How could he do this to me? I kept asking myself. On an intellectual level I knew he couldn't help it, but it really hurt emotionally. Finally, I faced up to the fact that I would never be able to help him get off drugs. It would have to be his battle.

I worried about his loneliness instead, for I hardly saw him When Martin found out he had gone straight back on the gear within two days of leaving, he blew a gasket.

'Right that's it,' he moaned. After all the help we've given him what with him polluting the caravan with his hepatitis and cigarette smoke no way is he welcome in this house . . . blah, blah, blah, blah

I hit on the idea of getting a kitten as a companion for Joey so he would not feel so alone. He has always been a cat lover and reasoned that it would be therapeutic for him if he had another life to worry about and some responsibility, so we set off on a quest for a black kitten. It had to be black, no other colour would do.

We drove miles across the country, Martin getting more pissed off with every journey. (He's dyslexic and finds it vexing trying to read road signs.) We tried pet shops, animal sanctuaries, shop windows but did not find one that tugged at us. In the end, I got sick and tired of looking at Martin's miserable bloody face beside me as we drove, his effing and blinding each time he took a wrong turn, his refusal to listen to me or Joey when we alerted him that he was about to. He was shouting at me in frustration after going round a roundabout for the third time looking for the correct turnoff. When he got out of the car to fill up with petrol Joey, who had been sitting quietly in the back, said he was sick and tired of having to sit and listen to him yelling abuse at me.

'One more time. Just one more word and I'm gonna say something,' he fumed.

'Leave it Joey, he can't help it. It's only because he can't read—it upsets him.'

'Yeah, but it's every fuckin' time. He expects me to sit and listen to him, you're me mum for fuck's sake.'

Joey never, ever interfered in a domestic, as he termed it, so I felt it was time to abandon the quest.

Sandra, one of my volunteers, came up trumps. Martin drove us to pick her up and she lent us her cat carrier while we went to collect a kitten her son Alan had managed to locate for us. Alan ushered us into his sitting-room and sat on a chair at the dinner table, a big smile on his face.

'Well, what do you think?'

The three of us stood like idiots, scanning the room.

'Where is he?' Sandra asked, losing patience. 'C'mon, we haven't got all day. Stop messing about.'

Alan smiled broadly and pointed to his black leather sofa. Sandra, Joey and I leaned forward peering. Nothing, only a rolled-up sock. The sock stretched and a tiny bundle of black fur sneezed, gave us the once-over from a pair of beautiful amber eyes, then curled into a sock again with disinterest.

'Aahh.' Three people instantly fell in love.

When we got to the car Martin got out and placed the catbox in the back window, feigning disinterest in the occupant. When we arrived at the flat I got out of the car to talk to Joey. Martin got the cat carrier from the back window and I caught him taking a sly peek through the ventilation holes while I was getting the rest of the stuff out.

'He's dead cute, isn't he?' I said, as we drove away.

'He's a cat,' Martin answered abruptly.

Yeah. Joey's cat equals jealous pig.

An inquest was held every day for weeks following the adoption. Every aspect of the orphan's life was recorded in roll after roll of film, every detail of its daily doings raked over in phone calls between the three of us; progress reports also had to given in person when Sandra called to the shop unannounced. Visitation rights were granted. A small fortune was spent on bedding, toys, cat box, cat loo, vet's fees, food.

The christening was a solemn occasion. A lot of discussion, though lacking in inspiration, went in to naming him. Sandra wanted Guinness because he was black. I suggested Shadow for the same reason. Joey said he would feel a fool shouting Guinness if he had to go looking for him when he strayed so we settled on Smudge, because he had the faintest smudge of grey under his chin.

I would ring Joey.

'Hello?'

'How's Smudge?'

'You used to ask how I was,' he joked.

'Yeah well, he's cuter than you.'

I adored Smudge. He truly was the cutest kitten you ever saw and I was a little jealous he wasn't mine. I was still grieving for Toby who had had to be put down due to heart trouble and was severely missing a pet in my life.

Joey loved him to bits of course, who wouldn't? Even the vet said Smudge was an unusually friendly cat, very talkative. I would call to the flat and Joey would be trapped in the armchair unable to move for fear of disturbing Smudge, who'd be curled up fast asleep on his chest with a paw resting on his face. It was lovely to witness. But I can't say that having Smudge changed anything for him. It had been naive of me to expect otherwise.

One day Joey rang to cancel a lunch date we had agreed on for my day off work. I asked him where he was and he said he was calling from Liverpool.

'Liverpool! What about poor Smudge?'

'I'll be home in a few hours. He'll be OK 'till then.'

'He's only a baby. You can't leave him all day!'

'He'll be fine Mum. I fed him this morning and left him lots of food and milk.'

'Don't be ridiculous, anything could happen to you and he'd be on his own, poor little thing, he's my baby too.' Notice I wasn't worrying about the 'anything could happen to my son' bit.

'No Mum, please.'

'I'm on my way,' I said, brushing aside his objections as I cut him off.

I hurried through my chores, loaded up my shopping trolley with his clean washing, groceries and cat food and set off to the flat. I was bent over the trolley fishing in the outer pocket for the keys when the door opened and a man came out wheeling a bicycle. We eyeballed each other. He had a bunch of keys in his hand and made as if to lock the door after him.

'Don't lock that door.' I said stonily.

'Joey's not here,' unsmilingly.

'I know he's not, he just rang me from Liverpool. I'm his mother.' I glared at him. He glared back at me.

'Where's the kitten?' I demanded, resisting the urge to slap his arrogant face.

'Upstairs,' he replied, with a tilt of his head.

I pushed past him and opened the door and he shouted something I did not catch. I walked backwards up the stairs pulling my shopping trolley after me and kept eye contact with him all the way. He looked like a bleached out Puff Daddy, enough bling to open his own pawnshop. He shouted up a warning that Joey's mum was on her way, then closed the front door and locked it from the outside. I could hear scuffling above me but I was so furious it never occurred to me to be afraid.

As I entered the kitchen, a guy ran into the bathroom and locked himself in and I heard the toilet flush. I called out for Smudge and he launched himself at me from nowhere, mewing.

'Oh my little bambino.'

I picked him up, kissing and stroking him as I took his food out of my trolley. I opened up a sachet of kitten food and looked around for his dish. It was empty. Swines. Over my left shoulder, I spotted his milk dish, almost empty. I bent down and picked it up. Bastards!

The man came out of the bathroom and walked past me without speaking and went into the living-room and sat down in the armchair. I followed him in and stood with my hands on my hips, breathing fire from my nostrils.

'Could you not have the decency to give the cat some bloody milk?' I said, through clenched teeth.

'I did, I gave him some earlier,' he protested.

'It's set to bloody custard! There's a bloody heatwave on in case you hadn't noticed,' I screeched.

Neanderthal shifted in the chair but did not open his mouth. He was young, red-faced, big-nosed, weak-chinned, piggy-eyed; and looked scared, which did not mollify me.

'Bloody, fuckin junkies,' I spat at him over my shoulder as I walked back to the kitchen.

My hands shook as I filled a cereal bowl with water and the cat dish with milk and set them on the floor. Smudge went straight to the water; I stroked him as he lapped. Poor little sod. He paused, talked to me a few seconds, took a couple more laps, then moved on to the milk.

I heard the front door being unlocked, and Puff Daddy re-appeared. He must have just done a deal in the snicket because it was only a matter of minutes since he had left. I may as well have been invisible. He went straight to the living-room without acknowledging me. He picked up the remote control and flicked the switch at the TV and settled himself comfortably on the settee. Right. That's it!

I walked into the room with all guns blazing and addressed them both.

'Look, you morons, it's 90° Fahrenheit today. Every living, breathing thing needs water. I know it's not your flat, or your kitten, but you could have shown a little humanity by giving a living entity some food and drink. You're both filling your faces I notice.' I snarled, indicating the pizza packaging and lager cans.

Neanderthal's head was going from left to right like an oscillating fan, anywhere but in my direction. Puff looked at me like I was a piece of shit, jumped up, strode to the kitchen and took an open can of salmon off the top of the wall unit and offered it to me saying:

'I gave him half of it this morning.'

'Maybe you did,' I conceded ungraciously, 'but he's only a baby. He needs lots of little regular feeds, and his milk has congealed. He'll be dehydrated.'

He rolled his eyes, sighed, leaned back against the wall, folded his arms across his chest, smirked with the left side of his face and said:

'My mum had a cat for nine years. Don't tell me how to look after a cat.'

'Your mother may have had a cat for nine years,' I said through a red mist, 'but if it was left to you to look after it she wouldn't have had it for nine bloody minutes. What good is a tin of salmon on the top of the wall unit? He's only fuckin' nine weeks old for fuck's sake. He can't fuckin' climb yet!'

I yelled at the top of my voice. It was like a bloody spaghetti western standoff as we stood glowering at each other, my heart thudding, my mouth dry, my hands shaking. He tilted his head back and regarded me through narrowed eyelids. He opened his mouth to speak but decided against it and pushed himself off the wall and went back into the living-room. He eyeballed me again, this time smirking from the right side of his mouth, as he lowered himself on to the settee.

I simmered down a little and finished unpacking the stuff I had brought with me and did a little tidying up around the kitchen, keeping up a two-way conversation with Smudge who was rubbing against my ankles as I worked.

I was undecided whether to leave the food I had brought; I didn't want to feed the enemy. Then I thought, sod it, I didn't want to be mean, so I put it away in the cupboard. I offered the men an orange.

Neanderthal boy declined, 'No ta.'

Puff totally ignored me.

There were a couple of callers while I was there but I did not see who they were because Puff Daddy answered the door. I could hear whispering so I knew they were conducting business. I did give a thought to what could happen should the police decide on a drug bust while I was there and I silently cursed Joey from a height.

I toyed with the idea of taking Smudge home with me, I hated leaving him with them. I would have needed to take quite a bit of stuff with me—bed, cat loo, carrying basket etc.—so I decided I would wait till later and see if Joey showed up. If he didn't I would have had to ask Martin to drive me round to the flat to fetch kitty.

I told Martin that the flat was being used as a drug den again, with Smudge as an accomplice. He asked me what did I expect from a junkie son. I told him he was supposed to be on my side, not going 'told ya, told ya', like a kid in the playground.

People will say, why tell him then? The simple truth is I needed to talk about it. There was no other ear to listen to me, and I trusted him implicitly.

'Just make sure I don't end up with the cat,' he said prophetically.

I had been home two hours when Joey rang to say he was back at the flat. I fired off a salvo of complaint the second I heard his voice, for all the good it did. He listened in silence until I was through. Then he attempted to explain his actions. He said he had kept quiet about the dealers being in the flat because he knew how I would react.

'You lied to me Joey. You told me you'd only gone this morning, now I find out you've been gone two days. Two days you left Smudge with those bastards.'

'Ah Mum.'

'Bloody good job I did go round, or Smudge could have died of thirst, poor little bugger.'

I finally accepted that Joey would always let me down and would continually allow dealers to use his flat. I vowed I wouldn't go to the flat as long as that was taking place and I kept to it. I missed Smudge severely.

Joey met me from work a few weeks later to tell me he was getting rid of the dealers because originally he had been under the impression they were travelling away from the flat to meet with the buyers, but he had arrived back unexpectedly one night and found around a dozen addicts loitering in the snicket eight houses down from the flat. They were waiting to score, and when he asked who their dealers were he was told they were his two lodgers. Talk about not shitting on your own doorstep. He was uptight because a lot of youngsters hung around the area and were taking it all in.

'Yeah well, why should the dealers care, they are not their kids—and it's not their flat', I was quick to point out.

I had already warned him they were dealing from the flat when he was away.

It did not take much sleuthing to discover the reason why the dealers wanted to keep close to base. Apparently, they had been ripped off a couple of times by addicts wielding dirty syringes. Neanderthal had handed over his stash when he'd had a knife held to his neck by a skint junkie. It had also been raining constantly for days on end, real Noah's Ark stuff, and they were fed up going out on their bikes in the rain. The flat was littered with wet clothes. And they kept losing their stash. Neanderthal kept forgetting where he hid it, he had a bad memory. I'm amazed he had one at all.

Puff mislaid £1,000 worth of heroin which he half-heartedly accused Joey of stealing. That was ludicrous because Joey was scouring the city from dawn to dusk trying to score, relations between him and his resident dealers having deteriorated due to them bringing sundry mates to stay uninvited. One such unwelcome guest had done a runner with some of Joey's clothes and his mobile phone charger.

Mr Big was issuing widespread threats about such a large loss. He threatened the dealers who in turn threatened Joey. Who lost it, finally, and booted the lot of them out of the flat. Hallelujiah.

18

I took to visiting the flat again. A couple of weeks went by. Joey rang me at home one evening around 8.00 p.m. to ask if I would meet him round at the shops as there was something he had to tell me. I panicked. If he could not talk on the phone, it must be serious. He could not call to the house because Martin had turned real nasty and would not let him darken the doorstep. I threw my coat on and grabbed my umbrella. Martin said, 'More trouble,' as I walked past him and opened the front door. I ignored him. I hurried round the corner, my pulse racing.

One look in Joey's eyes told me Martin was right.

'What is it?' I asked, my stomach churning.

'Y'aint gonna believe this mum, but remember when I left you at the bus stop today and I was soaking wet?' I nodded.

'Well when I got home I was looking for a dry jacket to change into but they were all wet after all that rain we've been having, so I put this one on the Scousers left and I found this in the pocket,' he said raggedly, and held out his hand.

'Oh Christ!' I said, recoiling in horror. 'Tell me that's not what I think it is. Please.'

He nodded mutely. I put my hand over my mouth. Wordlessly our eyes met, then dropped once more to the 'lost' heroin, with its street value of £1,000 he held in his outstretched palm. The sight could not have been more unwelcome had it been a handful of snot.

Instinctively we looked around us furtively in case we were being watched. I began to shake with fear.

'I don't know what to do,' Joey said bleakly. 'I'll obviously have to get out of the flat quick.'

We both knew that giving it back was not an option. I wasn't naive, so didn't suggest it. Not to a junkie.

I was scared. Really scared. Joey was too, I could see it in his eyes. I had not seen him as frightened since he was a little boy.

I tried to think. Joey was no help—he was too afraid.

The dealers and their boss were still making threats, both directly to Joey on his mobile phone, and indirectly to other dealers and users. They weren't 100 per cent sure he'd had the gear though. At the time he had been on the attack, ranting and raving at them for dealing directly from the flat while he was away, and leaving the place in a mess and so on. And because he was still foraging for gear every day he certainly wasn't acting guilty.

I cautioned him that were he to act any differently now it would be big trouble for him. These guys didn't mess about. Only recently they had carved up a girl who owed them a tenner for a bag they had given her on the slate. Even if he left the flat, he would only go to Liverpool and all the druggies knew each other there. The ones dealing here would know before his feet had hit the platform. The wonder of mobiles.

I had long ago stopped lending him money for drugs but I now found myself in the surreal situation of lending him money to buy heroin from the careless Scousers while he sat on £1,000 worth of their stuff.

It was not long before the pressure became too much for him and he decided he would go to Liverpool and sell it on. While he still had some to sell. Of course, it was party time for him and he was hitting up with abandon. 'The condemned man ate a hearty meal' sort of thing.

He saw it as his 'One Big Chance' to hit the 'Big Time'. Oh my son, my son.

I felt like Kay in *The Godfather*. When the book ended, she was kneeling in the chapel praying for the soul of her husband, Michael Corleone.

I don't honestly think I have ever made a sensible decision in my whole life. It's as if common sense is just not in my genetic make-up. I decided that with Joey gone I would move into his flat. My excuse to Martin was that I was moving in to look after Smudge, because he was destined to be a house cat. I explained that had I taken him to our house we would have had difficulty keeping him from escaping out the back door to the garden, and we were plagued with feral cats.

Also, I wanted to do my worrying in peace, away from Martin's accusing eyes. Of course I had not told him about the drug find, but he knew something real bad was going down because I was dead jittery, jumping out of my skin when the doorbell rang, pacing up and down the landing when I should have been sleeping, not eating, snapping every time he opened his mouth to speak. The truth of the matter is I wanted to be away from him because we argued constantly, every single day, whenever Joey's name cropped up.

It got really silly. I'd be going to the flat and I'd have to say I was visiting you know who instead of the word Joey. How could I not talk about him with his life now in jeopardy? I was obsessed with his safety, it occupied every waking moment.

I understood perfectly Martin's entitlement to the anger he felt concerning the whole sordid drug-infested mess I was in, we were in. What I could not endure was the hatred that blazed from his eyes at the mere mention of my son's name. I have yet to meet anybody who does not like Joey, in spite of him being an addict. He's so quiet and unassuming. Martin's detestation cut me to the quick.

Martin went ballistic when I told him I was going to stay at the flat, and said that if I went and slept in Joey's hepatitis-infected bed I needn't come back home, because he would view it as the ultimate betrayal. Men never learn do they?

I'd gotten to the stage where I didn't give a damn what Martin thought and off I went. Martin being Martin drove me there. He would never see a woman struggling and I had a small suitcase with me, along with a pocket full of hopes for a bit of peace and quiet. His last words as I got out of the car were:

'I can't believe you're doing this. This is the end of us.'

That night I put two duvet covers on the quilt and doubled up on pillowcases and clambered into Joey's 'hepatitis-infected bed' in gratitude, with Smudge snuggled up behind my knees. Heaven, I thought, surprising myself, not realising how much I had missed some personal space in my life.

Martin was not an intrusive or needy man, yet at the same time a glance, or the set of his shoulders, spoke volumes, and I had gradually been ground down by the whole Joey–Martin–Joey–Martin situation.

When I finished work I would call to see Martin and cook dinner for us. I didn't't stay long because Smudge would be waiting for me. I was fine but Martin was very morose during these encounters.

Joey's dreams of the big time were diminishing faster than my waistline because he was doling out his 'find' left, right and centre to people who let him crash at their places. Friends he wasn't aware he had were hanging on and he felt sorry for them when they were turkeying and he was dishing out freebies willy nilly. He had come up with some cock-and-bull story but he knew if he kept his mouth shut no-one could prove where the gear he was 'selling' originated. He was only gone a couple of days when he spilled the beans.

He was lodging with a user who knew a dealer who knew Joey's dealers etc. and each time he spotted one or another of them he ducked down below the parapet until the user he was with copped on. When the two of them got drunk, he kept badgering Joey until in the end he got peed off and told him the whole story.

The death threats came on the fourth day via Joey's mobile.

I was at work, sharing a joke with Glenda, as we sat at the till eating our lunch when my mobile rang. I stood up to stretch across Glenda to reach it.

'Hello my blue-eyed boy. How are–?'

'Get out of the flat Mum.'

'What?'

'Right away.'

I had to sit down.

Glenda was gabbing away. I stood up and said I had to make a quick call and I'd be right back.

'Joey?' asked Glenda.

I nodded.

'Ah bless him,' she said.

I went out of the shop and called him back. He told me he'd just had a call from Puff Daddy who'd heard he was in Liverpool. He was making threats to kill him. And me.

'D'you want me to show you what a hammer will do to your

mother's fuckin' head? I'll show her what fuckin dehydration is,' Puff had promised.

I slumped against the shop window and held onto the sill for support. Customers coming and going looked at me strangely.

When I got back, Glenda was having a joke with one of our regulars and tried to bring me in on it but I could not focus. I had this whooshing in my ears, like waves crashing against rocks near the sea.

Somehow, I got through the day. I know I snapped at Glenda a few times, but I don't think she noticed. I could not tell her because I did not want to scare her. I was worried in case trouble came to the shop, scared for my mostly frail volunteers.

After much soul searching, I decided against moving out of the flat. I wasn't being heroic—I was rattling in my high heels. I just did not see how I could go back home to Martin with my tail between my legs, armed with a trunk-full of major trouble. I still had to get through the ordeal of filling him in on what had been going on and warning him to expect trouble at the house. I had asked Joey if Puff knew I was staying at the flat and he'd said no. They probably figured no-one in their right mind would be stupid enough to stay in a place earmarked for a hit. They didn't know my MO obviously. Death Wish: the Sequel.

I went to the house to cook dinner just as I had the previous three days. After twelve years, you know someone pretty well and Martin was only in the house five minutes before he asked what was wrong. The dinner went uncooked. I told him everything. He heard me out in silence. When I had finished he shook his head wearily, then said:

'I can't protect you in the flat. Let's go and get your stuff.'

I argued that it wasn't his problem but mine. Me and mine.

'D'you know Lyn, for the first time in my whole life I feel like hitting a woman. It's our problem. They'll come here, this is where they think you are, so I'm involved anyway. I can't be in two places at once.'

He had a point. He knew I was wavering and he shot the bolt home.

'You do know the bastards will kill the cat don't you?' he said, looking at me as you would a child who refuses to believe they are in danger when they get too near the edge of a cliff.

'Oh my God—Smudge!' I had forgotten all about him, caught up in the intense drama as I was.

I opened my mouth for further protest then closed it again.

I'm a talker—everything that happens to me I dissect—yak, yak, yak—but as we drove the short distance to the flat, I never uttered a word. I swore when I left Dublin I would never again do anything I had to feel ashamed of. Twenty years on and here I was, endangering the life of a decent man whose only crime was to fall in love with a woman who had the savvy of a gnat. I felt a deep sense of remorse as we drove. He did not deserve me, that's for sure.

When we arrived, Martin sat outside in the car armed with a baseball bat while I went into the flat and gathered all my belongings and put them at the foot of the stairs. I put Smudge in his carrying box, quickly grabbed the rest of his paraphernalia and carried them downstairs and opened the door. Martin got out of the car watching the street like the nightclub bouncer he had been when he first had the misfortune to meet me. We loaded up the car and drove home in silence.

He spent the best part of the evening standing with his arms outstretched gripping the kitchen sink staring out of the window at the caravan in complete silence. With his shaved head, he always reminds me of a silverback gorilla when he stands like that, all neck and shoulders, pure alpha male. I can only guess what his thoughts were.

I tried to small talk a little but the atmosphere was too icy.

'You know Lyn,' he said as he turned from the window, 'out of all this the thing that really gets me is you did not trust me enough to tell me he found the drugs.'

My eyes watered and I had to look away.

'That's what really hurts,' he said sadly, as he picked up the baseball bat and left the room, closing the door softly. His tread was slow and heavy as he climbed the wooden hill.

I was transported back in time as I lay awake on Red Alert, waiting for an assassin. Dawn was breaking when I finally drifted off to sleep. On my own, in the spare bedroom.

19

I'm so regretful of my past that I hadn't had a copy of *Lyn* for seventeen years. I didn't want it accusing me each time I saw it, or to live with the fear of discovery should someone see it on my bookshelves. Recently I gave in to pressure from someone close to me who insisted on reading it, and I bought a copy.

Anxious to see how it might be perceived I decided to read it myself. I read it in one sitting, and I was amazed at the things I'd forgotten. As I read, I realised amnesia is a powerful tool for anaesthetising oneself against painful memories. I had nowhere to hide as I turned the pages.

It's an unpleasant feeling reading about yourself, to see your failures and your shortcomings in black and white, to think 'I don't think I'd like me if I wasn't me.' I could barely bring myself to turn the pages. I was sickened by the content, and so ashamed of myself. For instance, it leapt at me from the page how much I had revered the 'hard' man, and I was mortified at the cynical way in which I had portrayed Willy O'Donnell because he had not measured up to my idea of a 'protector'.

Yet there he was in print, the man had saved my life the night John Cullen stabbed me and Tommy Carlyle. He could have decided that it was every man for himself and done a runner, leaving me to be slaughtered, instead of staying to lead me to safety. The same goes for his brother. And Tommy Carlyle. How could I have been so blind? Who are the heroes now?

There too was gentle Róisín, kind-hearted and mischievous, with an innocence about her in spite of her profession.

'I'm only twenty-six,' she'd said when I had a go at her for letting me down. 'I'm only twenty-six, and I don't want to die yet. I haven't done anything, seen anything yet.'

I had expected her to stand alongside me and give evidence in court, and had fallen out with her because she hadn't. Her life had been in mortal danger, what had I expected? I must have caused them both much grief, for which I will be forever saddened and repentant.

Another thing that struck me forcibly was the jealousy I had shown when betrayed by the men in my life. As sex is so unimportant to me, I wondered fleetingly why it had mattered at all. Of course it hadn't; I should have phrased it differently in retrospect. Where the jealousy really lay was in facing the knowledge that they loved someone more than me.

As the offspring of two people who hated kids I have wasted most of my life wanting to be number one to somebody. Anybody. Each time I found out that I wasn't, I felt about six years old, just as I did when I realised that my mother preferred my sister to me.

Along the way I came to the conclusion that while it is possible to be the most important person in the life of another, it isn't all it's cracked up to be. Even if it happens it is still a heavy burden to bear, so I stopped searching. A truly liberating experience.

Then there was the self-delusion, the belief that I could handle dangerous situations, mixing-it with the bad guys, when in reality I had been utterly out of my depth.

Repeated reading of what I have written here has been an enlightening experience also. I realise I still have a distorted take on life. What a sarcastic mouth I have. I use humour as a shield when gravitas would better suit the occasion. I'm still debating whether I like myself any better now.

June rang me after reading the first rough draft to inform me that life wasn't all a laugh. As if this was a major revelation to me.

'What do you want me to do, crucify myself on every page?' I'd replied defensively.

All the women I worked with on the streets of Dublin used cynicism and humour as coping mechanisms. We were bitterly cold, scared a lot of the time, sick and tired of living in a goldfish bowl as decent people averted their heads as they passed, or let loose a string of expletives. We were sick of being outcasts, anxious, weary of our bad career choices. Caustic one-liners, wry observations, sarcasm and the ability to laugh at each other and ourselves kept our spirits up, and were our armour. What else would prevent us from throwing ourselves into the canal and ending it all?

Though I've been on the straight and narrow for twenty years, my view of the world is too ingrained for me to do things any differently. Besides, I'm not one for whining, feeling bitter, wallowing in bouts of self-pity or feeling hard-done by. I never expected anything from life, so I wasn't disappointed.

Now, if someone had told me the whole 'drugs-for-my-son-saga', I would have thought 'bloody fool, why did she do that?' Or 'Why didn't she stop and think?' Any idiot would see where such and such would lead. Or 'She's completely barmy.' It's all so obvious with hindsight. But each of our actions and decisions are taken in isolation, and it's only when they are added together that we realise what a bloody balls-up we have made of the big picture.

Retrospection brings great wisdom. I am in danger of drowning in a sea of 'if onlys'.

It was indeed the end of us as Martin had predicted. Though there would be another three weeks of hell to be got through before that would happen. As a couple, we went through the motions of living: going to work, shopping, cleaning, cooking, and eating. But there the pretence ended. Martin could barely bring himself to look at me, and when he did I wished he hadn't because his eyes reflected my transgressions.

He was the most tactile person I have ever met, always having to touch me, however fleetingly, as he passed, as if to reassure himself that I wasn't a mirage. It made me feel loved and wanted, though sometimes it did get on my nerves. Now he avoided me as if I was contagious.

It was so out of character for Martin to be uncommunicative and downright moody; he was normally so carefree, easy-going and smiley. His life was governed by *Top of the Pops* (he liked to boogie), *Red Dwarf* (he liked to laugh) and cannabis (he liked to get out of his face every night after a hard day's work).

I walked around in a daze of self-recrimination and regret. Frightened to attempt conversation I went about my business silently, tiptoeing around the house, preoccupied with worries about all of us. I don't think a complete sentence was uttered by either of us in the whole three weeks. A Norman Rockwell photograph of family life it was not.

The only saving grace about those weeks was that Smudge hadn't done a runner, in spite of one or other of us forgetting to shut the back door, so I suppose he'd decided we were OK. They do say you don't own a cat, they own you. I would catch Martin playing with him when he thought I was not looking, which was a relief. But there was no danger that Martin would treat him unkindly, it is not in his nature.

I went to visit Daisy, one of the volunteers, in hospital after work one evening. She was ninety-one years old and had fallen and broken her arm, and was very shaken up. Though worlds apart culturally—Daisy's so refined, an opera lover, olde worlde manners and graces—we always got on very well and I wanted to cheer her up.

(I used to tease her gently about her cut-glass accent. When she'd be telling me a tale I'd feign incomprehension, then when she'd finished I'd say:

'Oh, I think I know what you're trying to say, it's that sodding BBC accent of yours. Now if youda said it in plain English I'da understood ya. You gotta forget the letter aitch, just use short, staccato sentences with the first word lopped off. Now, what you meant was . . .' and I'd overdo the slang as I translated.

She used to find it hilarious and we had fun when she tried it for size. I once asked her had she ever used the F-word, expecting her to answer in the negative, and she admitted she had, once, when her husband had told her he was leaving her for his secretary. Good on ya Daisy.)

I rang Martin at 6.00 saying I'd be late and not to cook as I had called in to M&S for a lasagne. Though well intentioned and approached with great enthusiasm, his culinary skills are even more atrocious than mine, which is saying something.

Don't rush, he told me, and said he was going to have a few beers with a mate from work as soon as he had showered. Which was something he never did, he's a real homebody. I was relieved, to be honest, because it was like living in a morgue when we were in the house together since I had moved back from the flat, and I looked forward to soaking in the bath, and having the house to myself.

I bathed, heated half the lasagne and carried it to the living-room on a tray. I had just sat down on the settee to eat it when I heard the kitchen door open. I looked at the clock. It was 7.30. So much for a night in on my own. Martin poked his head round the door to see where I was. Something must have shown on my face because he said:

'You don't mind if I come home do you?' Real sarcastic.

I threw my fork onto my plate and put the tray down on the settee beside me. Well, since you're asking, yeah, I do mind. What I said was:

'No need to be so snotty. Of course I don't mind.'

He closed the kitchen door and I heard cupboard doors opening and closing then the sound of the kettle switching itself off. My lasagne went uneaten as I sat fuming at his sarcasm.

He came into the living-room and sat on his recliner with his feet up drinking a cup of tea. Unfortunately the TV was off because I had been planning on reading a book and the silence was deafening.

Even today, thinking back, I don't know how events spiralled out of control so quickly. I heard myself telling him that I could not carry on with the way things were between us and that I was going to find myself a place to live. Who said that? Sounded like my voice. Where did that spring from?

'I just knew this would happen,' he said, nodding his head in an air of finality. 'I knew you'd leave me.'

He looked small all of a sudden, as if the chair was devouring him, or he was melting into it, and a terrible melancholy came over me. I lowered my eyes and studied my hands.

I sat, dazed, by my unpremeditated announcement, wondering what would happen next. I was trying to think of something to say to lessen the pain which hung in the air and surrounded Martin like an aura when I saw Joey through the window. I got up and opened the window to ask what he wanted. His bike had just got a puncture, he said, and he wanted to borrow our pump to put enough air in the wheel to get him home where he could fix it properly,

'You've come at a real bad time Joey,' I told him. 'We're in the middle of an argument.'

'Sorry,' he said and turned and walked away.

'Tell him to fuck off,' Martin said, his face suffused with anger. 'Tell him to fuck off out of my life.' Drunken pig.

'Don't be so bloody nasty,' I said as I leaned out of the window and shouted for Joey to come back. 'He only wants to borrow the pump. I'll tell him to go round the back so you don't have to see him.'

I unlocked the back gate and Joey wheeled his bike through and propped it up against the wall under the kitchen window. I reached in behind the kitchen door and retrieved the keys to the garden shed and the flashlight which hung on a hook and set off down the garden with Joey following. I opened the shed door and took the box of bicycle doings off the shelf and asked Joey to shine the lamp in it.

'What's going on?' Joey whispered, inclining his head back in the direction of the house.

'Oh stop!' I said wryly, as I knelt on the floor and poked around in the box. 'I'd just told him I was leaving him when you came trooping down the path. Impeccable bloody timing, son.'

'You're not really are you?' he asked in surprise. 'Frigging hell Mum. What are you doing?'

'No, course not. Well . . . I don't know what I'm bloody doing, tell you the truth.' Which was the truth.

I was growing impatient and started throwing things out of the box trying to find the pump. I heard a sharp intake of breath and Joey stiffened and moved the beam of light away from the box. I thought he'd spotted a mouse or something and I scrambled to my feet instinctively, looking all around me.

'What is it?' I asked, searching the floor uneasily.

'Him,' he replied, nodding back at the house. 'What the fuck is he up to?'

I followed his gaze. Martin was standing in the doorway of the kitchen with his air rifle in his hands.

'He ain't gonna use that thing on me is he?' Joey asked, in mock alarm.

I looked at Joey. Then back at the house, from there to Joey, back again to the house. Martin broke the gun, loaded it with pellets then clicked it shut.

'Nah,' I laughed dismissively, and turned to face Joey. 'He uses it to fire into the air to scare magpies away. They bully all the baby birds in the nests. Poor little sods never even get the chance to take their first flight.'

'Phew! Had me going for a bit there', he widened his eyes dramatically.

'Least I don't think so,' I grinned at him with affection.

We both laughed, easing the tension. I located the pump, put the box back on the shelf and left Joey to lock the shed up.

'Are the magpies here again Martin?' I asked, smiling, in an effort of reconciliation as I walked up the garden path to the house, but it was getting dark so I don't think he saw me.

As I approached Martin took aim with the rifle, squinted along the sights and stood motionless, with his finger on the trigger. He was always so careful, and had a healthy respect for firearms, being a farm boy. He always stressed that one never pointed a loaded gun of any description at anyone. What the hell was he playing at? A tremor of fear ran through me. He did not answer. He could have been carved in stone. As I got near the house I saw that the rifle was not pointing at the trees as I had thought. The rifle was pointing at me.

'Jesus Christ, Martin,' I said, shortening the distance between us. 'What are you doing?'

I grabbed for the gun, but Martin tossed me aside with one hand and raised the rifle again in a firing position and aimed it down the garden path. He squeezed the trigger.

'No.' I screamed. I grappled for the rifle again but he elbowed me away.

'He's ruined my fucking life, the fucking junkie!' Martin raged, spittle flying everywhere, as he broke the rifle again to reload.

The ensuing few minutes are just a blur of insanity. Everything is jumbled up and I didn't really know what was happening. I remember screaming as Martin levelled the rifle to take another shot at Joey, who came running towards the house ducking and weaving, with Smudge in pursuit. I recall standing in front of Joey to shield him. I held him behind me with my left hand as I held the barrel of the rifle with my right hand. I was screaming at Martin and trying to push the barrel toward the sky.

'Leave him! Leave him alone! Don't you dare! Don't you dare fire that at him!'

Martin was veering left and right trying to get to Joey. I was doing the same thing in an attempt to keep them apart. We were like two footballers marking one another on the pitch.

'Get . . . out . . . of . . . my . . . fucking . . . way,' Martin said very slowly, through clenched teeth.

I was edging backwards towards the gate still shielding Joey and holding the barrel of the rifle. I was screaming at Martin to leave Joey alone. Martin was shouting that he was going to kill Joey, who was returning the promise.

'Leave him alone. Don't you dare, you bastard!' I screamed as Martin tried to push me aside. I tried to kick him, but my legs were too short to reach him as he dodged me.

'Go Joey,' I shouted hoarsely, as I turned quickly to look over my shoulder at him, while trying to keep an eye on Martin, at the same time. 'Open the gate! Quickly! Go! Go! Go! Go!'

As Joey was opening the gate I was pushed towards Martin. I doubled my effort to push the rifle aside. Joey took off down the entry yelling threats at Martin as he went. Martin, realising his quarry was getting away, went even more berserk and tried to follow but I shot the bolt quickly and stood in front of the gate like a snow angel with my arms outstretched and my feet wide apart for balance. Martin did his best to pull me out of the way, but strong as he was I would not budge. I don't know where I found the strength, but I knew with certainty he would have to kill me before I would let him go after Joey.

Martin took a step back, then turned towards the house and I knew where he was headed. I flew past him like greased lightning, into the kitchen, through the living room and out to the hall. I grabbed the keys from the front door and stuffed them in the pocket of my dressing gown. Martin was on me in a flash trying to wrestle the keys from me. He was yelling at me to give him the keys, and that he was going to kill Joey.

'No! Leave him alone! Get off me! Leave him! Don't you dare, don't you dare! Get off me, you bastard!' I shouted hysterically. I just could not stop. I was squeezing the pocket of my dressing gown with two hands so he couldn't get at the keys, and he had his hands on top of mine trying to prise my fingers apart.

He stood back suddenly, releasing his grip, and I stumbled back against the front door. We stood facing each other in the cramped space breathing heavily, sweating like pigs. I was shaking from head to toe. He stood for a few seconds to catch his breath.

'That's not the end of it. I will get him.' He turned and walked away.

I ran up to the bedroom, took my dressing gown and nightie off and pulled a pair of jeans, a shirt and a cardigan, then rummaged in the bottom of the wardrobe for my old dog-walking shoes. Next I rushed in to the bathroom and splashed cold water on my face, then held my wrists under the cold tap to cool myself down. I looked at myself in the mirror of the medicine cabinet while I waited for the cold water to do the trick and realised I was crying. I wasn't really sure what exactly I was crying about. Joey? Martin? Myself? Life?

I went to my bedroom and sat upon the bed with my head against the headboard. My throat hurt from shouting. I was overcome with exhaustion. I badly wanted to lie down, close my eyes, and sleep for ever, but I was too frightened. Of Martin of all people!

I still find that hard to believe. He'd worshipped the ground I walked on and would have done anything in his power not to hurt me. He used to say he wished he could get his hands on any of the men from my past who had beaten me and do likewise to them.

Not that I ever did the 'old woe is me' bit, looking for sympathy, but any idiot could see my nose was broken and I've more than a few scars on my face. His view was that no woman should ever be slapped around, Lyn especially. Lyn of the big heart, caring, generous, kind, Lyn. Well, they do say love is blind.

Though the altercation had seemed to go on for an eternity in reality you couldn't have fried an egg in the time it had taken for all our lives to be changed forever. Of course it was the alcohol which had unleashed Martin's temper in the first place. He wasn't a great drinker and as he'd only been at the pub an hour it didn't occur to me that I'd have to keep my mouth shut. I knew he had only capitulated because he hadn't wanted to hurt me, but it didn't make me feel any safer, and I felt like a prisoner under house arrest (well, bedroom arrest), as I waited out the storm.

I sat on the bed straining to listen for sounds of movement. I knew Martin would be sitting in his chair, staring into space, probably amazed by his own rage. I needed to get my mobile as I wanted to check up on Joey. After what seemed like an age, I deemed it safe to go downstairs. I entered the living room stealthily, crossed to the kitchen door and put my ear to it, holding my breath in case he heard me. Silence. I pushed the door open slowly, still holding my breath.

Sure enough he was sitting in his chair, his eyes sunk in the back of his head, with Smudge, the little traitor, fast asleep on his lap. As soon as he saw me he swivelled round on his chair, picked up the remote control and pointed it at the TV, the Music channel, what else? Madonna filled the silence. 'Ray of Light.' Ha!

He kept his back to me as I opened the fridge and got myself a chunk of cheese, then picked a mug off the stand and filled it with milk, closing the fridge door softly. My mobile was on the work-surface under the TV stand and as I reached for it he swivelled his chair in a semi-circle and sat looking at the wall. Miserable bastard.

I sat on the bed and lifted the flap on my mobile. Seven missed calls, all from Joey. So, Martin hadn't seen fit to tell me. I rang Joey, but though he'd calmed down a bit he was still angry and full of threats against Martin.

'I know you Mum, I know you'll try and talk me out of it just to keep the peace, but I'm not going to let him get away with it,' he said. 'I've had all this crap before with men in your life but I was only a kid then. I ain't gonna put up with it again.'

I closed my eyes as a flash of guilt washed over me and swallowed hard, trying to push it back down. I tried to reason with him, but he wasn't having any of it.

'I'll wait for him in the entry when he's coming home from work,' he declared.

'I'm so sorry Joey. I'm so sorry I've caused all this for you. Please, try and calm down a bit.' He didn't answer, I could hear him breathing on the other end.

'Just settle yourself in for the night and relax. Perhaps things won't look so bad in the morning.' The stupid things we say when we are at a loss.

Too frightened to undress for bed in case all hell erupted again, I lay fully clothed on top of the bedclothes until daybreak. I must have dozed off in spite of my intention of keeping watch because morning came too fast. I had heard Martin in the bathroom sometime during the night, then the sound of his bedroom door closing, so I knew he was in the house.

I sat on the edge of the bed trying to figure the best course of action to take. My throat seemed to have closed up from all the screaming and yelling. I ached all over, probably from grappling for the rifle. I was wary of going downstairs to fetch myself a cup of coffee because I didn't know what would greet me and decided I would wait until Martin left for work at 6.45 a.m. It was a Saturday so he would only have to work until two.

'Bye babe, love you,' were the last words I had heard daily for twelve years as he'd left for work. Even if we'd been bickering we made it a point never to part without a loving word. As you get older you realise how uncertain life can be and we harboured a dread of some calamity befalling the other, without having said those last caring words. I was curious as to whether he would talk to me before he left the house. I heard the front door slam.

I did my ablutions and my usual chores around the house. I changed the cat litter. I saw that Martin had already fed Smudge, and filled his dish with milk. I was thinking, thinking, thinking, but still couldn't reach a decision as to what to do for the best.

In the end I thought, sod it. I put my coat on, knelt down and stroked Smudge, picked up my mobile, got my handbag from the settee and walked to the front door. I hesitated. I threw my handbag to the floor, took my coat off and ran up the stairs to the bathroom. I picked up my make-up bag (first things first), grabbed some toiletries, a towel and face cloth then went to the bedroom and took a skirt, blouse and cardigan from the wardrobe. I opened the dressing-table drawer and grabbed a few pairs of panties and ran back downstairs. In the kitchen I opened a drawer and fished out a carrier bag and stuffed the whole lot in.

I paused to stroke Smudge again on my way out to the hall. I slid my arms into my coat, picked up my bags and opened the front door, stepped out and put my key in the lock. I placed the palm of my hand flat on the door to say goodbye to the house, then turned the key.

As I walked for the bus it came flooding back to me that I'd heard people shouting over the fences to one another during the commotion, asking what the hell was going on, wanting to know who was making all the racket. I was mortified at the memory but at the same time I didn't want to slink away, so I pulled my shoulders back, lifted my head, stuck my chin out and carried on to the bus-stop.

As soon as I got to work, I rang Women's Aid and asked for help in finding a place to stay. I had money, but, unsure of the future, I didn't want to go squandering it.

I didn't mention Joey, only that my partner had threatened me with an air rifle. I said I didn't feel safe going back to the house, I wasn't lying. She suggested that if I could manage to find somewhere to stay for the weekend, the council would help me when they opened on Monday morning.

Sandra invited me to stay with her for the weekend, and I accepted gratefully. I couldn't just disappear off the face of the earth so I rang Martin in the afternoon to tell him I wasn't going home. It was one of the worst phone calls I've ever had to make. He did not try to persuade me not to leave, but his voice was filled with pain as we talked. He said the only problem we had was Joey. I was too exhausted to argue the point. He was mistaken. The only problem we had was heroin.

He said he was worried that I hadn't taken my asthma inhalers with me. I assured him I kept a spare pair at work. He asked what I was going to do about Smudge, as he didn't want to be left with him. I bubbled up. I asked if he'd mind him until I got a place. He said he would and promised he'd be well cared for. I never doubted it. I warned him Joey had threatened to wait in the entry for him when he arrived home from work. I had to. I couldn't just let him walk into a trap.

'I hope he does. I'll have something waiting for him.' There was a pause. 'Thanks for warning me.'

We tried to be civilised and discussed what we were going to do long term. But we were both too raw for that.

'Let's just wait and see.' I said tiredly. 'Let's get the next few days over then we'll see.'

The silence stretched out, neither of us wanting to be the one to sever the connection. Eventually Martin was the one to break it.

'The gun wasn't loaded,' he said, so softly I barely heard him.

'Whatever . . . It hardly matters now.'

He lied. I had seen the little blue flash as he'd fired and the wisp of smoke curling out of the barrel afterwards. But it really was of no importance. The fact that he had pointed the gun was enough. I'd had my fill of extreme violence in the past and knew I couldn't live with it again.

A flash of understanding came to me as I put the phone down and I realised I was the trouble—I was the lynchpin which united the two warring factions. While I stayed with Martin there would always be strife for I would never sacrifice my relationship with Joey. I'd warned Martin repeatedly that it was not negotiable; there was no telling where it might all end up. Up until then it had always been Martin versus Joey, but now that Joey had taken up the gauntlet I decided it was time to remove myself from the equation.

I wasn't at all sure I was going about it the right way, with no proper plan of action. I just did not know what else to do. I could have gone to stay with Joey, but in a strange way the events of the night before had altered everything and something deep inside told me I should not involve him, and that I should go my own way. No more Joey. No more Martin. No more piggy-in-the-middle.

20

I hung around the shop at closing time to give Sandra time to get back to her flat; I didn't want to be waiting on the doorstep. I straightened hangers, polished the counter and ran the old carpet sweeper over the floor. I could hear myself sighing repeatedly.

Normally on a Saturday closing time I'd have been looking forward to Sunday, my one day off. I was only contracted to do four days, but we were a shop manager down so I filled in at our other stores. The extra money was handy and helped pay the mortgage, which was something else I now had to think about. I knew Martin couldn't manage to pay it on his own.

Sundays were usually spent car-booting, coming home with bicycle parts for Martin, books for me. Martin mended bikes for all the kids who lived on the road. It had all started when we'd found an old kid's bike in the canal when we were out walking Toby. Martin had climbed in and dredged it out and carried it home as pleased as punch, dripping wet. He loves tinkering, making something out of nothing, and he spent his free time rebuilding it and presented it to two boys down the road whose dad had done a runner.

The two boys were always squabbling with other kids whose bikes they'd borrowed. It gave us a warm feeling to see the pair with their own bike. But, brothers being brothers, they often came to blows over it. So Martin bought two rickety bikes at a car-boot sale for a tenner each then did a bit of mix and match to make one good one and gave it to the two boys. Before long Martin was fixing every bike in the neighbourhood.

He'd come home from work, knackered, to be greeted by a posse of kids with punctures, bent wheels and broken gears, sitting on the grass verge outside the house waiting for him. I'd be looking out of the window laughing at the expression on his face. I'd told them he'd be too tired, but he never turned them away. He'd tell them to wait until he'd eaten, then they'd all troop down the entry to the back garden and sit around the fish pond, waiting.

I was so used to it that if I looked out the window and saw a kid with a push bike opening the gate I'd just give him the thumb to go round to the back garden. Sometimes I made them something to eat while they waited.

Of course all the kids thought Martin was a hero. We'd be walking down the street and it'd be 'Hi Martin' all the way. His fame spread and a lad arrived with a bike with a bent wheel whom we'd never set eyes on. Martin asked him where he lived, it was miles away. He'd come on the recommendation of one of the girls around the corner.

'Can't your dad fix it?' Martin asked.

'No. He told me to ask you.'

As I pictured Martin, on his first Sunday alone I felt grief-stricken and I hoped 'my gang', as he laughingly referred to them came calling to fill the day for him.

*

Sandra used to volunteer at the shop but I'd 'sacked' her three times. It was all a matter of trust and reliability. The volunteers weren't allowed to work alone, there always had to be two of them for safety reasons, but when it was Sandra's morning for work she wouldn't show up and would go shopping instead. I'd be at home or out shopping on a rare day off and I'd get a call saying the shop was unattended and I'd have to drop what I was doing and go to work.

At only forty years old she was the youngest volunteer and was a good worker when she chose. She'd have the stock priced, put on hangers and hung on the rails in a flash; it was getting her there that was the hard part. I just accepted that's the way she was. She has a real wicked sense of humour and is good fun to be around when she takes her tablets. Unfortunately, when I accepted her invitation to stay I didn't know she'd decided to stop taking them.

I didn't want to put her to expense so I bought us M&S ready meals to tide us over and four bottles of wine, in anticipation of a couple of girly nights in. We were getting pretty sloshed, midway through the first evening, when I realised that things weren't right. She was talking about her boyfriend trouble. Her eyes were abnormally bright and her speech was manic as she harped on and on about the same things over, and over. If I tried to talk she'd shake her head and say 'No Lyn, I'm right. I'm right.' I asked her if she was still taking her medication.

She informed she'd never taken medication in her life, and asked what I was insinuating, staring at me unblinkingly. In the end I just sat there nodding off intermittently through the night as she did her one-woman monologue, pausing only to refill her glass or use the loo. Ever the optimist I hoped she'd be over it the next day.

I kept out of her way all day Sunday. I went in to town for a few hours wandering around aimlessly; I daren't risk spending because I didn't know what the future held. I called by the shop on the way back and spent a few more hours cleaning and dusting. I was hoping Sandra would be in when I'd finished as owing to my phobia, I had to be indoors before the witching hour. Luckily she was. Or rather, unluckily. I stopped on the way to her flat and bought her forty ciggies as a peace offering.

She didn't look overjoyed to see me when she opened the door, and I followed her up the stairs with a sense of dread. I knew I should have turned on my heel and left but I didn't want to risk being too confrontational; I'd seen her go off on one, in the past.

The Sunday night proved to be an even bigger nightmare. We were on our third glass of wine when she began giving me an ear-bashing for leaving Martin, and for having a drug addict for a son. She really let rip. She had a tiny insect bite on her arm which she was convinced had been made by a syringe filled with heroin, which she imagined Joey had injected in her arm. Nothing would convince her it wasn't true. The fact that she hadn't seen him for six months was irrelevant.

I knew it was her paranoid psychosis—she wasn't responsible for her actions—so I bit my tongue and hoped she'd get tired and go to bed. Not a bit of it. All through the night she ranted non-stop, two red spots on her cheeks, eyes bright with passion.

As morning approached I suggested rather timidly that perhaps we should try to get some shut-eye because I had to work the next day. Another bad mistake. If looks could kill I'd have been a goner; it seemed to further incense her. This is my property. My property. My property. She repeated it over and over and over, staring at me wide-eyed, insanity near the surface.

'I take it this is your property then?' I smiled, trying to appeal to the Sandra I was used to, the one with a sense of humour. It only spurred her on to another tirade.

I wasn't frightened of her, I was frightened for her. I worried what would happen to her when I left the next day, although I'm not trying to pretend I wasn't also very pissed off, because I was. It took some doing to sit and listen to her crap. Ten years ago I would have been out of there, but maturity, which came late to me, brings with it a sense of responsibility and I was reluctant to up sticks and leave her to her own devices. What if she wandered off, half-clothed as she had been the best part of the evening? Anything could have happened to her.

She grew more manic as the night progressed and I never closed my eyes the whole time. And I smoked my first cigarette in ten years.

She went to bed, finally, at 6.15 a.m. I didn't bother washing. I gathered my carrier bag of possessions together and left. Never again, I vowed, as I walked to the shop.

I put the kettle on in the back room and when it boiled washed myself as best I could in the tiny hand-basin in the loo. I made a cup of coffee and while I sipped it I contemplated ringing the psychiatric hospital where Sandra was being treated, to ask them to go and visit her, but decided against it. She wouldn't have thanked me, and it would have given her a legitimate grievance against me.

Bang on 9.00 I rang the council and made an appointment with a housing official. My wonderful Evelyn and Monday Marjorie as I called her (we had a Tuesday one too), covered the shop for me while I went to the housing department. I was gone for hours.

The upshot of it was that because I half-owned a property they could not give me a permanent place to stay. But as my home was no longer a safe environment they could offer me temporary accommodation, though it could take a week or two for a vacancy to arise.

The housing official asked me if I could afford a hotel for that length of time. They did have a hostel, she said, but it would not have been suitable for me. I asked why not. She said I would find it too rough, they housed problem families there. Christ! That wouldn't do, would it? I almost smiled.

I felt a little worried that they could take longer than two weeks to come up with a place and I could see my savings being frittered away so I said I thought I should go to the hostel. As I was at work six days a week I wouldn't see much of the other people.

'Trust me,' she said, shaking her head. She leaned back on her chair, took a deep breath, and said, 'You really do not want to go there.'

She raised her eyebrows and crossed her arms as she studied my face.

'I perhaps shouldn't say this . . . but they are really not very nice people. It's certainly not suitable for such as yourself.' Blimey!

So it was agreed that I would go to a hotel. They had two which they used when people were in a similar situation to me. The council paid for the hotel if you were on welfare, but as I was working and had savings I had to pay. The cheaper one was £25 a night. That was OK, wouldn't break the bank. Once again the navy ankle-length Laura Ashley dress and the low heeled shoes proved my undoing.

'Oh no, you wouldn't like it. It's a dreadful place.'

I assured her I would be fine. She shook her head again.

'Really, no. There's drug addicts and everything staying there!'

Oh well, in that case then. Well, I couldn't very well say it would feel like home from home could I?

On a serious note I had had a belly-full of drug-users so I said I would go to the better hotel, which I was assured was run by a lovely, homely lady. Sounded ominous.

Ah well, on reflection 'homely' had a comforting ring to it. I felt in need of warmth and kindness. The price was £48 a night but the council paid it up front then billed you for it, rather thoughtful of them really, as most women who are forced to flee don't have time to grab their cheque books or credit cards on the way out.

Marjorie and two other volunteers offered me a home until I got myself fixed up. It made me feel terribly weepy. In fact I did cry when little Dorothy asked me, but I didn't take them up on their offers.

Over-riding everything was the need to lick my wounds in private and I'd have slept under the stars sooner than spend a night under someone else's roof after the two nights I'd spent with Sandra.

At 5.00 I went into the back room to choose a book to take with me to the hotel. I've taken a book to bed with me since I was at primary school, and knew I wouldn't have a hope in hell's chance of sleeping without one. I didn't want anything too heavy, just something to take me out of myself. I chose a Clare Boylan, an author whom I had read before and knew I could rely on. I glanced at the title which didn't register, but even if I'd read it before I knew from experience she'd be worth a re-read.

I took my time closing the shop. Usually I would have been out of there, hurrying for the bus, rushing home to cook dinner as I had every night for the past eight years. The thought saddened me. I wondered what Martin would eat when he got home. Probably fried egg sandwiches, his usual standby. I felt tears prickling my eyes and blinked them away. I was starving but didn't know what to do about eating. What did women with no man, no home, no cooking facilities do about food?

I'll stop at a pub on the way home. No, perhaps not. I was too old to be mistaken for a woman waiting for a pick-up, and I had never eaten a meal alone in a pub. A restaurant then. Sit there like some sad old biddy with no friends or family to share a meal with? It was only tea-time, it wouldn't look so pathetic. Don't fancy it. Have a stomach ulcer, got to eat.

I set the burglar alarm and stepped out of the shop quickly, locked the door and stood for a couple of minutes with my back to it staring at the ground, reluctant to take those first steps of my new-found freedom. Why didn't it feel like liberation? It would have been so easy to turn right, up the road, on to the bus, home, cook dinner. Home. Martin would be so happy at my change of heart he wouldn't even pass comment, he'd be too scared to break the spell.

I thought of all the times I'd passed offices and noticed the odd person working late, after everyone else had left. It always seemed to be the same one or two, and I used to feel sad for them because they obviously didn't want to go home.

I mentally shook myself out of my indecision and forced my feet to turn left and start walking. My shop-worker's feet—corns on both little toes—were killing me, and just for good measure my arthritic knee was starting to give me a hard time. I was limping before I'd gone a few yards. I walked slowly, and slowed even further each time I passed a bar or restaurant, surreptitiously peeking in to see how full it was, trying to get up the courage to go in. In the end I bottled it. If you don't eat now you won't get anything until breakfast at the hotel. Once you check in you can't go out, it'll be night-time. OK. Look for a chippy then.

I never ever went out at night. I had lived in the city for ten years and only left the house twice at night in all that time. Both times were to Weight Watchers Christmas dinners, and both times I suffered panic attacks and had to ring Martin to come and fetch me. We'd stopped at a shop and bought a ton of chocolates on the way home and I'd pigged out for two days after on both occasions.

I have had two proper holidays in forty-seven years. Once with June and her husband when they took me to a hotel in Wicklow for a long weekend, and the other in 1982 when I stayed with my mum in a caravan in Brighton for a week. I have tried to rid myself of the phobia about being away from home, under a lot of pressure from other people, but can't seem to do it. I always end up hyper-ventilating, having panic attacks, asthma attacks, migraine and crying for days afterwards.

I asked a woman where I could find a chip shop and she said I had passed it so I retraced my steps, but when I got there it was closed, it being Monday. Oh sod it. Be glad, only another two inches on the thighs anyway. I was beginning to sound like Pollyanna to myself, so cheered myself up by repeating the word 'fuck' like a mantra as I limped resolutely to the end of the street. When I reached the corner I had a brainwave. Send out for a take-away. I don't know why it hadn't occurred to me before. Probably because it was something I rarely did; it always seemed a waste of money to me. Best get going to the hotel anyway. I had no Martin to rescue me if I had a panic attack. I also had no home so I hadn't a clue what would happen about the phobia. I felt a rare flash of self-pity which took me by surprise. Steady on old girl, I told myself, smiling at the sound of the words.

The hotel was welcoming in a country cottagey kind of way. All hanging baskets, frilly curtains, flowers in tubs, brass doorknob, sparkling clean windows. Even a 'Welcome' mat.

My tough facade began to melt like ice-cream in a heat-wave and I felt like an orphan who'd found a foster family as I walked up the three steps to the front door. It was as if the place was giving me permission for the tiredness I had kept at bay all day, and I rang the doorbell in weary gratitude at my good fortune.

A few minutes later Attila the Hun opened the door and eyed me suspiciously.

'Yes? May I help you?' she enquired, in the tone of voice which indicated she hoped she wouldn't have to. Her eyes raked over me and the carrier bag I was holding.

I explained who I was. She managed to arrange her face into what passed for a smile and ushered me into the hall. Wait there, she bade me. For the sake of poetic license I'd like to be able to say I considered doing a runner, but I didn't, I was too exhausted. As I awaited my fate I felt a deep sense of betrayal at the lousy descriptive powers of the housing official who had sent me there.

Attila returned in a few seconds holding two keys in her hand. She was heavily built with very short, mousy hair, obviously cut by the local barber, and skin devoid of make up, probably scrubbed with carbolic before being buffed to a high-gloss finish. Her eyes reminded me of a cow's: big, brown and unblinking. She was bursting out of her beige acrylic sweater, definitely not from the milk of human kindness flowing from her breasts, and I saw that the leather strap of her Edinburgh Woollen Mills kilt was done up on the last hole. She wore a pair of black Hush Puppies on her feet. She put the keys in her pocket and stood smack in front of me, and said:

'Right. I will just take a minute to run through the house rules with you.'

I stood to attention. Feet together, shoulders straight.

'This is a no smoking hotel.' I don't smoke. 'No food to be brought to the room.' Fine. 'No laundry to be done in the rooms.' Fine. 'No visitors allowed in rooms. Tea and coffee are provided. If you need more just ask.' Fine.

'Now. I will give you a brief layout of the hotel so you will know your way around,' she said briskly.

She positioned herself in the middle of the hall, squared her shoulders and began pointing to each room, palms up, like an in-flight air stewardess. Dining-room on my left. Telephone on my right. Residents' lounge downstairs. I half expected her to point over her shoulder and say 'Front door behind me.'

As she talked, I felt a fit of the giggles coming on so I chewed on the inside of my lip to stop them escaping. Eventually, the geography lesson over, she rearranged her face in a 'smile' and said she hoped I would enjoy my stay. As she took the keys out of her pocket a lipstick fell to the carpet. Probably confiscated. The giggles bubbled to the surface and I took a deep swallow and chewed on my lip a bit harder.

'Breakfast is from seven thirty until nine. In the dining-room.' In case I was memory deficient she waved her arm in the general direction.

Then, as if trying to remember her manners she gave an odd little upper-body shake and said:

'Do make yourself at home. Please feel free to use the communal lounge . . . just like any normal person.' This was accompanied by an alligator smile. Patronising bitch.

'Right. Upstairs. Two flights. Room 18.' She eyed my M&S carrier bag. 'You won't be needing a hand.'

I gave her a smile which made no attempt to reach my eyes and said good night. What a bloody cow. The Laura Ashley hadn't cut much ice with her, nor the greying hair and wrinkles.

I wasn't annoyed because she had presumed I was a welfare case. Or rather I was precisely because of that. It was the sheer snobbery of the woman. A socialist in my veins I despise people who think they are a cut above. I've met my fill of moralistic, holier-than-thou, I'm-better-than-you people, and there wasn't one of them good enough to tie the shoelaces of most of the women I had known who walked the streets for money.

It was the thought of the other women who were at her mercy that most incensed me, women running from a bad situation, tearful, frightened and lonely, looking for a safe harbour. The poor sods would arrive expecting Lady Liberty, the Angel of Mercy, just as I had done. Attila could stick her breakfast up her self-righteous arse. I would starve sooner than see her disdainful face before my day had even started.

In the sixteen days I would stay there I never once sat at the breakfast table. I existed on M&S sandwiches and chips from the local chippy. Nor did I step foot in the residents' lounge, where the normal people congregated. Months later, when the bill arrived, it was with grudging reluctance that I signed the cheque.

Room 18 was chintzy, but comfortable enough. I unpacked the carrier bag and put everything away. My skirt and blouse looked very lonely in the wardrobe. I put the kettle on to boil and shook a sachet of coffee into a cup along with two of sugar. As I sat on the bed waiting for the kettle to boil I opened the bedside locker. There was a Gideon Bible there. I wondered if Attila had read it. 'Blessed be the merciful' . . . probably not.

I made myself a cup of coffee and toyed with the idea of sitting on the bedspread with my shoes on just to spite Attila, which made me smile, but the bedspread was pretty so I folded it up, laid it on the chair, kicked my shoes off and sat back on the bed.

I was surprisingly alert considering how weary I'd felt on the way. I knew from the past that I wouldn't get much sleep. I never could when anything was bothering me. I can shrug anything off with a joke when I have an audience, then spend the twilight hours worrying myself sick. Migraine, asthma, eczema, duodenal ulcer and insomnia are my chosen weapons of self-punishment.

I had a migraine starting, wavy lines in front of my eyes, probably brought on by not eating. And worry. I thought of Joey and how he would fare without me to run to when he needed help. I would still be there for him, but I wouldn't be on tap, round the corner from him.

Miraculously, the trouble with the drug-dealers had blown over. Fate had smiled on Joey for once in his life because Puff Daddy had got himself stabbed by a dealer in Liverpool whose toes he had trodden on. Rumour had it that Puff had been on his way to make good his threats to kill Joey when the stabbing occurred, but that's probably only people upping the hype.

On the day Puff signed himself out of the hospital he set up shop again, only to be battered unconscious with a bicycle chain by an addict who had mistaken him for another dealer who'd sold him a dodgy deal—brick dust mixed with corn-flour starch. How else can dealers get rich quick?

Two more of the dealers had found themselves similarly outclassed, stabbed (both of them on the same occasion by one desperate addict), hit with a full bottle of Coca-Cola, a golf ball in a sock on another occasion, finally with a steering wheel lock on yet another, and had moved on to pastures new. Well that's what I'm presuming. I can't see them having the wherewithal to give it all up and go legit. All the aforementioned occurred in the space of a week. With a high mortality rate, they have short careers in the drug trade. Mr Big, that seller-of-death, had moved on to another town.

Joey had briefly called to the shop that afternoon. He looked as if he'd holidayed on the Riviera; he was deeply tanned from walking in the sun for hours trying to score. He had found the motivation to spruce himself up and to the casual observer he could've passed for any ordinary Joe. He wasn't emaciated, unlike most junkies. He's no different to any other addict of course, food is last on the list, drugs are all. It was Mummy who fed him.

'Your eyes are as clear as a baby's,' I'd said enviously, 'How the hell do you do it? Your whites are real white, why haven't you got red blood vessels like you used to? You look like you've used those blue eye drops.'

It was the heroin, he told me. It had destroyed every vein and blood vessel in his body.

'Must act like embalming fluid then, formaldehyde or something. Don't suppose they market it as a beauty cream do they?' I'd said, not wanting to depress him.

And I'd had a huge lump in my throat as I'd watched him walk out of the shop door. As soon as he'd gone, I burst into tears.

I was mulling all this over, and over, and over again, and it was doing my head in. Then I thought of Martin all alone in the house for the first time in twelve years. I've jumped into every relationship I ever had without thinking, only to fall flat on my face. With Martin it was the only time in my whole life I landed on my feet and the guilt of leaving him bore down on me heavily.

I knew that the pain I was feeling about the future loss of us was not entirely altruistic. I had been cocooned by his love for so long, his love was the mirror I saw myself in daily. I was his Lou-Lou, as he called me, adoring me with his eyes, his perfect significant other. I wasn't sure I could face being just me.

Then I thought of Smudge, poor little unlucky black cat. I had abandoned him too. I read once about a woman whose partner didn't like cats because he felt they were alien beings come to spy on us. I liked that idea. I wondered what Smudge would be thinking.

The idea of sending out for a takeaway had of course taken a nosedive, as soon as I'd set eyes on Attila. It would've meant contact with her and I'm not that much of a masochist. I was starving, (which had started my ulcer up), my throat still hurt, as did my knee, the pain in my head and behind my right eye was intensifying and I'd left my Migraleve at home in my other handbag. Home.

I wanted my mum. I've never asked for help when I've been in trouble, even in the most life-threatening situations I always felt it was down to me, but there's been a couple of times in my life when my self-sufficiency was a bit wobbly and I've resorted to ringing my mum just to be able to talk about it. It would have to be a real emergency mind you. Mum always loved a bit of drama, a piece of the action to brighten her day; she had a low boredom threshold. To Mum it was irrelevant that it was probably more than just a drama and that I might not make it to the next day; she welcomed the diversion, loved the excitement. The apple doesn't fall far from the tree.

I thought of Chris, my first born, coming to the end of his second ten-year jail sentence for bank robbery. Last time I'd visited him he was doing his Cool Hand Luke bit, laughing, joking, entertaining the troops. But I wasn't fooled; it was like looking in the mirror. I know the despair that envelops him, the dark places he travels to when he lies on his bunk after lock-up.

I know he won't thank me for saying so, but the only good thing to come out of his long jail sentences is that he wasn't there to bring up his kids. I know it broke his heart, but at least the cycle of crime and imprisonment will not be perpetuated by this next generation. Gill married a good man, a paramedic, and together they're doing a good job of raising my grandchildren who have turned out to be great kids and a joy to me.

I thought about my daughter Fiona, with her Obsessive Compulsive Disorder—scrubbing, bleaching, scouring—in an attempt to make things how she wants them to be, to have some control in her life. I've tried to build bridges since the time she and her good-for-nothing boyfriend tried to relieve me of my meagre savings, but she's too full of hate, for me, for everything and everybody. Who could blame her? We only shared a life for three years. It wasn't enough to build a relationship that could withstand the repercussions of the life I've lived. If only.

I thought about my mother, lost in the shadows of Alzheimer's. She'd looked really well last time I'd seen her: pink cheeks, masses of curls, years younger than her eighty-three years. She'd been sitting on a chair playing with a pink plastic bracelet on her wrist with intense concentration on her face, like a happy little girl. There was a terrible poignancy to the scene, for Mum's main goal in life had been to amass as much gold jewellery as she could. (She and Puff Daddy would have made a good team.) Someone had nicked a ring from my mum's room so my sister had taken the rest of it home with her for safekeeping, and had bought her trinkets in replacement. My sister later gave it all to me. Neither of us is in to jewellery, but I treasure it, it's the essence of Mum.

'Hello Mum,' I'd said as I stood in front of her chair.

She'd looked right through me then leaned left and right on her chair trying to see something behind me.

'Someone to see you Bridie,' the care worker said. 'Your daughter Lynda,' but mum may as well have not heard.

As I knelt in front of her and took both her hands in mine for some rather odd, unexplained reason I had a flashback to the young woman who had acted out the whole of *Rebecca* for me, when as an eleven-year-old, I'd waited up for her to come home from the pictures. Mum became very agitated and tried to pull her hands away, straining to look over my head. I released her hands and got to my feet.

'Mum? Hello Mum. Mum it's me Lynda. Mum? Mum?' I stood like a little girl, willing her to notice me. She never had. Now she never will.

I think Mum missed her vocation. She was in the same beauty contest that Maureen O'Hara went on to win and I often wondered how Mum's life would have turned out if she had won it. Would it have been Mum up there on the silver screen with John Wayne? As someone who'd watched, enchanted, on the linoleum of my bedroom floor, I can attest to the fact that Mum would have made a fine actress. She was wonderful as Mrs de Winter, so convincing as the wicked Mrs Danvers.

I made another cup of coffee and put it on the bedside locker. I contemplated washing my face to remove my make-up, but decided not to break the habit of a lifetime; it would only keep me awake. I showered quickly, then realised I had nothing to sleep in, so put my cardigan back on and climbed into bed very carefully, so as not to move my head too much. I closed my eyes for a few minutes willing the pain to go away.

I told myself to get a grip: all was not lost, I still had my job, still had Ann, my lovely volunteers, even my customers. They'd been like a second family through all the trials and tribulations off the past eight years; it had always been more than just a job to me. I felt a little more cheerful.

I picked my book up off the locker and laid it on the bed while I had a swig of coffee then settled back. As I reached for the book, I noticed the significance of the title for the first time: *Room for a Single Lady*. The shadow of a smile passed my lips at the irony of it. I didn't know whether to laugh or cry.

21

The ground floor flat I moved to was in a corner plot with a snicket running at the side leading to the local junior school. There were garages and sheds at the rear, mostly burnt out, long abandoned to vandals. Gangs of teenagers gathered there after dark, messing about, shouting, scrapping, drinking, smashing empty bottles against my bedroom wall out of boredom. Weekends were the worst. On the one hand, I felt sorry for the teenagers, they had no place to go. But the young are so scary these days and I was not brave, or stupid enough, to go out and tell them to shut up.

I hated the place. I don't think Dolores rated it either although she wasn't around when the kids were kicking up a racket. After a cup of coffee and a cig, I ventured round the back each morning to sweep up the broken glass, lager cans, dog ends and miscellaneous items of doubtful origin and binned them before I left for work.

A young woman walking a Scotty dog stopped one morning to tell me, 'You're wasting your time there, love. Let the council do it, it's what they're paid for.' That sort of attitude always mystified me. People laughed when Maggie Thatcher was filmed picking rubbish up off the road, but that was the only time I actually admired her for something.

When I came back through the snicket, the dog was squatting, depositing the previous day's dinner on the pavement, the woman standing daydreaming. I paused; I was interested to see whether the young woman would pick up. No such luck, the two vanished into the darkness.

I had been used to walking to work, but I now had to get the bus. Some nights I did not get home until almost 7.00. To top it all I measured the width of the UPVC internal doors in the flat, twenty-seven inches. It meant the new leather suite I had just bought would not fit through. It may seem a petty reason for moving house but money does not grow on trees. I asked for a move.

Strictly speaking, I was a property owner because of the house I co-owned so they could have told me to lump it. However, I asked nicely and the woman at the council was lovely, very understanding. Six weeks later I got a move. They said the house would have to be sold; the rent agreement listed me as a temporary tenant until then.

Oh, Lord. Martin, poor sod, would lose out there too, and I dreaded telling him we had to sell. It was his home. He was working his socks off to pay the mortgage and the bills on his own.

For almost a year, I buried my head in the sand, ignored letters from the council asking the state of play. I continued paying direct debits for water rates, insurance, TV licence for the house to lessen the burden on Martin. It was a bit of a struggle paying two lots of everything on top of rent for the flat, but I got by. The new flat was fine, near to town, so I could walk to work.

Dolores showed up a week or so later. I was hoping not to see her again, but it wasn't to be. I got into bed one night, leant over to switch the light off, and there she was at the foot of the bed. I scrambled out of bed, heart hammering, and she disappeared. I sat up all night with the lights on. I know that the visitations are but a visible projection of what's going on in my head. I hope. And yet, I don't think I imagine the sudden charge of electricity, the impression of soft movement in the room.

It took me a while to acknowledge that the constant lump that seemed to be lodged in my throat, which I romantically thought of as the loss of love, was in fact me old mate, guilt. I worried about Martin constantly. I felt that I was indispensable to him, that without me he would fall flat on his face.

I had not spoken to him since the day he had helped me to bring some of my clothes and kitchen stuff to my new flat. The short car journey had been painful for both of us. You'd never have guessed we'd lived together for twelve years. We sat like two strangers, staring straight ahead, not knowing what to say. I broke the silence to ask what had happened to his left arm; there were three ugly, deep gouges, about four inches long.

'Oh, just a little self-mutilation,' he said, face flushed with embarrassment

'Oh God.' I felt three swift arrows—pity, guilt, shame—like into a frigging dartboard.

'I'm over it now,' he said, softly. 'Won't happen again.'

He said he needed to stop at a hole-in-the-wall. I watched him tapping out the keypad. I'd always held his bankcards, done all his banking. He claimed he wouldn't be able to manage. If he did it his way, Martin would keep his money under the mattress; he didn't trust the banks.

Martin thought money was there purely to help others. As he was leaving the flat, he pulled a roll of money out of his jeans and handed it to me.

'There's £250 there. Take it, you'll need it,' he said quietly.

'Oh Martin. I can't take it, love. You need it.' Go on, make me feel even guiltier, why don't you.

'I have more than you. Got more than I ever had in my life . . . thanks to you. Take it,' he insisted.

My eyes felt damp.

'Only because before that you gave it all away. You're too soft-hearted. It's high time you looked out for yourself, Martin,' I replied, ignoring the money.

'Maybe I'll start,' he said unconvincingly. 'But not with you. I wouldn't have a penny in the bank if it wasn't for you, Lyn.'

'Oh, love,' I said brokenly, eyes fixated on his arm, the raw wounds an accusation. 'I can't.'

'You're the best thing that ever happened to me, Lyn.' His voice was low, thick with emotion.

'Take the money,' he said, unusually forceful, opening my hand, closing my fingers round the notes.

'Bet you don't think that now,' I said, my mascara had started to run.

'You always will be, Lyn. Best years of my life, these were. I can't make you come back, but I know you love me. And I told you I'd love you 'til the day I die. Please. Take the money.'

His face was wet too. I took the money.

We knew it was the last time we would ever see one another and we did not know how to say goodbye. Do you hug? Peck on the cheek? Shake hands? I could have hugged him, the impulse was there, but I could see his heart was breaking and he was trying desperately to hold it all together, so I stopped myself. We opted for fidgeting, looking round the room, trying to keep a check on the tears. I knew I had to be the one to do it. 'Bye, Martin.'

'Bye love,' he replied huskily. 'Take care. If you ever need me you know where I am.'

I dare not look at him. 'Ditto,' I whispered. 'Bye.'

I watched through the window as he walked to the car. He opened the driver's door, sat in, reached in under the dashboard, pulled some tissues out of the box, and blew his nose. I pulled a handful out of the box on the writing desk and did likewise. I watched him drive away. He did not look back at the flat.

I felt cold. Dolores turned from the window and looked at me, sadly. I think she liked Martin. I wasn't so frightened of her appearance in the day time and when I looked again, she was no longer there.

For such an unassuming man Martin left a large void. I have witnessed the darkness in people for too long to look up to anyone, but Martin was, is, uncontrovertibly a fine man, one of nature's gentlemen and it made what I was doing to him feel terribly wrong. I ran an eye over the past. The abusive Stockholm Syndrome relationships, and even when I had weaned myself away from those, the spilling my guts to a man, praying for his forgiveness for my past, neck on the block, like sodding Marie Antoinette waiting for the axe to fall. And not one of them worth a toss. Twelve years in a loving relationship—free from fear, without the threat of violence, jealousy or control—had helped me to discover myself as a person. I am indebted to Martin for that.

*

Total freedom takes some getting used to, but at least I was free to devote my energies to Joey, now I no longer had Martin's needs to distract me. This took the form of nagging, cajoling, cursing, crying, beseeching, along with an occasional dollop of emotional blackmail. Joey came to dread coming to see me; that he came anyway is to his credit. I knew before I started that the battle was lost. However, hope is what makes us human. However hopeless the future may seem, we never give up trying to alter the inevitable.

The next twelve months was the 'year of the leg'. Joey had one blood clot after another. I was convinced it was the same blood clot, though he said it was not. He never once completed the course of antibiotics prescribed, so how would he know?

He was in and out of hospital as regularly as the nurses, signing out at the first sign of the swelling subsiding. He caught MRSA during one stay, compounding the problem; it was revolting to look at and slower than slow to heal.

It's hard to keep a dressing on the lower leg, especially when you ride a bike. When Joey dropped in, he'd sit on the settee and the first thing he'd do was roll his sock down to ease the pressure and have a good scratch to relieve the itching.

The MRSA would get an airing, ugly suppurating tissue, marbled with black and navy woollen sock fibres. Joey has the highest pain threshold of anyone I've ever known, but I still don't know how he puts up with continuous ill-health.

After work I would make the daily pilgrimage to the hospital, money in the slot for a wheelchair, in the lift, up to the ward, help him into the chair, down in the lift, sit outside in the hospital car park for a couple of hours, smoking, hopelessly pleading with him to put an end to drugs. Once I asked why, if he had to use heroin, he could not have stuck to smoking it.

'Ah yes, well. I was only an apprentice then.' Self-deprecating grin. 'I enrolled in the College of Further Education after Dawn left me. Took an intravenous course, joined the rest of me classmates.'

'Ha ha. You'll graduate ahead of the rest of the class in your alma mater that's for sure. Summa cum laude . . . highest distinction possible for fucking up the body God gave you.' I wanted to strangle him. I wanted to protect him.

Mostly we sat silently, watching the world go by. Then I would wheel him into Oxfam for books, the shop for sweets and Lucozade. Joey would hold his right arm out, guiding the wheels of the thingamajig that held his drip alongside us. Then up in the lift, back to the ward, help him in to bed, back in the lift, wheelchair back in its slot, walk home in tears.

I grew so used to seeing him on crutches it became the norm. Sometimes, I would open the door, look down at the crutches, sigh, turn and walk to the kitchen to put the kettle on, leaving him to see himself in and close the door. I knew it was an unsympathetic way to act but the emotional pain, and the consequent anger was hard to handle.

I would make no mention of the crutches, studiously avoid looking at his lower body as we talked. On those occasions the anger in my eyes would betray me and after a quick cuppa, he'd make himself scarce.

Nine times out of ten, I'd ring him before he got out the hall door of the flats, say I was sorry, and ask him to come back. The tenth time I'd feel the loss, but let him go.

I could not help but feel sad and a little resentful, at the turn my life had taken since Joey came on the scene. Heroin had driven a wedge between Martin and me. The loss might have seemed more bearable if only I had found a way to help Joey clean up his act. The man I loved, for the life of my son. A worthy sacrifice, had I succeeded. But it was just the same old same old. The anger came from knowing it was all for nothing.

I still did not think though, that just because Joey had lost his way it meant it was OK to stand by and watch him commit suicide. The Joey before drugs is still there beneath his addiction, essentially a decent human being. Not all junkies lose every shred of human decency. Through Joey I have met a few addicts, three of whom I actually liked as individuals.

I bumped into Ellie, an addict who lived on our street, on my way to work one morning.

'Morning Ellie. You're up early,' I said. Her hair was a mess, looked like she'd slept in her clothes. I took it for granted she was on her way to score.

'Not really. I get me Gran up an' dressed an' do her egg on toast every mornin' 'fore the carer comes.'

Never presume. Must try to remember.

'Your Gran is lucky to have you.'

'S'pose,' ' 't in't that.' Ellie shrugged. 'Me Gran don't want no-one seeing her in her nightie. Dead old fashioned like that.'

We smiled at the modesty of old-fashioned women.

Ellie fell into step beside me; we walked to the end of the street.

'What happens at bedtime?' I asked curiously.

'Oh, I go back at eight and settle her down.'

I wouldn't be ashamed to have Ellie for a daughter, she may be an addict, but she'd put some respectable citizens to shame.

What happens to dead junkies was something I had never given a thought to until Joey brought it up. The truth is stark and terribly depressing.

When a junkie dies, the only people who mourn their passing are close family members, often not even them. Sometimes they have lost touch with the family. Often the deceased had caused such misery and heartache the family are relieved it's all over.

It's understandable; smackheads are not exactly a great loss to the community. All the same, you'd need a heart of stone not to feel moved when you hear tell of a junkie funeral without a solitary mourner. They are so young too, it is not as if they are elderly people, the last in line of their generation with none left to mourn for them.

Joey told me of one such incident, though there were many more. He and a mate were scoring smack. As the transaction was taking place, the supplier said to the mate, 'Sorry to hear about your brother.'

'How d'ya' mean?' the mate asked, barely interested.

'Don't ya know?'

Mate shook his head. 'Know what?' Impatient, anxious to inject the morning fix . . . feel the golden glow.

'Oh fuck.' Dealer pulled a face, scratched his head, choosing his words. 'He ODd last week. Sorry pal, thought you'd a known.'

After shooting-up, mate and Joey called in at the Chapel of Rest. Mate had to know who had been to view the seventeen-year-old dead boy. No one, it transpired. No one had signed the book of condolences either. On talking to the people at the funeral parlour, Mate learned that not a single person had shown up at the crematorium to show respect for 'our kid'.

Joey confided that, ever since, he's had a mortal fear that only the undertakers would attend his own funeral. Right then I couldn't think when I'd last heard a single more depressing statement. I swallowed a mouthful of gravel.

'You won't know much about it, will you?' I said logically.

'I know that. It's just a hang-up I've got. I can't seem to get past it,' Joey said, shaking his head. 'It's just . . . you live all those years and there's not one fucker in the whole world who cared.'

'Don't worry son. I'll hire some professional mourners. And if not, I'll make sure there's a football match on . . . mingle with the supporters when the hearse is passing.'

Joey's eyes cut to me, saw the anguish on my face, bit back whatever he was going to say.

'Should be like me . . . don't have one. I'm not having a funeral service at all,' I smiled brightly. 'Least that way I won't be embarrassed when no one turns up.'

You have to lighten things up when someone's going maudlin on you. Anyway, it was true. I'd already made my wishes known. The real reason was I didn't want people scratching their heads when the pastor asked for their thoughts for my eulogy.

I can't get that conversation out of my head. It's a terrible thing for a mum to say but in a sense, I wish I could outlive Joey, be around to make his funeral arrangements. If I had to drop in at a pub and offer free drinks all round I'd make sure he had a decent turnout.

Other people see the goodness in Joey; one person who'd mourn should Joey die before he did is Kenny, an old alcoholic who lives across the street from Joey's flat. Kenny used to sit out front on a rusty lawn chair chatting to passers-by, weather permitting. Nowadays, he spends as much time outdoors as possible. Kenny is dying. It began with liver cancer, the cancer then spread. That did not prevent local yobs from stealing his wheelchair, leaving him housebound.

Knowing Joey rode a bicycle, Kenny had sent a kid to knock and ask would he nip to the shops for some milk. Joey willingly obliged.

Lost on Planet H it wouldn't have entered Joey's head to 'neighbour' the old chap, but he had got on his bike and searched the area for the wheelchair; he came across it in the brook near the playing fields. He'd had a go at fixing it, but it was beyond repair; he's not exactly the practical sort anyway, but the thought was there. After that an odd relationship developed between the pair. A charity managed to procure another wheelchair for Kenny a few months later.

Kenny, a cantankerous old git, was forever sending Joey back to the shops if the bread wasn't soft enough, or he if felt there were too many eyes in the spuds. Joey felt mortified taking stuff back, but he did it.

Kenny thought nothing of ringing Joey at 7.30 in the morning with, 'Get up, lazy bastard. I'm waiting for me paper.'

'Sod off Kenny. I've only been in bed two hours.'

Kenny would keep ringing until Joey got out of bed.

Joey tried turning his mobile off once when he'd had a late night. Kenny got two men on their way to work to carry him over the road, where he sat, finger on the doorbell until Joey poked his head out of the upstairs window. Joey dressed, cycled to the shops, got the paper, dropped it off to Kenny, chuntering all the way.

'Here.' He slapped the newspaper in Kenny's lap. 'Why the fuck you couldn't wait 'til I got up. News is still gonna be there.'

Kenny gloated, triumphant.

Kenny was lonely. And powerless. Abandoned by his offspring—who knows why. He could have been a lousy father. He was a target of ridicule for the local yobs, an incontinent alcoholic, confined to a wheelchair, spindly legs jerking like a marionette's when upright, an easy target.

Joey understood that having his own personal lackey, especially one even lower down the food chain, empowered Kenny, increased his feelings of self-worth and validated his existence for the short time he had left. I don't know if Joey realised that it cut both ways.

I rang Joey one Sunday.

'Where are you?' I wanted to know.

'Tesco's'. Joey answered.

'Tesco's! What are you doing there?'

The supermarket was four miles away. Joey only had a push bike. 'I hope you're not shoplifting.'

'Don't be daft. I'm getting Kenny's prescription.'

'It's bloody lashing down! Are you on the bike?'

'Course. What else? I'm soaked as it happens. I could strangle the old bugger.'

'I don't understand. Why did you have to go all that way? Why couldn't you have got it at Boots? They open until four Sundays.'

'I know. You know what Kenny's like,' he laughed, 'Awkward sod. Waits 'til everywhere shuts, then decides he's gotta have it now.'

After hearing about Kenny for two years, I finally met him when he came to the hospital to see Joey. He came by taxi; a porter brought him to the ward in a hospital wheelchair. Joey was shocked to see him, but you could tell he was moved. I felt choked myself.

Straight away Kenny began to wind Joey up. I watched him covertly as he spoke. Kenny was straight from central casting, cadaverous face, yellow withered skin, wrinkles as deep as the Grand Canyon. The whites of his eyes reminded me of beef suet, yet the eyes themselves looked as though they belonged to a younger man.

After a while, I left them alone so Kenny could indulge in a bit of grumbling to cheer himself up. Joey shot me an 'I'll get you for this' look as I waved goodbye in the doorway. I grinned back at him. I was glad he had a friend—one who was not a junkie—and I went downstairs to the coffee shop.

The pair bickered like a couple of old maids most of the time, but they had a relationship built on dependency. Kenny needed a young pair of legs with a pushbike to run his errands. But it was more than that. Joey was his link with the world.

Joey, too, benefited from the companionship. He spent a lot of time at Kenny's, a drug-free zone, drinking tea, chatting. Apparently, Kenny was good company when he was sober.

On the other hand, he was a bit of a nuisance when drunk. He fell asleep and pissed on Joey's leather settee once. Joey phoned to ask me how to get rid of the smell of ammonia.

'You can't. Dump the settee.'

Last Christmas Kenny gave Joey a Christmas card two days before the festivities. Joey like most men has no interest in cards at all; he said he'd open it when he got home.

Kenny, cranky as ever, said, 'No! I want you to open it now.'

'Oh, bloody hell. Anything to shut you up.' Joey grumbled. He opened the envelope. Kenny had put a £10 note in the card. Joey stared at the note, then at Kenny.

'Didn't think I'd let Christmas go by did you son?' said Kenny, happy, smiling. ''preciate all you've done.'

Joey was on the phone to me as soon as he got home. Kenny who had nothing to give, giving what little he had, had made him feel bad. The thought of getting Kenny a gift hadn't entered his head.

The next day I bought a tin of biscuits and a box of Belgian chocolates from Marks & Spencer's, gift wrapped them, and gave them to Joey. I told him to say they were from him.

I rang Joey. 'Did you give them to him?'

'Yeah. Told him they were from you, he wouldn't believe I'd bought 'em anyway . . . knows where my money goes.'

'What did he say? Did'ya tell him I said thanks for looking after my baby?'

'Yeah. He just sat there bloody crying. He started when he was ripping the bow off the wrapping paper. Probably knows it's his last Christmas. I didn't know where to look.'

'Ah, poor old . . .'

'Don't start snivelling. He was pissed.'

'I thought he was off it.'

'He was. Said Christmas depressed him . . . ghosts of Christmas past and all that. Been on the piss for two days.'

'Don't talk to me about ghosts. I know how he feels.'

'Yeah. Me too. This time next year, I'll be in the nick. Kenny'll probably be dead . . . and I won't even be able to go to his funeral.'

Happy Christmas one and all.

*

I had tried dealing with Joey the hard way, after being told on the phone by June that feeding him and paying his heating and lighting was the wrong way to go about helping him.

'You wouldn't see your kids without food and heat,' I argued. She wouldn't. No way.

'Yes I would Lyn,' she snapped, 'because he hasn't a hope if you keep facilitating him.'

She then proceeded to demolish every argument I put forward. She said that the only thing I should facilitate was his treatment for drug addiction. A reasonable assertion, but things are different when you are at the coal face. Forcing an addict to accept help is just not do-able.

I reasoned that June, who is married to a psychiatrist and has an old friend who is now chief-psychiatrist at the Betty Ford clinic knew better than me, chained by motherhood. I should imagine it is easier for a camel to pass through the eye of a needle than it is for the likes of Joey to end up somewhere like that, but June meant well; the least

I could do was try it her way. I stopped buying him food and paying his gas and electric. After two weeks, my resolve crumbled and I called to see him, unannounced.

He'd lost weight, looked even sicker than usual and sat in an armchair wrapped in a duvet, a pair of crutches signifying another leg infection.

The flat was like a deep freeze, dirty dishes in the sink, no hot water, empty fridge, bare cupboards, candle stumps on the mantelpiece, windowsill, table, floor, TV.

He'd fallen asleep knocking a candle over, which had burnt a large hole in the carpet; the walls were smoke blackened. He'd slept through it all. Luckily, the fire had burnt itself out. On closer inspection, even that had been a fluke; the surrounding carpet was soaked through when he'd tripped over the mop bucket with his crutches.

I freaked out at the sight of the pale-blue smoky curtains. Smoke. Fire. Death. I'd dragged Joey out of one burning house as a child. Fuck the right way—the Betty Ford clinic, the Priory, tough love, the drug counsellors, all the stuff I had read—they didn't live with the ghosts of eight people who'd died by fire.

I went straight out and topped up his gas and electric cards at the post office, then next door to the Spar shop where I purchased microwave meals, milk, bread, butter, tea, sugar, cheese and a few chicken burgers. He was not one for cooking in normal circumstances and his leg was in a bad state.

'You really must go to the hospital,' I said, pointing to the crutches, and left it at that. I knew well he would do no such thing.

The infection dragged on for weeks. He obviously had a death wish and who was I to stand in his way? I had been at his side through so many identical traumas that I was sick and tired of his refusal to help himself. I was back to 'tough love'.

Days passed without contact. No news was good news and I buried my concerns by indulging in a flurry of writing. I could have rung his mobile, but I wanted some time out. Eventually, desperation forced Joey to come for help early one morning. I saw immediately that his condition had worsened, dramatically. The poison had travelled from his groin, stomach, leg, foot, to the left buttock, which had swelled to such an extent he looked deformed. Even his scrotum had swollen; he walked with his legs wide apart like an ancient baboon near to death, bent over, painstakingly slow.

I was so shocked by his condition constructive thought vanished. Inanely, I asked could I get him something to eat or drink. You'd think I'd offered arsenic by the horrified look on his face. He was vomiting anything that passed his lips, retching was painful, he said.

'I'm phoning a taxi. You're going to casualty. Don't argue.'

Frozen to the spot with pain, he stood motionless, propped up by the crutches, bent at the waist; he held his left leg away from his body, his eyes were closed, his face a mask of pain.

'Please Mum. I'm in too much pain to be hanging around in casualty. Please, I'm begging you . . . lend me enough for a couple of bags and I swear on your life I'll go the hospital.'

'Joey! Your system's being poisoned! You have a fever . . . look at the sweat on you. You need to go now!'

No response was forthcoming, apart from a slow intake of breath.

'Oh, God,' I groaned. I was desperate to do the right thing, my eyes told me this was no time for procrastination.

'You say it wouldn't be the end of the world to have a leg lobbed of . . . well look at you . . . it's everywhere. They can't chop your arse . . . your whole body in half.'

He was still standing in the same spot with his eyes closed. I was expecting him to keel over any second.

'OK.' I said in defeat. 'Only on condition you go to hospital the moment you've scored.'

His shoulders slumped; he closed his eyes as if in prayer. Still standing, he asked me to take his mobile out of his pocket for him. I handed it to him. He rang his dealer. The dealer was waiting for his dealer. There's never a dealer around when you want one.

Quickly, I fetched a duvet from the bedroom, threw it over the settee to protect it, and eased Joey backwards on his right side; he lay at an awkward angle, unable to sit, or lie back. He moaned softly. I fetched feather pillows and attempted to ease them under his left side to cushion the weight of his swollen, infected body. He indicated he was going to vomit so I fetched a plastic bowl from the kitchen and held it under his chin. He retched, in great pain, there was blood in the bile. He was sweating terribly, fiery to the touch.

I got a flannel and a bowl of cold water, knelt beside him, and gently wiped his face. He leaned back slightly with his eyes closed allowing me minister to him. More than anything that was a sure sign of how bad he felt.

He fell asleep as I stroked his forehead, just like when he was a child. I thought he had lost consciousness because his breathing was so shallow. I felt for a pulse. I noticed a damp patch spreading on the cushion behind his head. I gently prised his fingers from the sick bowl and emptied it down the toilet. I rinsed it out and splashed some Dettol in it, and put it on the floor next to the settee.

My instinct was to ring for an ambulance while he was sleeping, but I saw pictures of him refusing to go with them. He slept for twenty minutes before the pain woke him. He tried to sit up, but couldn't manage it. When I lifted the throw off him, it had doubled in weight with his perspiration. That really scared me.

His dealer rang, wanting to meet a few streets away. Joey pleaded with him to meet him on the corner near my flat. He wouldn't have managed any distance. I watched from the window holding my head in my hands as my elderly neighbour passed Joey on her walking frame. I tried not to let my mind wander to a dark place.

When he returned he locked himself in the bathroom to inject the devil's dandruff. I rang for a taxi. Joey shouted for me. He had dropped his syringe and lost most of his gear on the floor and couldn't bend to pick it up. I had to do it.

When the taxi arrived, I shouted at him to hurry.

'You'll have to help me Mum.'

I opened the bathroom door; he was leaning against the sink trembling, sweating, trying to tidy himself up. I assisted him as best I could.

'C'mon. Leave them! I'll pick them up,' I said, leaning over to pick up his crutches. I helped him out of the bathroom, steadied him on his crutches.

He nodded towards the kitchen. 'Just need me coat.'

'I'll get it. Taxi's waiting.' I grabbed his coat from the floor where he's dropped it. I felt a sharp pain.

'Ow!' I threw the coat from me, looked at the blood on my thumb in bewilderment. 'What was that?'

Joey looked at the blood. 'Oh fuck!'

'What?' I said, his tone scaring me.

He poked at his coat on the floor with one of the crutches. I looked down. I stared at the hypodermic needle poking through the material of the coat.

'Oh Jesus,' I said, shakily. I grabbed some kitchen towel from the roll, wrapped it round my thumb, lifted the coat gingerly by the collar, and handed it to him.

'God, Mum. I'm sorry.'

I watched, mesmerised, as he removed the syringe with shaking hands, searched the inside pocket for the plastic cap and put it on the tip.

'Taxi,' I said abruptly. The taxi driver was ringing the doorbell impatiently. It took longer to get Joey in the taxi than it did to drive there; I sat in the passenger seat holding the crutches. My thumb throbbed.

Once Joey had been through triage, the doctor saw him straight away. He asked Joey to drop his trousers. Furrows of pain etched in his face, Joey complied slowly, his hands trembling as he gently, painfully, carefully pulled his pants to the side. His body shook from head to toe with the effort.

Because of its location, I hadn't actually seen the source of the infection. I almost lost my breakfast when I saw the deep puss-filled crater in Joey's groin. It was the size of a golf ball. The surrounding area, lower torso and thigh were purple and swollen. I honestly do not know how he had borne the pain. It was the worst thing I had ever seen.

The doctor ummed and aahed, but kept his hands firmly in his pockets. You couldn't blame him.

The speed with which Joey was processed through Casualty was a scary indication of how seriously ill he actually was. While we waited for someone to collect Joey for the ward, I mentioned to the doctor I had pricked my thumb on Joey's needle. The doctor turned and looked at Joey as if he had just crawled out from under a rock. Joey was too ill to care. The doctor said he would send a nurse to take blood from us then left the cubicle.

The male nurse took mine easily, obviously, but couldn't find a vein in Joey. This all took time. It was dreadful to witness. Poor Joey, on the point of collapse was leaning forward over the trolley with his head on his arms, while the unfortunate nurse tapped, inserted the needle, tapped, wherever a vein should be. There were tiny drops of blood in half a dozen unsuccessful sites. Joey didn't utter a word of complaint in spite of the pain and his obvious discomfort.

When the doctor returned to the cubicle Joey asked him how much longer, he was desperate to lie down and take the weight off his body.

'We have to see to your mother first,' the doctor snapped. 'Your records show you have hepatitis. Got to do the blood work, see if there is anything else we should worry about.'

The wonderful nurse managed to get enough blood, after trying for twenty minutes, tapping, tapping, tapping, finally settling for a tiny capillary he located on Joey's ankle.

The nurse and I smiled at one another in relief.

'How did you manage that?' Joey roused himself enough to ask. 'I tried there one day for ages.'

He strained to look over his shoulder at the ankle, as if to commit the site to memory for future reference.

'I worked in Casualty in Glasgow and Liverpool,' the nurse replied by way of explanation.

While we were giving blood—both sporting plasters and bloody needle spots, silken threads of familial love binding us—possibly sharing the same disease, the same death sentence, I felt a strong bond with Joey. Strangest of all was the complete absence of fear I felt. Seeing him in this state I realised he was the entire focus of my life and I felt that should he die my life would be empty and worthless. If we got a bad result, we would be in it together. Joey would not be alone. I've never felt closer or loved my young son more than I did at that moment.

The doctor gave me a tetanus jab and told me the nurse would be back to give one for hepatitis. I would need another three hep jabs as a follow-up at monthly intervals to boost my immune system. I told him I'd come back for the first one, once Joey was settled in the ward. I helped the nurse get Joey onto a trolley and walked behind carrying the crutches.

When we got to the ward, Joey looked longingly at the bed. The few minutes he'd slept at mine was the most sleep he'd had in a week. I attempted to undress him, but he begged me, no, he could not bear to be touched, the pain was too great. The nurse popped her head round the curtain to say she'd be along in a tick to give him some pain relief. Joey knew that meant diamorphine, which brought the tiniest smile to our faces. I helped him on to the bed where he half lay, half sat, fully clothed, eyes shut, pain distorting his features.

'Go Mum, please. I can't talk. Go get your hep jab. Least I'm here now.'

I stroked his face for a moment; he was burning up. My hand was wet with his sweat; I leant over the bed and kissed his forehead.

'I'll come back when I've had it. I love you.'

Two doctors came to see Joey just as I was leaving. Walking down the corridor, I heard a loud crash. I threw my handbag on the floor and ran back to the ward with my heart in my mouth.

Joey was face down out cold on the floor with one of the doctors kneeling beside him and two nurses moving obstacles out of the way. The doctor and a nurse rolled him over on his side. Joey's jeans were down around his ankles; from his groin, an arc of poison sprayed the air, like a whale spouting water.

'Oh God. Nooo . . .'

The other doctor pointed his head at the door, one of the nurses put herself in front of me like a shield.

'It's a gusher,' I heard a doctor say as the nurse hurried me out of the room and guided me to a seat in the corridor.

22

I went to Joey's flat to fetch his dressing gown and pyjamas later that night. I was hit by a blast of warm air when I opened the hall door. Walking up the stairs, I came upon rows of hypodermic needles planted upright in the carpet on the top step, like crosses marking graves of unknown soldiers on a battlefield. I stood looking down at them in confusion. What did it mean? A threat? Junkie code for skull and crossbones, an addict's Jolly Roger? There did not seem to be any pattern or design to the artwork to this cenotaph for dead junkies. Was this junkie creativity? I shivered. My legs shook as I stepped over the hypodermics.

Then I noticed the 'sin bins', the black plastic tubes the chemist gives out with a needle exchange, stacked against the wall, along with the citric acid and surgical swabs. The sin bin is a tamperproof receptacle for used needles. I kicked one of the sin bins with the toe of my shoe; as it rolled over I could tell it was full. Oh, my God.

Walking into the flat was like entering a furnace. The central heating was on high, the gas fire at full pelt. You'd know Joey wasn't paying the bills. I switched all the heating off and opened the windows to clear the smell of vomit that filled the air. I stood with my back to the window and surveyed the room, in a state of shock. I was standing in a smack den.

Plastic syringe caps, unused syringes, bloody surgical swabs, empty citric acid sachets, tinfoil—these were all on the floor, the table, on top of the TV, on the coffee table. Along with these were empty drinks cans with holes punched in the side, drinking mugs, tops sealed with foil, dirty plastic tubing protruding, so someone had been smoking crack. There were overflowing ashtrays, dog ends, tinfoil, spent matches. The fireplace had been used as an ashtray; it was covered in cigarette butts and more had been extinguished on the carpet next to an armchair.

There was a mattress on the floor with its sheets and duvet covered in vomit. There was a large patch of vomit beside the settee. The floor had disappeared under a layer of clothing, bedding, trainers, newspapers, drinks cans and cider bottles.

I went to the kitchen to open the window. Kirsty Young the newsreader smiled at me from the wall over the sink; the photograph had been clipped from a magazine. I opened a drawer searching for a pen to write a list and found thirty-one almost full bottles of prescription antibiotics, dozens of loose strips of Ibuprofen, bandages, plastic pouches and compression stockings. I heaved a deep sigh of despair.

Back in the living room, I picked my way over the mattress to the bedroom. The bedroom was spotless. I searched for the dressing gown, but could not find it. I noticed a piece of checked material amongst the clothing on the mattress in the living room. I dragged it towards me with my foot. It was Joey's dressing gown. I saw that it was streaked with vomit. I kicked it aside in distaste. The smell of vomit was overpowering.

But what to do? Well, first things first, buy new dressing gown, slippers, and pyjamas. Sorted. Joey couldn't come home to this . . . all these germs waiting. Yet I was so distressed by now that I had not the wherewithal to face the clean-up. There were other more pressing things on my mind, like Joey's survival. Deal with it later then, when he's on the mend.

He will mend, won't he? God? Don't take Joey. Please, let him get better.

It wouldn't be the first time prayers were offered up in a crack den but I begged and prayed hard and while I wouldn't dare call it a religious experience I began to feel calmer.

Joey spent six weeks in the hospital. When I considered how speedily the National Health Service discharge patients these days, it drove home to me the gravity of this latest self-inflicted dice with death.

He was on morphine for a few days before the swelling began to subside. Then he was on Heparin injections and twenty-seven pills a day. He wasn't best pleased when the morphine was finally withdrawn.

He slept a great deal in the first few days. We didn't speak much when he was awake; he wasn't up to it, but we smiled a lot. At one point it looked likely he'd lose the leg. We discussed the practicalities, often with humour. We were just so glad he was alive.

The nurses liked him. They were very kind and brought him extra ice cream and titbits; they were trying to fatten him up. He'd hardly eaten during the weeks the infection had taken hold and was but a bag of bones. He seems to bring out the maternal instinct in women, the aura of melancholy that surrounds him probably accounts for that. People have often remarked on it. One of the older nurses told me he would have died had he not gone to casualty when he did.

'He's had a bad do. It was touch and go there for a while.'

The nurse turned to Joey and said, 'There might not be a next time. Think of your poor Mum.' She fluffed his hair affectionately. 'You don't want to put her through this again do you?'

Joey shook his head, embarrassed as hell.

He had the best of care. A full MRI scan every two days in the first two weeks, then twice a week. He had a tube inserted in his groin to drain the poison into a plastic bag that was taped to his leg. His pyjamas and sheets were stained with puss. I collected clean sheets from the nurses' station each day and changed his bed to help lessen their burden. He didn't have enough pyjamas to cope with the amount of seepage from the wound, so in the end he used hospital greens.

Each time things seemed to be improving, the infection started spreading again; they would restart the MRI scans. They had to deal with the MRSA on his other leg at the same time. He went two weeks without as much as a cigarette, too ill to get out of bed.

The doctors arranged for him to have methadone to cope with the withdrawal from smack. He may have been incapacitated, but you never know with a junkie. At least now he wouldn't be forced to attempt to get out of bed searching for drugs. He said that had he known they would prescribe methadone he'd have gotten there a lot quicker.

Two days later, he was moved to a room on his own, which is standard practice with addicts. This suited us both very well with Joey not being a mixer, and me having to spend so many hours there daily. In the early days, I took a book to read and sat beside his bed while he slept.

There was a sign outside Joey's door warning nurses, cleaners and catering staff to glove up before entering, because of the hepatitis.

The bloody Patientline cost me a bomb. Now I understand all the complaints in the media about it recently. It cost £3.50 a day for him to watch TV, and 50p a minute (35p off peak), to phone him from a landline. At least I was working; I felt sorry for people struggling to pay, already having to cope with their loved one's illness and a long hospital stay.

After a couple of weeks, I draped his dressing gown over his shoulders and wheeled him outside so he could smoke. We did not stay long; he weakened easily and conversation tired him. I stood looking down at his pale drawn face as he dozed off, heartbreakingly vulnerable. His hair had grown long, covering the scars on his head, evidence of so many batterings. He had lost the close-cropped heroin look. Oh how I hated that look. I don't know why he'd recently taken it into his head to affect the feral look—tracky bottoms, baseball cap—as he'd always dressed so conservatively. He was always the odd one out when I spotted him with other junkies.

My baby . . . and I almost lost him. I held onto the wheelchair and thought of all he'd been through in his life. Whatever I had done, Joey didn't deserve this life. Dolores would not have wished it on him. I followed his gaze: he was looking at the trees, their branches rustling gently in the slight breeze.

*

A sane person would expect Joey's discharge from hospital to be cause for celebration. I was under no such illusion. The week before I had gone to the ward, walking towards him, smiling like a fool, glad to see him. He was propped on crutches at the door of his room, laughing and talking to an unseen someone in the single room facing his. Drawing abreast, I'd looked in at the young male x-ray sitting on the bed. My smile quickly vanished. I knew a junkie when I saw one.

Joey introduced us; the junkie was a mate of his. I smiled politely, said hi. The guy was friendly and personable, but wired. He was waiting for a pal to bring him some smack Joey told me when he'd closed the door of his room.

I nodded to the wheelchair without speaking. I felt a bit of a shit as we made the trek to the ground floor in silence, but I couldn't help myself. We sat outside in the sunshine for a while without speaking.

Eventually Joey said, 'I can't help him being opposite me.'

'Oh Joey, I know that. It's not him. I'm not angry. It's just . . . my heart's breaking. You nearly died. I really thought . . . this time . . . you'd be . . . I don't know, scared I suppose, scared enough never to take heroin again. Seeing you with him all animated, talking about smack as if it was . . .'

'I'll be careful Mum. I promise. Please don't cry.'

'It's just that all this. . . all this has been for nothing. I know I'm going to bury you. I can see it.'

'You won't Mum. I won't inject it, promise.' He passed me a paper napkin.

I blew my nose, smiled weakly. 'So tell me,' I swallowed. 'What flowers do you want? Red roses?'

I already knew they were his favourite.

He'd smiled.

'Don't forget.' As if.

Up until then I had not said a word about the state of his flat. Mind you, I don't know how I managed it. I suppose I put myself in his shoes. The last thing he needed when he was fighting for his life was someone moaning that he had left a mess behind him, or about the company he kept. Everything was fucked up now anyway as far as I was concerned so I saw no point in holding back. I told him what I thought. He couldn't help vomiting, he'd been ill, he protested weakly, he couldn't clean up after himself.

'Jesus! I know that. I'm not talking about the illness. Your flat was like a bloody crack den in an American movie. I walk up the stairs and I'm confronted by an army of dirty syringes standing to attention in the carpet.'

He smiled at the imagery.

'Do you know how scared I was, picking those up? I had to clean up with industrial gloves on because I was scared of sinking my hands into something and getting jabbed with another of your bloody needles. Again. That's what I'm objecting to. Not the bloody sick. That's what mums do.'

'That wasn't me, Mum. That was my mates. We ran out of sin

bins so I told them to leave the needles in one place at the top of the stairs. I knew you'd go ballistic else.'

'Since when do you have "mates" round to do drugs?' I asked.

'I couldn't get out to score, so they came over,' he responded, his eyes pleading for understanding. 'They just sorta stayed, felt for sorry for me, I suppose. Pretty decent of them, actually,' he added nostalgically.

I gave up. What else could I do? Maybe Joey was right. Perhaps it was decent of them. Though why one of them didn't see fit to lift a finger to tidy the place I don't know; maybe they did not notice the mess, perhaps it was normal for them.

We all have our own circle of friends, associates and colleagues. I always watch the homeless people gathering outside the chapel of a morning for their tea and crusty bread roll, with their sleeping bags under their arms, backpacks on their shoulders, carrier bags holding all they own in the world. The alienated of the affluent west. They may look rough, dirty and unkempt, shivering in early-morning drug/alcohol withdrawal, but you can see the camaraderie all the same.

Three of them passed me the other day, they were laughing at something, real belly-heaving laughter. I marvelled at it. I felt tempted to ask them to share the joke. It must have been good for someone who has nothing in the world to feel so full of mirth. Another thing I noticed was each of them ran their fingers in the refund tray in the phone kiosk without breaking stride as they passed, even though two others in front had already done so. Hoping for Divine Providence I suppose.

I guess a junkie is entitled to have a junkie friend. I resolved to keep my nose out of Joey's business. I wasn't too sure if I could stick to it, but at least I was willing to try.

I could not shake the images of Joey's flat out of my head, the visual foretaste of what would become of Joey when I died. Without me to care, to go 'ballistic' as he calls it, Joey will probably meet his maker in a smack den.

*

The pain of childbirth is soon forgotten once you've given birth. When you try to recall it, you remember it hurt, but you can't relive the actual pain of labour. The same must have applied to Joey, his suffering and the brush with death was but a distant land where pain lay buried. His invalidity benefit had mounted up while he'd been hospitalised and was too great a temptation. He scored smack the first day out. The despair I felt almost flattened me. I wished I could crawl into the bed he had just vacated and have someone care for me.

He still had to rely on crutches when he signed himself out. Even after six weeks, poison was still seeping out of the open wound. The tube draining the wound, the plastic bag tied to his leg proved cumbersome out in the world, but hey, he was alive. He had gained a little weight in hospital and so did not look too bad.

I couldn't take comfort from appearances any more. Remembering the nurse's struggle to draw blood from him, I knew Joey was like a car that had had its odometer turned back. It might look fine, but it's still on its second time around, ready for the knacker's yard.

*

Joey's physical condition did not prove to be as much of a hindrance as one might have expected. I almost fell off the chair when he informed me he'd fallen in love.

'Is she a junkie?'

He nodded.

I sighed. I knew the terrain. More problems. More heartache.

'I'm not being funny, Joey. But please, I don't want to meet her.'

'I knew you'd say that. Don't worry, I won't bring her here.'

'I'm sorry . . . I just can't bear it. It'll be the same as with Dawn, all over again.'

I told him that if they were still together in three months time I would welcome her to my home. It was an easy promise to make; I knew it would not happen.

I only caught a fleeting glimpse of her once, when I happened to look out the window and saw the pair passing by, him walking, she riding his bicycle, pale faced, red curls flowing behind her. Botticelli's Venus. Apart from the scabs round her mouth. Venus was obviously wise enough to stick to smoking the drug.

Now that Joey had two habits to feed, he was under double the pressure for money. By that stage he was so well known in town by store security that he ran out of options. The moment his (or any known shoplifters) feet hit the city pavement, store detectives alerted each other by walkie-talkie, adhering to a new policy of following them everywhere until they got out of town. At the end of one such day, suffering withdrawal and listening to Venus nagging him to come up with the money to score, he broke into three houses in a row. His love waited for him in the alley at the back.

Because he was still struggling to walk properly he made a pig's ear of the first two burglaries. He heard someone moving about so he so he got out as quick as he was able to, empty-handed. In the third house, he found a plastic bottle of loose change and a few computer games on a shelf underneath the TV. Mission accomplished. He shoved the games down his jumper. His mouth was dry with nerves and withdrawal so he opened the fridge where he found a bottle of Coca-Cola. He glugged a third of it, then clambered out the window, taking the bottle with him. He picked up his crutches and limped to the garden fence, bottle of change in one hand, cola in the other. He had another swig of the drink and then threw it on the grass, lobbed the crutches over the fence to Venus, and pulled himself up and over after them.

I was given the full blow-by-blow account of the foray the next morning. It was rare for me not to see Joey's point of view, or at least to make allowances or excuses for his actions because of his addiction. I heard what he had to say without comment.

'You're not very happy with me, are you?' he said, quietly.

I didn't reply.

'I know you think it's wrong, but I was desperate.'

I gave him such a tongue-lashing it's a wonder his ears didn't drop off. I've been burgled myself so I knew how it felt; the idea of someone rifling through your personal possessions, their sticky paws touching your clothes, tossing the family treasures aside, is almost like being raped. Almost. I didn't condone his shoplifting, but I'd done it myself in my teens so it would have been hypocritical to go overboard about it. I grew out of it. But there is a distinction between taking from a store and invading someone's personal space.

For lack of hard news, the break-ins headlined the next day's evening paper. There had been a few other burglaries, unconnected to Joey. I suppose it was the three in a row that did it. Joey was a nervous wreck, hiding, shaking and breaking out in cold sweats. I wasn't far behind him. His new love left him as soon as the coins from the plastic bottle and the £35 they got for the computer games was spent.

The crooks who'd bought the games from Joey's new love were arrested and charged within a couple of weeks. They sang like the proverbial canary. When the police came for Joey, the only hard evidence they had was the DNA they lifted from the bottle they retrieved from the back garden of the burgled house.

'How could you be so stupid? I asked him. 'You know about DNA. Don't you watch *CSI*?'

'Of course I know. I looked at before I threw it, then thought . . . ah, fuck it. I think I wanted to get caught. I'd had enough.'

I offered up silent prayers of thanks that he'd been arrested. Blow me if he didn't go and get bail, a first for him and a complete shock to both of us. The bail dragged on. He had been warned by his barrister to expect three years' imprisonment. He started bringing a couple of bags of books and videos over each day for me to look after until he got out. I had to get rid of some of my books to make way for his. I emptied my linen chest to make way for his videos, which held every TV documentary screened over the past three years.

I groaned aloud at the mention of a large cardboard box containing three years' worth of newspapers he wanted me to mind. Joey's a bit eccentric like that. He is a hard news fanatic so they were all what some call the 'quality papers': *The Times*, *Guardian*, *Telegraph* and so on, stolen or discarded by the public of course. I had no room to store them, but said I'd find a way if he got them to me, they were too heavy for me to lift. Why he could not snip the articles he wanted I do not know. Still, one man's junk: he also brought eighty-nine *National Geographic* magazines, anthropology being another thing he has a passion for. Soon I could hardly move for his stuff.

It was not the thought of being locked up that Joey was bothered about. Now suffering from combat fatigue and weary of the daily fight for survival he was actually looking forward to his stretch. But after six years of continuous heroin use he was scared stiff of cold turkey for weeks without relief. However, Joey had come up with a 'Plan'.

*

When the day of the court case arrived, I arranged to meet him outside the Crown Court at 10.30. By eleven, there was no sight of him. I rang, rollicking him.

'I'm just buying some sleepers for the nick.' His phone cut off before I could respond.

I could not understand what he needed them for. Knowing he was definitely going inside he had put his plan into action. For four weeks before the trial, he had been selling small amounts of smack for some heavy dealers. He had given them all the proceeds a few times so that they would begin to trust him with larger amounts. He had to make his losses up from his benefits because he still trusted 'mates' who went into hiding when pay-back time arrived. The day before court, he'd given the dealers £250 and received the equivalent in heroin back, supposedly to sell. He omitted to tell the dealers he was going to prison on the morrow.

He reckoned on the smack lasting three weeks in the nick because he would have to smoke it. He would feel obliged to give some away to other prisoners; it's the way things work. The sleeping pills were for when the smack ran out, he explained.

It was 1.00 by the time he'd sorted his affairs. I was seething, hanging around outside the court, ashamed to make eye contact with anyone, worried they might be the witnesses. I couldn't take myself off to a café in case I missed him. Joey rode up on his pushbike, slowly, as if on a Sunday jaunt, yawning all the way to the steps of the court, smiling like a naughty schoolboy. He had his best clothes on, the preppy look he favoured: blue button-down shirt, clean jeans, crew necked navy Burberry sweater. Heaven knows where the cashmere Burberry came from; I did not ask. He could have passed for an office worker on dress-down Friday were it not for the lump slap in the middle of his forehead, like an extra eye, a red drop of blood drying in the centre of it. The latest injection site, so much for all the promises.

'For Chrissake's Joey. Talk about the late Marilyn Monroe. I've been stood here since 10.30,' I snapped. I felt like yanking him off the bike.

He grinned sheepishly. 'Sorry. Kenny wanted me to stock him up with groceries before I went inside. You won't have to put up with me for the next three years, relax. I didn't want to rush. What for? I'll be in the nick soon enough.'

'You look like a bloody Cyclops with that thing on your head,' I said, shaking my head. He grinned. I snatched the can of lager out of his hand, put it in the bin and nodded towards the court doors.

As soon as we opened the doors, a man with a real miserable expression on his face strode across to us, grabbed Joey by the wrist, and none-too-gently slapped a pair of handcuffs on him.

'There's a warrant out for your arrest,' the man snarled. 'You should have been here at 10.30.'

Joey twinkled his eyes at me as if to say 'Temper, temper'. I smiled too. You could almost see the steam coming out of the chap's ears. I had seen the same man hanging around most of the morning and presumed he was a court official. The man, obviously a cop, shoved Joey through the metal detector, then told him to empty his pockets onto the table.

Joey yawned, took his mobile phone and a paperback from his jacket pocket, and placed them on the table. I tilted my head to look at the title. Solzhenitsyn's *Gulag Archipelago*.

'Bit OTT aren't we?' I grinned. 'It won't be that bad. Least you'll have central heating.'

Joey smiled back. 'I want to finish it. I'm on the last chapter.'

'Move it,' the cop said tersely.

Joey, a little embarrassed, pulled his dentures out of his pocket, and placed them on top of the book, two pairs of Irish eyes smiling. The cop stood stony-faced. I took £50 out of my purse and asked the cop if it was OK to give it to Joey.

'He's not convicted yet,' he replied sourly.

He is as far as you are concerned, I thought. I pushed the money across the counter. Joey shoved it in his pocket, handed me his mobile and house keys, retrieved his dentures and the book, and was yanked away by the handcuffs. I went to follow them through the door; the cop pushed me back.

'You can't come in here. I'm taking him to the cells.'

'Where do I go?'

The servant of the public let the door swing back in my face without speaking.

I looked around but couldn't see a sign for the public gallery. I sat on a bench for half an hour. People started coming back to court after the lunch break. I asked one of them where to go and she pointed to a door to my left. I went in, walked up the stairs to the gallery. The accused was sitting in the dock, head down, reading, or so I thought.

The judge hadn't arrived yet. There were only half a dozen people in the courtroom, mainly clerks and solicitors. Sourpuss, the cop, sat on one of the benches to my left. I stared at the back of Joey's head. He was so still. I leaned forward to get a better look. The defendant was fast asleep in the dock, obviously overwhelmed with respect for court proceedings. He looked so defenceless. I couldn't help but smile. I looked around the court. Everyone was smiling in Joey's direction, all except for Sourpuss.

I did not know then that Joey had swallowed six sleeping tablets on the way to court. Six! Why junkies have to take everything to extremes beats me.

Joey's barrister entered the court, walked over to the dock and shook Joey awake. They talked for a while. The barrister beckoned me down the steps and shook my hand. He was a lovely man, impeccable manners, very well spoken, what I call 'genuine posh'. He asked if I could think of anything he could offer to the judge in mitigation for Joey.

Where do I start? I sighed deeply, closed my eyes for a moment. By default I was the guilty one. I should have been in the dock on a charge of failing to protect my son, but of course, the barrister didn't want to hear that.

I shook my head, sighed, and said, 'No'.

I sighed deeper. 'Joey has had a dreadful life.' Thanks to me. 'But whatever I tell you the judge will have heard a million times before, abuse, abandonment . . . you name it, he's had it . . . and worse. You know Joey's a heroin addict?'

The barrister nodded.

'To be honest, it may not be what you want to hear, and he won't thank me, but this day . . . this prison sentence will probably save his life.'

The barrister nodded sympathetically. 'I can see that things are not good for him at this point. He looks rather frail.'

I looked at Joey in the dock; he'd fallen asleep again.

'A few weeks ago he almost died. Six weeks in hospital. Still has a bag taped to his leg draining the poison out.'

'You know, I suppose he's told you, that he can expect three years today?'

I nodded. 'I only hope it's long enough.'

The barrister's face was full of compassion. I couldn't imagine him working as a prosecutor; he came across as more your liberal humanist. Joey had requested him to tell me that he'd decided to plead guilty and that as I'd been there all day I should go home. The barrister promised to ring with the verdict when the court closed.

I looked at Joey's bike propped against the wall of the courthouse as I left, no lock on it of course. I had no way of getting it home; I've never ridden a pushbike. I hope whoever came across it was poor. All the weight lifted from my shoulders. It's true when people say that. I felt as if I'd just got my gold star at Weight Watchers. For the first time in years, I knew where Joey was. I knew he was safe. He would not be able to get his hands on another damn hypodermic needle, no more devil's dandruff. He would be fed and clothed and have light, heat, access to medical care, work to fill the days. Most important, he would have people around him. No more sitting alone on a park bench in the dead of night.

A few times, when taking Toby for his late night walk I had looked across the river and seen Joey sitting on a bench on his lonesome, the tip of his cigarette glowing in the dark. He cut such a lonely figure, it used to break my heart. I would concentrate on sending waves of love across, hoping that at some level, he caught them.

*

I could hardly believe my ears when the barrister rang and told me Joey had copped for eighteen months.

'What went wrong?' I asked, disappointment slowing my response.

'We were lucky to get the travelling judge. The usual judge is ill at the moment. He most certainly would have treated Joey less leniently. Joey has previous convictions.'

'Um. I know. Was he awake for the trial? Joey, I mean.'

The barrister chuckled. 'I'm afraid not. The court usher did manage to wake him at one point, but he nodded off again.'

'Oh dear. I bet the judge was furious.'

'Well, no. I explained to him that Joey was not long out of hospital, and that he was still taking medication, so he made allowances for him. I did go to talk to Joey in the cells afterwards, but they were unable to rouse him.'

Three years would have meant Joey served eighteen months, allowing for remission. Now he would only have to serve nine months. Three months of that you can say would be taken up with heroin withdrawal, leaving only six months which was not, in my book, long enough to change a mindset.

Joey says he does not remember any of it. The first he knew it was over was when he woke up in the meat wagon outside the prison. When he got to reception, he asked the screw how long he had received. The screw shouted across to his mate, 'Hey, Rip Van Winkle here wants to know how long he got! Had a kip in the dock.' Screws and prisoners had a good laugh. For the first couple of weeks they addressed Joey as 'Hey, Rip Van'.

Joey could not believe his good fortune. He rang from the nick a couple of days later to ask what the judge had said when passing sentence. I told him I did not know, he had asked me to go home, remember.

'I can remember a miserable fucker cuffing me, that's it.'

'You should have left off the sleepers if you were that interested in the judge's comments.'

'Nah . . . Wasn't that bothered. Knew I was going down anyway . . . just wanted to make sure I was out of it. I'm well happy with eighteen months anyway.'

'You were out of it alright. You were snoring in the dock at one stage. Talk about living your life under anaesthesia!'

Joey laughed.

'Anyway, I'm glad you're well happy, as you say. Can't say as I am. I'm happy on your account, but it's too short for the smack.'

'Uh. Gotta go Mum, they're calling me for lock-up. I'll ring you in a few days.'

23

Apart from a blip on the radar screen when Joey stayed in the caravan, I mostly felt younger than my biological age. I expected to feel like a thirty-year-old once Joey went away and was surprised when the opposite happened. I missed him terribly and felt quite superfluous, as if every bit of energy had been sucked out of me.

For weeks I put off going to his flat to tidy up before handing the keys back to the council. The flat was only a mile from mine but it felt like a marathon when I eventually mustered the motivation to go. I sat for a long time and looked around me. It was as if I had come aboard the *Marie Celeste*. On the coffee table in front of me was a half-drunk cup of tea, an egg sandwich on a plate, perfect teeth impressions on one corner, a *Time* magazine open beside them. Joey's old trainers, socks poking out the top were on the floor next to the chair as if waiting for their owner to come bounding in at any moment.

When Chris left prison, he always had a woman and a home lined up. For Joey, it would mean back to living in a hostel. At one time this would have instilled despair in me, knowing how rife drugs are in hostels. Now I know that it is as easy for prisoners to get drugs in prison as it is outside and I could not bank on Joey being clean when he got out.

I was shocked when I learned that Chris had left prison with a heroin addiction. There has to be something seriously wrong with the system when prison officials have to make arrangements for a long-term prisoner to attend drug counselling on their release. I do not know where the answer lies. High-security prisons have strict visiting, searches, sniffer dogs etc. but still drugs get through.

Melissa, the woman Chris had gone to live with when he got out after his ten stretch, rang me last summer to tell me she'd just had a phone call from a park ranger in Glasgow, who had found a carrier bag containing Chris's driving licence, passport and some damp mouldy clothes. My heart skipped a beat with the shock. I thought he was safe and well, happy with his new family. On the contrary, Melissa informed me. She wanted no truck with drugs—she had two children to consider—and she had kicked Chris out when he began using again.

The police had been to Melissa's house to arrest Chris for violating his parole a couple of days before she rang. She was furious at having police on her door-step; they would not believe she did not know where he was. Chris's parole was on condition that he attended drug counselling and reported to his probation officer twice a week. He complied for a few months, but once heroin got a grip all deals were off, by his reckoning. He knew he had screwed up and expecting a recall, he had gone on the run. It meant he could not sign on the dole so the authorities had no way of knowing whether he was dead or alive. After the discovery of his stuff he was being treated as a missing person case.

Melissa told me they had been fine for the first six months. Chris attended drug counselling, took driving lessons and passed his test and got a passport with a view to a family holiday with her and her kids. She was angry, giving vent in a long monologue about heroin, how it had destroyed their relationship. Her anger spent, we talked and worried what could have happened to Chris, agreeing the circumstances of his disappearance seemed sinister.

Being naturally pessimistic, I thought that he was dead and for months I lived in dread of a knock on the door which would bring me the news that his body had been found.

My misery had only come to a end when a letter arrived from Durham jail. Chris spent last Christmas inside on a parole recall.

For short periods of my life, I forget to hate myself. Slumped on Joey's settee looking around at a life abandoned, I was filled with self-loathing. It was all my fault. Surely every one of my children would have been better off if one of my exes had done a proper job and finished me off.

Fiona may have steered clear of arrest and imprisonment, but the only positive in her life is that she is a teetotaller and a non-smoker. She is so damaged by the fallout from her parents' shortcomings that she has nothing but anger and hatred for us both. I am heartbroken that I can do nothing to change the way she feels about me.

When Colin, the boyfriend, went to prison for GBH on a neighbour, Fiona and I talked most days and we were closer than we had ever been. She would ring asking how to cook something, or what to do when one of her kids was invited to a schoolfriend's birthday party. What did one send as a pressie? These were the little things most children are taught at their mother's knee, and which she—with an absentee mother and brought up by an anti-social father—had missed out on. Though she could not have known it, most of the time I had tears in my eyes as we talked. I felt happy my daughter was asking me these things, while filled with pain for her that she had not a clue about them.

When Colin got out, everything returned to normal. Pity he hadn't got ten years. If I wanted to talk to her I had to put up with his whiny voice first, bragging about his latest scam. When she came on the line she was cold and distant. The trouble with my belated attempt to be a mother to my daughter was that they came as a pair, and to get to Fiona I had to go through Colin. Twice, he had rung me in the early hours of the morning, drunk and abusive. I told him to ring back the next day, that I had to get up for work, then put the receiver down and unplugged the phone. That was viewed by them as a declaration of war. I switched the phone back on the next day and discovered Fiona had left hate messages on my voice mail and sent texts to my mobile letting me know exactly what she thought of me and my past. She promised to let John Cullen know where I was living. I no longer felt safe. I moved house again, and changed my SIM card. They did likewise. I lost not only my daughter, but also my two grandsons. I wish, I wish, I wish. More than anything I wish it were possible to put an end to the hostilities and turn the clock back to when she was three. We both know that all hope for reconciliation has passed, but that said, I would be there like a shot if I heard Colin was back in the nick.

I had managed to put myself on that much of a downer, thinking abut the kids and what a bloody mess I had made of it all, that the gas fire was starting to look tempting. How easy it would be to switch it on without lighting the pilot light. Then again, that would take guts. I dragged myself out of the chair and began sorting Joey's belongings.

Joey had kept his promise to me; all traces of drugs had been removed. I threw a few more books into a bin liner and filled another two with clothes. I scooped up all the medicines and surgical supplies and threw them in a carrier bag; these I would take to the chemist. Tidying only took me half an hour, but I was loath to leave, aware it would be for the last time. I took a last look at the flat before saying good-bye. I had put so much time and energy into the flat, it had all been for nothing. Joey had dirtied his bib as far as the council were concerned; the rent was long overdue and they would not countenance re-housing him. Whatever happened, never again will Joey have the chance to live in such close proximity to me.

Joey's letters from prison were extremely positive. After turkeying for three months, he had emerged happy, fit and healthy. He was able to sleep and was now playing football, exercising, rediscovering the joy of simply being alive. Prisons are a lot cushier than in my day, a deterrent and rehabilitation rather than punishment. The way it should be in a civilised society. Even so, the average prisoner goes through dark periods once deprived of their liberty. They miss their significant other, their children, the family, mates, home. Joey's only real enjoyment of life had been reading and watching TV documentaries and prison provided those gratis.

It took a while before my contentment caught up with his. Then he wrote to me that he was to be tagged and sent home on early release providing he had a secure address to go to. In this case, Mummy's. He promised that it would only be for a few days. Then he would tell the probation officer we were not getting on and they would move him to a hostel. Oh, and by the way, he was off the gear so I did not need to worry about that; he would be going to the gym instead. He had been inside for four months. My equilibrium took an instant nosedive. I was ambivalent about Joey coming to mine. I wanted to keep him close, but the thought of living with heroin again was more than I could bear. I knew bloody well that he would be using in no time. I would say no. Maternal conscience is hard to live with all the same and I pondered how to break it to him.

A week later I capitulated. I pushed the letter through the letterbox and walked home bowed under the weight of my decision. It is a great pity that life is not like the Gwyneth Paltrow film, *Sliding Doors* where we have a choice of endings. I knew which door I had opened. I began counting the days off my calendar. And then this letter came.

HMP Alcatraz. Without the sea!

> Hi, Mum,
> My luck's run out. I lost my tagging. I'm really sorry mum; I know you've made arrangements etc. I had a scuffle with some idiot at the servery. He started mouthing off, I tried to ignore him, but he kept on, everyone on the wing listening, we had a scuffle, screws broke it up. I only got seven days chokey! Done five of them. I should have been out today but F it. I hope these here let you know in time. Last Tues screws unlocked me and said, 'Shoes on, MRI.' Complete news to me. Anyway, took me to Royal Hosp for an ultrasound scan on my groin, been having trouble with it for a few weeks now. Some days I can't walk at all, been laid off work for three weeks too, on RIC, rest in cell. I was put in a space wagon with four screws, cuffed to two of em, whisked off. The great thing about it was I didn't have to hang around, we went straight into ultrasound, all five of us, ha! They scanned all over my leg, groin, stomach, up to my chest. I'm not sure what they meant, but they said I've got lots of old scar tissue, and old clots, and still got clots in my groin and leg. They've put me on Warfarin; I've got to stay on it the rest of my life! We left here at 7.40, and were back for 12.30. I enjoyed my day out. They even let me have a smoke outside the hosp, still cuffed obviously. I can NEVER touch a needle again. So getting nicked was the best thing for me. I'll ring when I get a new pin number, which won't be till I'm back on the wing. At least now, you will have another four months' peace, so make the most of it! Only joking. I'm still well

> happy—made some good mates in here—loads of books—food is not too bad, though I miss a fried egg sarnie. I'm out Jan 17 by the way, in time for your birthday, I'll take you somewhere nice.
>
> Take care mum,
> I love you.
> Joe.
> xxxx

All of a sudden, he's Joe?

Though I haven't said so to Joe, not wanting to upset well happy son, I'm freaked out that his release date is 17 January. The anniversary of the murders.